A HANDBOOK OF DICTION FOR SINGERS

A HANDBOOK OF DICTION
FOR SINGERS

Italian, German, French

Second Edition

DAVID ADAMS

OXFORD
UNIVERSITY PRESS

2008

OXFORD

UNIVERSITY PRESS

Oxford University Press, Inc., publishes works that further
Oxford University's objective of excellence
in research, scholarship, and education.

Oxford   New York
Auckland   Cape Town   Dar es Salaam   Hong Kong   Karachi
Kuala Lumpur   Madrid   Melbourne   Mexico City   Nairobi
New Delhi   Shanghai   Taipei   Toronto

With offices in
Argentina   Austria   Brazil   Chile   Czech Republic   France   Greece
Guatemala   Hungary   Italy   Japan   Poland   Portugal   Singapore
South Korea   Switzerland   Thailand   Turkey   Ukraine   Vietnam

Published by Oxford University Press, Inc.
198 Madison Avenue, New York, New York 10016

www.oup.com

Oxford is a registered trademark of Oxford University Press

Library of Congress Cataloging-in-Publication Data
Adams, David, 1950–
A handbook of diction for singers : Italian,
German, French / David Adams. — 2nd ed.
p.   cm.
Includes bibliographical references and index.
ISBN 978-0-19-532558-4; 978-0-19-532559-1 (pbk.)
1. Singing—Diction. 2. Italian language—Pronunciation.
3. French language—Pronunciation. 4. German
language—Pronunciation. I. Title.
MT883.A23 2007
783'.043—dc22   2007001876

11   13   12   10

Printed in the United States of America
on acid-free paper

Dedicated to the memory of Italo Tajo

Acknowledgments

I wish to thank the University of Cincinnati for granting the sabbatical leave that made the writing of this book possible. Thanks also to Professor Kenneth Griffiths, esteemed colleague and linguist, for reading the manuscript and providing many valuable suggestions; and to Professor Lorenzo Malfatti for his peerless expertise in matters Italian. Finally, thanks to the many students who have given me the experience over the years which resulted in this book.

Preface to the Second Edition

In spite of the positive reception of the first edition of this book, no sooner was it published than I wanted to revise it. A subsequent reprint corrected most of the typos, but more work needed to be done. I am grateful to Oxford University Press for providing the opportunity to address the book's shortcomings with this second edition. I have attempted to organize the material in a more logical fashion. Page formatting has been adjusted with the goal of greater clarity. IPA usage has been updated. Some individual sections have been reorganized or rewritten. Sample texts have been added at the end of each chapter, with IPA transcription and notes about fine points.

The ultimate aim of the book has always been to present the material as thoroughly as possible for the needs of the singer. As a result, many fine points are discussed that may not be relevant for some classes or individuals at their particular stage of development. Nevertheless, students who aspire to a professional level of classical singing must become sensitive to subtleties of the languages in which they sing. Diction classes and texts can only strive to instill this realization in student singers and hope to inspire them to continue perfecting their linguistic skills.

Preface to the First Edition

This textbook is intended for voice students taking classes in the lyric diction of the Italian, French, and German languages. It is written for the student whose native language is American English. It is also intended for voice teachers, vocal coaches, conductors, and anyone else who deals with the singing of these languages. It can, of course, be used for self-study and reference.

The distinctive aural qualities of any language can be gleaned only imperfectly from a book. It is crucial that students of singing hear Italian, French, and German sung by a variety of native singers. It is likewise important to experience the inflections of the spoken languages to the extent possible, and to gain at least some expertise in speaking them. It is absolutely essential to study the grammar of each language as thoroughly as possible. Fluency is not required, but developing an ear for the cadences, modulations, and phrasings of a language will make a significant difference in the authority with which it is sung.

The study of "diction" can encompass at least three levels:

Beginning: Mastering the basic rules of pronunciation, what sounds result from what letters in what contexts, such as when *s* is voiced or unvoiced.

Intermediate: The above, plus mastery of those characteristics of a language that are different from one's native language, such as purity of vowel sounds uncolored by English diphthongs, nonaspiration of consonants in Italian and French, and relative length of sounds (single and double consonants in Italian, vowels in any language), to name a few of the more important examples.

Advanced: All of the above, plus a subtle understanding of stress and inflection over longer phrase groupings.

This book is ultimately aimed toward helping the student achieve an intermediate level of proficiency, as would be expected in a graduate level diction course. It can also be used for a beginning class, if used selectively. Achieving an advanced level usually requires spending a prolonged period in the country where the language is spoken and much practice speaking it oneself. Nevertheless, it is hoped that some of the fine points discussed will at least make the student more sensitive to various nuances of language. Taken together, such nuances comprise a potentially powerful expressive arsenal for the singer.

Since "diction" is a word that often has negative connotations (classroom exercises, learning rules) it might be better called "skill with a language." For a singer, having inadequate language skills is equivalent to having inadequate intonation; the music just does not sound right. The sensitive listener will be put off by one just as much as the other, no matter how beautiful the voice.

THE INTERNATIONAL PHONETIC ALPHABET

The International Phonetic Alphabet (IPA) is an indispensable tool in any discussion of the sounds of a language. Learning IPA symbols is not difficult, at least within the scope of diction texts such as this one. The student unfamiliar with them can learn them as they are presented.

While there is general consistency in the usage of the major IPA symbols among the texts and dictionaries that employ them, there are a number of small discrepancies and inconsistencies. An example is the treatment of German diphthongs: the word **euch** is found transcribed [ɔç], [ɔyç], or [ɔøç] depending on the book. Glides, also called semi-consonants, are represented in different ways, so that the glide in the Italian word **guerra** can be transcribed [gwɛrra], [gŭɛrra], or [gu̯ɛrra].

Such inconsistencies from one book to another are ultimately unimportant, as long as the symbols used within a given book are consistent and clear in what they represent. This book will explain its choice of IPA symbols when necessary. It will also present alternatives commonly found in other books.

Valuable as the IPA is, it is limited in the amount of information it can convey. This is particularly true of inflections over longer phrases. It also must be remembered that the IPA is a means to an end and not an end in itself. It is not uncommon to hear a singer who enunciates all sounds according to the "rules" and yet sounds stilted and unidiomatic. One needs to get past the IPA to the language itself.

/a/ and /ɑ/

Until recently it has been customary to represent the sound of the Italian vowel-letter *a* as /ɑ/. This symbol is also used by Siebs for the sound of the German vowel-letter *a*. In French, however, it has been customary to represent the bright sound of the vowel-letter *a* as /a/ and the darker version (as in **bas**) as /ɑ/. Since the Italian and German sounds are equivalent to the bright sound in French, it is logical to use the same symbol /a/ for all three languages and reserve the symbol /ɑ/ for the dark French version of this vowel. A number of recent books have adopted this format (e.g., Duden for German, Canepari's *Dizionario di Pronucia Italiana* for Italian), and this book also does so.

Some books use both symbols for German to differentiate length: /ɑ/ is long; /a/ is short. This text prefers to use one symbol (/a/), adding the colon /:/ when it is long, as Duden does.

Some may object to using /a/ in all instances for singing, arguing that this vowel sound is not "round" enough. This issue enters the realm of vowel modification (see below), an important consideration for all singers and voice teachers. This text prefers to make its points in reference to the spoken language, occasionally discussing modifications for singing, but always assuming reasonable and necessary adjustments for singing depending on context.

Symbols for *r*: /ɾ/ /r/ /rr/

The symbol /ɾ/ represents a single flip of the tongue for the pronunciation of the letter *r*. It is commonly used in diction texts for Italian intervocalic single *r*, though not all of them use it. Standard diction texts do not generally use /ɾ/ for other languages, however. The result is some inconsistency from language to language, since for the purpose of singing, intervocalic *r* is normally one flip of the tongue in all three languages: **caro**, **herauf**, **j'irai**.

For Italian double *rr*, which requires the roll, the symbol /rr/ is used. In Italian the symbol /r/ is used when the letter *r* is adjacent to another consonant and begins or ends a word. The reason is to differentiate intervocalic *r*, which should be only one flip of the tongue, from *r* in a consonant cluster, when it may be rolled or flipped. This text will use /ɾ/, /r/, and /rr/ for Italian.

French and German use the conventional symbol /r/ for virtually all situations, assuming the flipped sound (except when German uses /ɐ/, q.v.). Some texts use /rr/ for French in those few situations when a rolled, lengthened r sound is called for, and this text will follow that example.

The Symbol / /

The colon placed after another IPA symbol indicates that the sound represented by the preceding symbol is to be lengthened. It may be used for consonant or vowel sounds. This book employs the symbol only for long vowel sounds. For example, the two German words **Stadt** and **Staat** are differentiated in sound only by the relative length of the vowel sound. The sound of the vowel in **Staat** [ʃtaːt] is approximately twice as long as that in **Stadt** [ʃtat].

A problem arises with this symbol in IPA renderings of groups of words or phrases. While the examples cited above would not change, a word such as the Italian **mia** could change. This word is probably best transcribed [miːa] to show that the sound /i/ is longer than the sound /a/. The same word, however, is rather different in the phrase **mia madre** (normal inflection), because the stress of the phrase goes to the long vowel of **madre** and the duration of the /i/ in **mia** is reduced. Perhaps for this reason many texts dispense with the use of /ː/ altogether. This book uses the colon for all long vowels, even when the length may be reduced in the phrase.

For the purpose of singing, length of vowel sound is largely determined by the musical setting. Nevertheless, an understanding of relative duration of sounds as they occur in speech is crucial to virtually all kinds of singing.

VOWEL MODIFICATION AND THE IPA

Every voice teacher and reasonably experienced singer is familiar with the need to modify vowel sounds in different parts of the voice. This was referred to above under /a/ and /ɑ/. The needs are different for different voice types. Many books with IPA transcription for singers attempt to address this issue by altering IPA vowel symbols standard for speaking to different ones for singing. A few such instances are universally accepted, such as French **les** having /e/ when spoken but /ɛ/ when sung. Most such changes, however, run into the problem that a given modification may work for one voice or voice type, but in another may sound exaggerated or affected. The aim of any vowel modification is to give the illusion of the required vowel sound while keeping the sound beautiful.

Just as a page of music is nothing more than a blueprint for ultimate performance, which can differ from one performer to the next, so IPA transcription is a blueprint, a skeleton, for the singer's realization of language. It is best to use the IPA for singing as it is used for speech. The teacher and intelligent singer will understand that adjustments must be made, but it is not for an artificially imposed IPA symbol to dictate an adjustment.

There is a certain amount of repetition and redundancy built into this text. The basic reason is that repetition will drive a point home, but there is also a cross-referencing purpose. If one wants to check on the vowel sound in the first syllable of the French word **dessein**, for example, it will be found under *closed e* because initial *dess*- results in closed /e/ in French, but the same information will be found under *open e* as an exception to the usual pattern of *e* before a double consonant resulting in open /ɛ/.

It is assumed that the teacher will supplement this text with materials of his or her own devising, such as homework of IPA transcriptions of complete aria or song texts, readings of texts in class, and listening to recorded examples

ITALIAN DICTION

Introduction 3

International Phonetic Alphabet Symbols for Italian 4

Italian Vowels 4

Specific Vowel Sounds in Italian 6

Glides in Italian: /j/ and /w/ 8

Italian Diacritical Marks 9

Italian Syllabification 11

Italian Word Sress 13

Apocopation 15

Italian Diphthongs 15

Italian Triphthongs 18

Phrasal Diphthongs and Triphthongs 19

Vowel Length in Italian 20

Italian Consonants 21

Consonant Combinations and Their Sounds 30

Single and Double Consonants in Italian 32

Characteristics of Double Consonants 33

More About Vowels 35

Ambiguous Spellings: Is It a Vowel or a Glide? 38

Phrasal Doubling in Italian 41

Articulating Italian Double Consonants in Singing 44

Singing Consonant Clusters 45

Musical Settings of Italian Diphthongs 46

Italian Diphthongs: Vowel Distribution in Singing 48

Musical Settings of Italian Triphthongs 50

Singing Phrasal Diphthongs and Triphthongs   51

Vowel Distribution in Singing Phrasal Diphthongs   51

Patterns of Phrasal Triphthongs in Italian   57

Italian Word Underlay in Scores   60

Other Possible Assimilations of *n*   61

Italian Dictionaries   62

Sample Texts   63

Appendix: Guidelines for Determining Open and Closed *e* and *o*
   in the Stressed Syllable   66

GERMAN DICTION

Introduction   83

International Phonetic Alphabet Symbols for German   84

The *Umlaut*   85

Word Origin: Germanic and Non-Germanic   85

German Vowels and Vowel Length   86

Word Stem, Word Stress, Vowel Length   87

Specific Vowel Sounds in German   88

Diphthongs and Adjacent Vowels   100

The Glide /j/   101

German Consonants   102

More about Syllabic Stress and Vowel Length   115

More about German Word Structure   116

Certain Consonant Clusters and Vowel Quality   121

German Monosyllablic (Some Polysyllabic) Word Patterns for Vowel
   Quality and Length   122

Words of Non-Germanic Origin   125

Glottal Separation in German   128

Glottal Separation versus Legato Connection in Singing German   129

Phrasal Consonant Clusters in German   133

Possible Assimilation of Consonant Sounds in German   136

German Dictionaries and Pronunciation Reference Books   139

Sample Texts   140

FRENCH DICTION

Introduction   145
International Phonetic Alphabet Symbols for French   146
French Diacritical Marks   147
Definition of Terms Relating to French Diction   148
French Syllabification   150
Word Stress in French   155
Vowel Length in French   155
French Vowel Sounds and How They Are Spelled   157
Mixed Vowels   167
Nasal Vowels   172
Glides in French   176
French Consonants   180
Liaison   197
Musical Settings of Mute *e* [ə]   202
Musical Settings of Glides   208
French Dictionaries   212
Sample Texts   213

Bibliography   217

Index of Sounds by Spelling   219

General Index   225

A HANDBOOK OF DICTION FOR SINGERS

ITALIAN DICTION

INTRODUCTION

Italian is widely assumed to be an easy language to sing, the easiest of all the foreign languages. This assumption may derive from the fact that beginning voice students usually sing in Italian as their first foreign language; thus if beginners sing Italian, it must be easy. While Italian is grammatically easier than German, and much more phonetic than French (and English), it is difficult to speak and sing Italian well. Indeed, singers who have perfected French and German are often surprisingly unskilled in Italian.

Any language has distinctive sound characteristics resulting in its own unique color. Italian has always been justly praised for the purity of its vowel sounds. Just as important to the overall sound color of Italian, however, is how it treats consonants.

In order to achieve an intermediate level of proficiency with Italian diction, the following points need to be mastered on a consistent basis:

1. Purity of vowels, with particular attention to unstressed syllables.
2. No diphthong in pronouncing /e/, /ɛ/, /o/, and /ɔ/.

3. Appropriate "lift" or brightness to /a/ and /ε/.
4. Long sustained vowels in stressed syllables before a single consonant.
5. Proper linking of vowels between words.
6. Basic understanding of open and closed *e* and *o*.
7. Short single consonants.
8. Long double consonants.
9. Forward articulation and nonaspiration of consonant sounds.
10. Relative lengthening of *l*, *m*, *n*, and *r* when initial in consonant clusters.

International Phonetic Alphabet Symbols for Italian

Vowels
/a/ **amo, fama**
/e/ **vedo, stella**
/ε/ **bella, gelida**
/i/ **mio, addiritura**
/o/ **colore, dottore**
/ɔ/ **sposa, memoria, povero**
/u/ **tuo, crudele, fortuna**

Fricative Consonants
/v/ /vv/ **evviva**
/f/ /ff/ **farfalla, buffo**
/ʃ/ /ʃʃ/ **scendo, lascia, pesce**
/s/ /ss/ **sasso, stesso**
/z/ **rosa, smania**

Lateral Consonants
/l/ /ll/ **libro, giallo**
/ʎ/ /ʎʎ/ **gli angeli, figlio**

Affricate Consonants
/tʃ/ /ttʃ/ **cerco, caccia**
/dʒ/ /ddʒ/ **gemo, fuggire**
/ts/ /tts/ **zio, pazzo**
/dz/ /ddz/ **Zerlina, mezzo**

Glides
/j/ **pianto, patria, buio**
/w/ **sguardo, sangue, tuoi**

Plosive Consonants
/b/ /bb/ **abate, babbo**
/p/ /pp/ **popolo, gruppo**
/d/ /dd/ **Alfredo, freddo**
/t/ /tt/ **tutore, tutto**
/g/ /gg/ **fuga, fuggo**
/k/ /kk/ **seco, secco**

Vibrant Consonants
/ɾ/ /r/ /rr/ **caro, carta, carro**

Nasal Consonants
/n/ /nn/ **pane, panna**
/m/ /mm/ **ama, mamma**
/ŋ/ **fianco, languire**
/ɲ/ /ɲɲ/ **gnocchi, agnello**

Other Symbols
/ː/ lengthen preceding sound
/ˈ/ syllabic stress
/‿/ phrasal diphthong

ITALIAN VOWELS

Italian has five vowel-letters and seven vowel sounds. Some vowel-letters have additional functions.

1. The vowel-letter *a* always represents the sound /a/:

   cara [ˈkaːɾa]   **amara** [aˈmaːɾa]

2. The vowel-letter *e* represents either the closed vowel sound /e/ as in

   vero [ˈveːɾo]   **segreto** [seˈgreːto]

   or the open vowel sound /ɛ/ as in

   prego [ˈprɛːgo]   **estremo** [esˈtrɛːmo]

3. The vowel-letter *i* has three possible functions:
   the *vowel* sound /i/:

   gigli [ˈʤiʎʎi]   **infinito** [infiˈniːto]

   the *glide* /j/:

   pietà [pjeˈta]   **fiato** [ˈfjaːto]

   silent after *c*, *g*, and *sc* when preceding another vowel (softening *i*):

   bacio [ˈbaːʧo]   **lasciare** [laˈʃʃaːɾe]   **Giovanni** [ʤoˈvanni]

   also silent after *gl* when preceding another vowel:

   figlio [ˈfiʎʎo]   **scegliere** [ˈʃeʎʎeɾe]

4. The vowel-letter *o* represents either the closed vowel sound /o/ as in

   voce [ˈvoːʧe]   **sonno** [ˈsonno]

   or the open vowel sound /ɔ/ as in

   sposa [ˈspoːza]   **donna** [ˈdɔnna]

5. The vowel-letter *u* represents either the vowel /u/ as in

   tuo [tuːo]   **futuro** [fuˈtuːɾo]

   or the glide /w/ as in

   tuoi [twɔːi]   **guerra** [ˈgwɛrra]

SPECIFIC VOWEL SOUNDS IN ITALIAN

/a/

The bright Italian /a/ sound is often surprisingly difficult for English-speaking singers to find. The problems can be reduced to two:

1. *Italian /a/ is brighter than its English counterpart.* English-speaking singers tend to center this vowel (rendered as /ɑ/ for English) in the soft palate, which is often rather collapsed as well, giving it a darker, "lower" color. The Italian sound is oriented toward the hard palate, with the soft palate raised, and is consequently brighter and higher. While areas of register transition require the vocal technique to adjust vowel positions somewhat, this should not result in an unidiomatic vowel sound. The singer unused to this position may feel that this /a/ is "spread." The difference between "spread" and "bright" must be learned.
2. In unstressed syllables /a/ *must not lose its purity*—**amara, fatale**. In English, vowels in unstressed positions almost always neutralize to /ə/. English speakers unwittingly carry this habit over into Italian (**Figaro** becomes **Fi-guh-ro**). This problem can be especially difficult in longer breath groups.

/i/

English has both closed /i/ as in *seat* and open /ɪ/ as in *sit*. Italian has only the closed position for the vowel-letter *i*. It is easy for native English speakers to revert to the open position, making the Italian sound unidiomatic. Once again, this tendency is encountered mostly in unstressed syllables. In the word **finire** be sure that the first two syllables have the same vowel quality, though different in length: [fiˈniːɾe].

/u/

English has closed /u/ as in *boot* and open /ʊ/ as in *book*. Italian has only the closed position for the vowel-letter *u*.

The sound /u/ is subject to great regional variation in English-speaking countries. This fact can present problems when this vowel sound is sung. Usually the deviation from /u/ involves a variation of the mixed vowel /y/ as in French (**lune**) or German (**grün**). The problem is tension in the tongue. When the tongue is gently arched toward the oral pharynx, and the front of the tongue is relaxed, the result will be /u/. Rounding of the lips is appropriate, but only by gently tensing the corners of the mouth. There should be no tension in the muscles of the lips: **futuro** [fuˈtuːɾo].

Open and Closed *e* and *o*

/e/ /ɛ/ /o/ /ɔ/

The sound /ɛ/ occurs frequently in English (*bed, deck*), but see the next section for differences between English and Italian. An Italian word with the open sound of *e* is **bello** [ˈbɛllo].

The sound /e/ normally occurs in English only as the first part of a diphthong (*maid, gate*). An Italian word with the closed sound of *e* is **stella** [ˈstella].

The sound /ɔ/ occurs in English (*fought, awe*), though regional differences in pronunciation may affect when it occurs. An Italian word with the open sound of *o* is **cosa** [ˈkɔːza].

The sound /o/ is only approximated as the first part of English diphthongs (*go, toe, blow*). An Italian word with the closed sound of *o* is **come** [ˈkoːme].

The rather complex matter of when an *e* or an *o* is to be pronounced with the open or closed sound is discussed more fully on p. 35 and in the appendix to this chapter.

Appropriate Vocalization of /ɛ/

The comparison of /ɛ/ in American English and in Italian is similar to the comparison of /a/. The sound is common in English but, just as with /a/, the American pronunciation tends to be "back" and rather flat or low. In the languages of continental Europe this sound is generally pronounced with much greater height and forwardness.

American singers tend to position this vowel where they speak it, just as they do with /a/. Furthermore, American singers often equate this back position with vocal "space" and are reluctant to abandon the sensation. Indeed it often happens that when singers find a position for /ɛ/ with appropriate lift and height, they mistakenly believe they are singing /e/. It is essential that the student learn to maintain lift and height in both /e/ and /ɛ/.

Inappropriate Diphthongs

The sounds /e/, /ɛ/, /o/, and /ɔ/ are likely to have an inappropriate diphthong when pronounced by English speakers, since such diphthongs are characteristic of English: /e/ and /ɛ/ become /eːi/ and /ɛːɪ/, and /o/ and /ɔ/ become /oːu/ and /ɔːʊ/. Italian **se** should not sound like English **say**; Italian **lo** should not sound like English **low**. There must be no movement of the jaw or lips either in the release of the vowel or in the transition of the vowel to the next sound.

GLIDES IN ITALIAN: /J/ AND /W/

A glide is a very short vowel sound that yields immediately to a longer vowel sound within the same syllable. The terms "semiconsonant" and "semivowel" mean the same as the term "glide." Italian has two glides: /j/ and /w/.

The glide /j/ (as in English "yes" [jɛs] and "music" ['mjuːz:k]) is spelled in Italian with the letter *i*:

    pietà [pje'ta]   **fiore** ['fjoːɾe]   **siamo** ['sjaːmo]   **ieri** ['jeːɾi]

It can also be spelled with the letter *j* (called *i lungo* in Italian). This spelling can happen only between vowels or at the beginning of a word; it cannot happen after a consonant:

    Iago or **Jago** ['jaːgo]   **aiuto** or **ajuto** [a'juːto]
    muoio or **muojo** ['mwɔːjo]

Because English does not normally use the letter *i* as a glide, people inexperienced with Italian commonly mispronounce the /j/ glide as the vowel /i/: The letter *i* functions differently in the Italian word **piano** ['pjaːno] from that in the English word *piano* [pi'æno]. This is a common error that must be corrected.

The glide /w/ (as in English "was" [wʌz] and "twenty" ['twɛntɪ]) is spelled in Italian with the letter *u*:

    cuoco ['kwɔːko]   **guerra** [gwɛrra]   **quattro** ['kwattro]
    uovo ['wɔːvo]

In Italian, *u is never silent* as it may be in French:

French **qui** [ki]	vs.	Italian **qui** [kwi]
French **guerre** [geːr(ə)]	vs.	Italian **guerra** [ˈgwɛrra]
French **quand** [kɑ̃]	vs.	Italian **quando** [ˈkwando]
French **languir** [lɑ̃giːr]	vs.	Italian **languire** [laŋˈgwiːre]

In Italian, spelling alone does not always make clear whether or not a word has a glide. This matter is discussed on p. 38.

ITALIAN DIACRITICAL MARKS

- The *grave accent* (`) is the most common diacritical mark in Italian. In older printed Italian it is always found with stressed final vowels in polysyllabic words. Modern printed Italian employs the *acute accent* ( ) for stressed final *i, u,* and *e* (when closed).

beltà [belˈta]   **vedrò** [veˈdrɔ]   **lassù** (or **lassú**) [lasˈsu]
partì (or **partí**) [parˈti]   **perchè** (or **perché**) [perˈke]

Final stressed *e* is open in a few words. The grave accent is used:

caffè [kafˈfɛ]   **ahimè** [aiˈmɛ]   **Moisè** [moiˈzɛ]

In three-letter monosyllabic words spelled consonant-vowel-vowel, the grave accent over the final vowel indicates that the first vowel is either a glide or a "softening" *i*:

può [pwɔ]   **piè** [pjɛ]   **diè** [djɛ]   **più** (or **piú**) [pju]
già [dʒa]   **ciò** [tʃɔ]

Such words without an accent are to be pronounced as a diphthong:

pio [piːo]   **tuo** [tuːo]   **mie** [miːe]   **sia** [siːa]   **fia** [fiːa]   **mai** [maːi]

The grave accent is also used to differentiate monosyllabic words that have different meanings but are otherwise spelled the same:

là (there)	**la** (the, it)
sè [se] (oneself)	**se** [se] (if)
è [ɛ] (is)	**e** [e] (and)
tè [tɛ] (tea)	**te** [te] (you)
nè (or **né**) [ne] (nor)	**ne** [ne] (of it, of them)
sì (yes)	**si** (one, oneself)
dì (day)	**di** (of)

The same may occasionally happen with polysyllabic words:

àncora ['aŋkoɾa] (anchor)   **ancora** [aŋ'koːɾa] (again)

In polysyallabic words ending in *i* plus a vowel, the grave accent may sometimes be found over the *i* to indicate that the vowels form a diphthong (that is, the *i* is not a glide or softening *i*):

Lucìa [lu'ʧiːa]   **follìa** [fol'liːa]   **librerìa** [libre'riːa]

Use of the accent in such cases is unfortunately inconsistent; these words are just as often found without accents.

- The *circumflex accent* (ˆ) is very occasionally encountered in older Italian. It indicates that a letter has been omitted. It has no effect on pronunciation, and its use is not obligatory:

  dormîa [dor'miːa] = **dormiva** [dor'miːva]
  côre ['kɔːɾe] = **cuore** ['kwɔːɾe]

  Masculine nouns that end in *-io* normally have a plural form in *-i*. In literary texts the plural may be spelled *-ii*, and sometimes *î* is encountered. All possibilities of the plural form are pronounced the same, as a single *-i*.

Singular	Usual Plural	Alternative Plural Spellings	
gaudio	gaudi	gaudii, gaudî	['gaːudi]
esercizio	esercizi	esercizii, esercizî	[ezer'ʧittsi]

- The *dieresis* (¨) is occasionally seen in Italian orthography. When two adjacent vowels are to be separated over two syllables (instead of being pronounced as a diphthong in one syllable), sometimes two dots are found over one of the vowels, usually the first (**vïole**) but sometimes the second (**Aïda**). Both the act of separating the vowels and the symbol itself are called dieresis. The symbol is found in French spelling and is also known as *trema*. It is not to be confused with the German *Umlaut*, which looks exactly the same but has a different function. Poetic Italian sometimes requires dieresis for the requirements of the verse, and often composers follow suit in the music.

ITALIAN SYLLABIFICATION

It is important to understand syllabification as an aid in determining relative length of vowel and consonant sounds. Italian, like other Romance languages, is characterized by *open syllabification*. An *open syllable* is one that ends in a vowel. A *closed syllable* ends in a consonant. These terms are not to be confused with open and closed vowels.

- A *single consonant* occurs between two vowels and begins the next syllable:

    a-mo-re [a'moːre]   **po-po-lo** ['pɔːpolo]   **fe-ri-to** [fe'riːto]

- A *double consonant* is the occurrence of two of the same consonant together. Syllables divide between the two consonants:

    trop-po ['trɔppo]   **mat-to** ['matto]   **bel-lo** ['bɛllo]

- A *consonant cluster* is two or three different consonants together. The cluster will divide after the first consonant if it is *l*, *m*, *n*, or *r* (the *lemoners*):

    al-to ['alto]   **tem-po** ['tɛmpo]   **con-te** ['konte]   **par-la** ['parla]

When the letter *s* begins a cluster, there is not universal agreement as to how the cluster divides. For the purposes of this book it is useful to group it with the *lemoners* and divide after the *s*:

    tes-ta ['tɛsta]   **cos-tan-te** [kos'tante]   **bas-ta** ['basta]

unless, of course, it begins a word:

    stu-den-te [stu'dɛnte]

- Some consonant combinations are spelled like clusters but act like double consonants. Printed Italian shows the entire combination beginning the syllable:

-sci-, -sce-	**pe-sce** ['peʃʃe]	**la-scia-re** [laʃ'ʃaːre]
-gn-	**so-gno** ['soɲɲo]	**ma-li-gno** [ma'liɲɲo]
-gli-	**fi-glio** ['fiʎʎo]	**pe-ri-glio** [pe'riʎʎo]

A few words have rare, atypical clusters which divide between the consonants:

tec-ni-ca ['tɛknika]   **ab-di-ca-re** [abdiˈkaːɾe]

Almost all other cases are two-letter clusters ending in *r*. The cluster *bl* is also possible. The entire cluster belongs with the vowel following it.

    a-pri-re [aˈpriːɾe]   **a-vrà** [aˈvra]   **la-dro** [ˈlaːdro]
    ve-tro [ˈveːtro]   **o-bli-o** [oˈbliːo]

- *Adjacent vowels* are usually considered to be in the same syllable. Sometimes the first vowel of a vowel cluster is a true vowel, sometimes it is a glide, sometimes it is silent. This will be further discussed later in the chapter.

    mio [miːo]   **miei** [mjeːi]   **sua** [suːa]   **suoi** [swɔːi]   **già** [dʒa]

Adjacent vowels separate into *different syllables* in the following circumstances:

1. When *i* comes between two other vowel-letters. The *i* (pronounced as the glide /j/) begins a new syllable:

    a-iu-to [aˈjuːto]   **bu-io** [ˈbuːjo]   **gio-ia** [ˈdʒɔːja]
    muo-io [ˈmwɔːjo]

2. When *a*, *e*, or *o* is immediately followed by a stressed vowel. Such combinations are called *second-vowel syllabic diphthongs*:

    pa-u-ra [paˈuːɾa]   **be-a-to** [beˈaːto]   **le-o-ne** [leˈoːne]
    po-e-ta [poˈɛːta]

3. When a prefix is followed by a vowel and within the prefixes *dia-* and *bio-* (no glide):

    riuscire (ri-u-sci-re) [riuʃˈʃiːɾe]
    bienne(bi-en-ne) [biˈɛnne]
    dialogo (di-a-lo-go) [diˈaːlogo]
    diaframma (di-a-fram-ma) [diaˈframma]
    biografo (bi-o-gra-fo) [biˈɔːgrafo]

Note that some words might have similar spellings that are not prefixes and therefore have a glide:

diavolo ['djaːvolo]   **biondo** [bjondo]

4. When a consonant cluster ending in *l* or *r* is followed by two vowels (no glide):

biblioteca (bi-bli-o-te-ca) [biblioˈtɛːka]   **oblio (o-bli-o)** [oˈbliːo]
cruente (cru-en-te) [kruˈɛnte]

And a few other words that begin with *l* or *r* followed by two vowels (no glide):

ruina (ru-i-na) [ruˈiːna]   **Luigi (Lu-i-gi)** [luˈiːdʒi]
rione (ri-o-ne) [riˈoːne]

5. In some words with *u* plus vowel (no glide). Some sources present
some these words with glides, others do not:

te-nu-e ['tɛːnue]   **man-su-e-to** [mansuˈeːto]

ITALIAN WORD STRESS

Understanding patterns of word stress, or syllabic stress, in Italian is important for understanding the character of the language. While musical
settings usually make word stress clear, such is not always the case. In IPA,
the symbol indicating stress is placed before the stressed syllable.

- Most Italian words of two or more syllables take the stress on the
penultimate (second-to-last) syllable (**parola piana** in Italian):

  Roma ['roːma]   **Milano** [miˈlaːno]   **Venezia** [veˈnɛttsja]
  Firenze [fiˈrɛntse]

- Some words take the stress on the final syllable (**parola tronca** in
Italian). The final vowel will have either a grave or an acute accent:

  beltà [belˈta]   **perché** [perˈke]   **amerò** [ameˈrɔ]   **partí** [parˈti]

Some words end in a final stressed diphthong. No accent is used. This includes words that end in stressed *-ia*, *-ie*, and *-io* (see further discussion of
such words on p. 38):

  an-drei [-ˈdrɛːi]   **cer-cai** [-ˈkaːi]   **co-lui** [-ˈluːi]   **ma-lia** [-ˈliːa]
  fru-scio [-ˈʃiːo]   **buf-fo-ne-rie** [-ˈriːe]

- A large minority of words take the stress on the antepenultimate (third-to-last) syllable (**parola sdrucciola** in Italian). Rarely is an accent given, so unknown words must be checked in a reliable dictionary:

anima [ˈaːnima]   **timido** [ˈtiːmido]   **lagrima** [ˈlaːgrima]
gelido [ˈʤeːlido]   **incognito** [inˈkɔɲɲito]

Certain recurring word endings result in the antepenult stress pattern. Some of them are:

Adjectives

-ˈabile	**amabile** [aˈmaːbile]	**inesorabile** [inezoˈraːbile]
-ˈibile	**possibile** [posˈsiːbile]	**visibile** [viˈziːbile]
-ˈevole	**piacevole** [pjaˈtʃeːvole]	**colpevole** [kolˈpeːvole]
-ˈesimo	**ventesimo** [venˈtɛːzimo]	**undicesimo** [undiˈtʃeːzimo]

Adjectives, Adverbs

-ˈissimo	**prestissimo** [presˈtissimo]	**felicissimo** [feliˈtʃissimo]

Nouns

-ˈudine	**solitudine** [soliˈtuːdine]	**abitudine** [abiˈtuːdine]
-logo	**prologo** [ˈprɔːlogo]	**catalogo** [kaˈtaːlogo]

Many verb forms take the antepenult stress, particularly some infinitives in -*ere*, and third person plural forms:

Verbs

ridere [ˈriːdere]   **credere** [ˈkreːdere]   **parlano** [ˈparlano]
conoscono [koˈnoskono]   **amavano** [aˈmaːvano]

- A fourth-to-last-syllable stress (**parola bisdrucciola** in Italian) is rare but possible in the third person plural of -*are* verbs that have an antepenult stress in singular forms:

dimenticare [dimentiˈkaːre]   **dimentica** [diˈmentika]
dimenticano [diˈmentikano]
meritare [meriˈtaːre]   **merita** [ˈmɛːrita]   **meritano** [ˈmɛːritano]

and in some compound forms where pronouns are attached to verbs:

portamelo [ˈpɔrtamelo] (bring it to me)

APOCOPATION

Apocopation or truncation (**troncamento** in Italian) is the elimination of (usually) the final vowel of a word. This happens frequently in literary Italian. The word stress does not change:

an'cora = an'cor   fe'dele = fe'del
a'more = a'mor   'amano = 'aman

It is interesting to note that apocopation can occur only if the result is a final consonant of *l*, *m*, *n*, or *r* (the *lemoners*), the same consonants that can end a syllable in a cluster (though *s* is not included here). Thus **andiamo** can become **andiam** and **vanno** can become **van**, but **andate** cannot be altered.

As with **van** above, sometimes more than just the final vowel is removed:

sanno = san   danno = dan   fanno = fan   hanno = han

A family of Italian nouns has a complete form ending in -*de* and an apocopated form ending in a stressed vowel. The shorter form is the norm in modern Italian; the longer form is antiquated but found in vocal texts:

pietà = pietade   piè = piede   fe, fé, fè = fede
mercè = mercede   beltà = beltade   virtù = virtude
libertà = libertade amistà = amistade

Other than words taken from other languages (including many proper names), the only common Italian words that end in consonants are a few small words such as **il**, **con**, **per**, **non**, **nord**, **sud**, **est**, **ovest**, and contractions such as **del**, **nel**. *Any other word ending in a consonant does so as a result of apocopation.* It is incumbent upon the student to know the complete form of any apocopated word.

ITALIAN DIPHTHONGS

A diphthong is the occurrence of two adjacent vowel sounds in the same syllable. Sometimes a glide-vowel combination is called a *rising diphthong* and a vowel-vowel combination is called a *falling diphthong*. In this book, glides are treated separately; this section will deal only with vowel-vowel diphthongs.

English pronunciation frequently requires diphthongs in syllables that have only one vowel-letter (e.g., *by* [bɑːi]). Since Italian vowels are always pure, diphthongs must be spelled with two vowel-letters.

When the diphthong occurs in the stressed syllable, one vowel sound is longer than the other; that sound is called *syllabic*. Usually the first vowel is syllabic (**aura** [ˈaːura]), but sometimes the second vowel is (**paura** [paˈuːra]. The syllabic vowel is stressed and the vowel length is determined by syllabification rules (e.g., **maestro** [maˈɛstro] has a stressed short vowel). When the diphthong is in an unstressed syllable, both vowel sounds are short and approximately equal in length (e.g., **aurora** [auˈrɔːra]).

Diphthongs occur frequently in Italian, much more so than in French and German. Here is a list of all twenty possible diphthong combinations (not all of which actually occur) with examples of first-vowel syllabic, second-vowel syllabic, and unstressed diphthongs where they occur in Italian.

ae:	first-vowel syllabic:	**aere** [ˈaːere]	
	second-vowel syllabic:	**paese** [paˈeːze]	**maestro** [maˈɛstro]
	unstressed:	**maestà** [maeˈsta]	
ai:	first-vowel syllabic:	**mai** [maːi]	**avrai** [aˈvraːi]
	second-vowel syllabic:	**aita** [aˈiːta]	**Aïda** [aˈiːda]
	unstressed:	**ahimè** [aiˈmɛ]	
ao:	first-vowel syllabic:	**Paolo** [ˈpaːolo]	**Menelao** [meneˈlaːo]
	second-vowel syllabic:	**faraone** [faraˈoːne]	**Aosta** [aˈosta]
	unstressed:	**Paolino** [paoˈliːno]	
au:	first-vowel syllabic:	**aura** [ˈaːura]	**causa** [ˈkaːuza]
	second-vowel syllabic:	**paura** [paˈuːra]	**baule** [baˈuːle]
	unstressed:	**aurora** [auˈrɔːra]	
ea:	first-vowel syllabic:	**idea** [iˈdɛːa]	**rea** [rɛːa]
	second-vowel syllabic:	**beato** [beˈaːto]	**teatro** [teˈaːtro]
	unstressed:	**realtà** [realˈta]	
ei:	first-vowel syllabic:	**lei** [lɛːi]	**vorrei** [vorˈrɛːi]
	second-vowel syllabic:	**veicolo** [veˈiːkolo]	
		bey [beˈi] (*L'Italiana in Algeri*)	
	unstressed:	**deità** [deiˈta]	

eo:	first-vowel syllabic:	**trofeo** [troˈfɛːo] **Orfeo** [orˈfɛːo]
	second-vowel syllabic:	**leone** [leˈoːne]
	unstressed:	**Leonora** [leoˈnoːra]

eu:	first-vowel syllabic:	**feudi** [ˈfɛːudi] **neutro** [ˈnɛːutro]
	second-vowel syllabic:	does not occur
	unstressed:	**Euridice** [euriˈdiːtʃe]

ia:	first-vowel syllabic:	**mia** [miːa] **osteria** [osteˈriːa]
	second-vowel syllabic:	usually /j/ glide **pianto** [ˈpjanto]
		but **dialogo** [diˈaːlogo]
	unstressed:	usually /j/ glide **piacere** [pjaˈtʃeːre]
		but **diamante** [diaˈmante]

ie:	first-vowel syllabic:	**mie** [miːe] **gallerie** [galleˈriːe]
	second-vowel syllabic:	usually /j/ glide **fiero** [ˈfjɛːro]
		but **bienne** [biˈɛnne]
	unstressed	/j/ glide **pietà** [pjeˈta]

io:	first-vowel syllabic:	**mio** [miːo] **addio** [adˈdiːo]
	second-vowel syllabic:	usually /j/ glide **azione** [atˈtsjoːne]
		but **rione** [riˈoːne]
	unstressed:	/j/ glide **fiorito** [fjoˈriːto]

iu:	first-vowel syllabic:	does not occur
	second-vowel syllabic:	usually /j/ glide **fiume** [ˈfjuːme]
		but **liuto** [liˈuːto]
	unstressed:	usually /j/ **chiudete** [kjuˈdeːte]
		but **riunione** [riuˈnjoːne]

oa:	first-vowel syllabic:	**boa** [bɔːa]
	second-vowel syllabic:	**soave** [soˈaːve] **cloaca** [kloˈaːka]
	unstressed:	**soavità** [soaviˈta]

oe:	first-vowel syllabic:	**eroe** [eˈrɔːe]
	second-vowel syllabic:	**poeta** [poˈɛːta]
	unstressed:	**poesia** [poeˈziːa]

oi:	first-vowel syllabic:	**voi** [voːi] **poi** [pɔːi]
	second-vowel syllabic:	**gioire** [dʒoˈiːre]
	unstressed:	**ohimè** [oiˈmɛ]

ou: does not occur

ua: first-vowel syllabic: **tua** [tuːa]   **sua** [suːa]
          second-vowel syllabic: /w/ glide **uguale** [uˈgwaːle]
          unstressed: usually /w/ **guanciale** [gwanˈtʃaːle]
                                        but **ingenua** [inˈʤeːnua]

ue: first-vowel syllabic: **tue** [tuːe]   **sue** [suːe]   **bue** [buːe]
          second-vowel syllabic: /w/ glide **guerra** [ˈgwɛrra]
                                        but **cruente** [kruˈɛnte]
          unstressed: /w/ glide **guerriero** [gwerˈrjɛːro]
                                        but **assidue** [asˈsiːdue]

ui: first-vowel syllabic: **lui** [luːi]   **altrui** [alˈtruːi]
          second vowel syllabic: usually /w/ glide **guisa** [ˈgwiːza]
                                        but **ruina** [ruˈiːna]   **Luigi** [luˈiːʤi]
          unstressed: /w/ glide **guidare** [gwiˈdaːre]

uo: first-vowel syllabic: **tuo** [tuːo]   **suo** [suːo]
          second-vowel syllabic: /w/ glide **buono** [ˈbwɔːno]
          unstressed: /w/ glide **fuorché** [fworˈke]
                                        but **ingenuo** [inˈʤeːnuo]

The most common diphthongs are the following:

those with first-vowel syllabic *i* (*-ia, -ie, -io*):

    sia   **mie**   **Dio**

those with first-vowel syllabic *u* (*-ua, -ue, -ui, -uo*):

    sua   **due**   **cui**   **tuo**

first-vowel syllabic diphthongs ending in *i* (*-ai, -ei, -oi, -ui*):

    mai   **lei**   **voi**   **lui**

first-vowel syllabic *au*:

    aula   **aura**   **aumento**   **esaurito**

ITALIAN TRIPHTHONGS

Strictly speaking, a triphthong is the occurrence of three successive vowel sounds in a word. Three successive vowel-letters do not always result in a true triphthong. If the first vowel-letter is an *i* after a *c* or *g.* as in **ciao** [tʃaːo], the *i* is silent and the result is a diphthong. In all other situations either the first or second vowel-letter must be a glide.

- If the first vowel-letter is a glide, all three vowels are in the same syllable. This pattern is found in five common words:

  tuoi [twɔːi]   **suoi** [swɔːi]   **vuoi** [vwɔːi]   **puoi** [pwɔːi]   **miei** [mjɛːi]

  and in a few less common words:

  quei [kweːi]   **guai** [gwaːi]

- If the second vowel-letter is a glide (this can happen only with /j/), the triphthong separates into two syllables. The syllables divide before the glide:

  paio ['paːjo]   **buio** ['buːjo]   **aiuto** [aˈjuːto]

Four successive vowel-letters in a word result in one of two possibilities:

1. glide-vowel-glide-vowel, as in **muoio** ['mwɔːjo]
2. softening *i*-vowel-glide-vowel, as in **gioia** ['ʤɔːja]

Four successive vowel-letters always separate over two syllables.

PHRASAL DIPHTHONGS AND TRIPHTHONGS

Most Italian words end with a vowel; many begin with a vowel. Consequently many words are linked by contiguous vowel sounds. This is one of the primary elements in the legato flow of the language, spoken as well as sung. Such situations are called *phrasal diphthongs* or *triphthongs*.

La donn*a è* mobile   . . . finchè l'ar*ia è a*ncor bruna

A characteristic of English is that words beginning with vowels are usually articulated with a glottal stroke. Students must learn *not* to do this in Italian, but to connect the words smoothly.

Vocal music presents a variety of situations involving such vowel combinations. They are discussed later in the chapter.

VOWEL LENGTH IN ITALIAN

Unstressed vowels are always short, but they must remain pure. Long vowels are roughly twice as long as short vowels and are shown phonetically by the symbol /ː/.

- Vowels are considered long when they occur in *stressed open syllables*. An open syllable is one that ends in a vowel.

  amo [ˈaːmo]   **amare** [aˈmaːɾe]   **neve** [ˈneːve]   **padre** [ˈpaːdre]
  sopra [ˈsoːpra]   **vittoria** [vitˈtoːrja]   **Euridice** [euɾiˈdiːtʃe]

- In monosyllabic words with diphthongs and polysyllabic words with stressed first-vowel syllabic diphthongs, the first vowel is long:

  mio [miːo]   **hai** [aːi]   **aura** [ˈaːuɾa]   **amerei** [ameˈreːi]

Second-vowel syllabic diphthongs determine vowel length by the usual syllabification rules. If the stressed syllable is open, the vowel is long:

  paura [paˈuːɾa]   **soave** [soˈaːve]   **paese** [paˈeːze]   **teatro** [teˈaːtro]

If the syllable is closed, the vowel is short:

  maestro [maˈestro]

- Monosyllabic triphthongs have a long vowel after the glide:

  puoi [pwoːi]   **miei** [mjeːi]   **guai** [gwaːi]

There are some situations in which stressed open syllables contain *short* vowels:

- Stressed final vowels, including monosyllables:

  amò [aˈmɔ]   **amerà** [ameˈra]   **la** [la]   **più** [pju]

- Before -*sci* and -*sce* (function as doubled sounds):

  lascio [ˈlaʃʃo]   **pesce** [ˈpeʃʃe]

- Before –*gli* and –*gn* (function as doubled sounds):

  egli [ˈeʎʎi]   **ogni** [ˈoɲɲi]

- Before intervocalic *z* (single *z* pronounced as double):

  spazio [ˈspattsjo]   **letizia** [leˈtittsja]

Stressed vowels occurring in *closed syllables*, that is, before double consonants, or before consonant clusters beginning with *l*, *m*, *n*, *r*, and *s* (stressed closed syllables) are *short*.

petto ['pɛtto]   **ricco** ['rikko]   **bello** ['bɛllo]
colpa ['kolpa]   **tempo** ['tɛmpo]   **contro** ['kontro]
sordo ['sordo]   **arte** ['arte]   **testa** ['tɛsta]

There are two related situations in which a long vowel is less obvious:

- When pronouns *mi*, *ti*, *si*, *ci*, *vi* are attached to verbs, the original vowel length remains, in spite of the consonant cluster:

    amare [aˈmaːre]   **amarvi** [aˈmaːrvi]
    vedere [veˈdeːre]   **vedersi** [veˈdeːrsi]

- Apocopated words retain the vowel length of the complete form of the word:

    valore [vaˈloːre]   **valor** [vaˈloːr]
    andiamo [anˈdjaːmo]   **andiam** [anˈdjaːm]

Finally, compound words essentially retain the characteristics of their component parts, although the overall word stress is on the final component:

girasole [dʒiːraˈsoːle]   **capolavoro** [kaːpolaˈvoːro]

ITALIAN CONSONANTS

Idiomatic rendering of Italian consonants is as important as that of the vowels. The proper rendering of each is often mutually interdependent. Four basic points regarding Italian consonants must be mastered:

1. There must be a clear differentiation in the length of single and double consonants.
2. Consonants must be *unaspirated*: specifically *b*, *p*, *d*, *t*, and the sound /k/ release much less air than they do in English.
3. Consonants must be articulated *well forward*, more so than in English. Specifically, *d*, *t*, and *l* must be pronounced with the tongue in contact with the upper front teeth.
4. The two *r* sounds must be mastered (flip and roll of the tongue).

Many sources use /ː/ to indicate double consonant length (/tːt/). This text uses only the double consonant symbol (/tt/). Four sounds not spelled with double consonants are pronounced as doubled:

gli as in **figlio** [ˈfiʎʎo]
gn as in **sogno** [ˈsoɲɲo]
sce and *sci* as in **pesce** [ˈpeʃʃe] and **lasciare** [laʃˈʃaːre]
intervocalic single *z*, as in **pazienza** [patˈtsjɛntsa]

When initial in a word, these sounds are not doubled: **gli** [ʎi], **sciolto** [ˈʃɔlto], unless phrasal doubling applies.

Some consonant-letters in Italian are invariable in their sound and take the same IPA symbols as English. They are:

b /b/   *d* /d/   *f* /f/   *l* /l/   *m* /m/   *n* /n/   *p* /p/   *t* /t/   *v* /v/

The following consonant-letters or combinations are either variable (that is, they can have more than one pronunciation) or require specific explanation because of their difference from English:

r,   s,   z,   zz,   c,   g,   h,   sc,   gn,   gli,   nc,   ng,   nq

These letters and combinations will be discussed in the order given, following a discussion of Italian /l/.

The Italian /l/ Sound

A few more observations about /l/. Of the sounds that appear to be equivalent in English and Italian, this is perhaps the most problematic. English /l/ is usually pronounced with the tongue rather tense and making contact with the palate well behind the teeth, as well as with a collapsed pharynx. Many students have such an ingrained English /l/ position that it is very difficult to speak or sing an idiomatic Italian /l/, especially a short intervocalic /l/ as in **fatale** or **crudele**. The tongue must not only be forward, but the vowel shape of the preceding vowel must be behind the tongue as /l/ is pronounced, an aspect that is even more crucial for double *ll* and when *l* begins a consonant cluster. The sound must have resonance as well as forwardness.

R

Italian *r* has two pronunciations:

- *Flipped:* a single, quick stroke of the tip of the tongue against the front of the roof of the mouth.
- *Rolled:* two or more such strokes in rapid succession on a continuous release of breath.

In both cases the sound is voiced, that is, the vocal folds are vibrating.

As a single consonant between vowels *r* is *always* flipped and *never* rolled:

    vedere [ve'deːɾe]   **amore** [a'moːɾe]   **diretto** [di'rɛtto]

As a double consonant, *rr* is *always* rolled and *never* flipped:

    ferro ['fɛrro]   **torre** ['torre]   **bizzarro** [bid'dzarro]

Here are potentially tricky words, in which a distinction between single *r* and double *rr* must be made:

    orrore [or'roːɾe]   **guerriero** [gwer'rjeːɾo]   **irrorare** [irro'raːɾe]
    correre ['korreɾe]   **narrare** [nar'raːɾe]   **Ferrara** [fer'raːɾa]
    Carrara [kar'raːɾa]

The other possible contexts for *r* are the following:

beginning a consonant cluster:

    morte ['mɔrte]   **fermare** [fer'maːɾe]

ending a consonant cluster:

    trenta ['trenta]   **improvviso** [improv'viːzo]

beginning a word:

    roba ['rɔːba]   **ridere** ['riːdeɾe]

ending a word:

    per [per]   **andar** [an'daːr]

In general for the above four contexts, Italian speech employs the flip for nonemphatic situations and the roll for emphatic ones, although nonemphatic situations may still employ a light roll. The heightened expressive nature of singing tends to use the roll most of the time, although parlando and recitative singing certainly could employ the flip.

S

The letter *s* has two sounds (not including *sc*; see p. 30).

Unvoiced s /s/ occurs in these positions:

- beginning a word followed by a vowel:

    subito ['suːbito]   **sorella** [soˈrɛlla]   **solo** ['soːlo]

- preceding an unvoiced consonant:

    stella ['stella]   **testa** ['tɛsta]   **squarcio** ['skwartʃo]

- following a consonant:

    senso ['sɛnso]   **Alonso** [aˈlonso]   **forse** ['forse]   **falso** ['falso]

- doubled (the sound is also prolonged):

    stesso ['stesso]   **basso** ['basso]   **assistere** [asˈsisteɾe]

- final (rare, foreign words only):

    Ramfis ['ramfis]   **Amneris** [amˈnɛːɾis]   **Radamès** [radaˈmes]

Voiced s /z/ occurs in these positions:

- preceding a voiced consonant:

    sgelo ['zʤɛːlo]   **sguardo** ['zgwardo]   **sbilancia** [zbiˈlantʃa]
    fantasma [fanˈtazma]   **smania** ['zmaːnja]   **Amonasro** [amoˈnazro]

- single between vowels (intervocalic):

    sposa ['spɔːza]   **tesoro** [teˈzɔːɾo]   **naso** ['naːzo]

Italian dictionaries indicate that some words with intervocalic *s* use the unvoiced sound /s/ in the Tuscan manner. The most common of these words are **casa**, **cosa**, **così**, and adjectives ending in -**oso** (-*osa*, -*osi*, -*ose*): **pietoso**, **curioso**, **doloroso**. Most Italians pronounce these words with a voiced *s* /z/. This practice is standard in sung Italian. It is recommended that every intervocalic *s* be pronounced as /z/.

There are, however, three contexts in which *s* appears to be intervocalic but *functions as an initial s* and is therefore *unvoiced* /s/:

1. when the reflexive pronoun **si** is attached to a verb:

   > . . . **se potriasi star meglio in altro loco** [po'triːasi]
   > (**si potria**)—*Le nozze di Figaro*
   > **Pur mai non sentesi** ['sɛntesi] (**si sente**)—*Rigoletto*
   > **Credeasi, misera** [kre'deːasi] (**si credeva**)—*I puritani*
   > **Volisi l'offesa a vendicar** ['voːlisi] (**si voli**) - *La traviata*

   Attention must be paid to other forms ending in -**si** that are not reflexives added to verbs. In such cases the *s* is voiced:

   > **rimasi** [ri'maːzi], **promisi** [pro'miːzi] (*passato remoto* verb forms),
   > **estasi** ['ɛstazi], **brindisi** ['brindizi] (nouns), etc.

2. when the prefixes **ri-**, **di-**, and **tra-** occur before *s* plus a vowel:

   > **riserva** [ri'sɛrva]   **risorsa** [ri'sorsa]   **disegno** [di'seɲɲo]
   > **trasalire** [trasa'liːɾe]

   This is also true of **pre-** when it is a prefix, as in **preservare**. When it is not a prefix, a subsequent *s* plus vowel is voiced, as in **presente, presenza**.

   Note the difference between **di-** as a prefix and **dis-** as a prefix. When the latter occurs before a vowel, the *s* is voiced:

   > **disordine** [di'zordine]   **disonesto** [dizo'nɛsto]

3. in compound words, when *s* begins the second element:

   > **ventisei** [venti'sɛːi]   **trentasette** [trenta'sɛtte]   **girasole** [dʒiːra'soːle]

Z

The letter *z* has two sounds: voiced /dz/ and unvoiced /ts/. These sounds are called *affricates*, which means that two sounds are involved, which is reflected in the IPA rendering.

When it is intervocalic, *z* is pronounced as a double. IPA transcription reflects this pronunciation, either /ddz/ or /tts/. Double *zz* is always intervocalic and is, of course, always doubled. As part of a consonant cluster, *z* is transcribed as a single consonant.

The voicing or unvoicing of *z* sounds in Italian is perhaps the most unphonetic aspect of the language. Guidelines for determining which sound is used in a given word are of limited help, although unvoiced *z* is much more common than voiced *z*. Unknown words should be checked in a reliable dictionary. The guidelines, such as they are, are as follows:

- Intervocalic single *z* followed by *i*, usually (but not always) acting as a glide, is unvoiced (remember that it is also pronounced as a doubled sound).

  nazione [nat'tsjoːne]   **benedizione** [benedit'tsjoːne]
  grazia ['grattsja]   **pazienza** [pat'tsjɛntsa]
  polizia [polit'tsiːa]   **negozio** [ne'gɔttsjo]

  A rare exception is the word **azienda**, with voiced *z* [ad'dzjɛnda]

- Intervocalic single *z* not followed by *i* is voiced. This happens rarely, but it does occur in a number of proper names relevant to vocal repertoire.

  Suzuki [sud'dzuːki]   **Azucena** [addzu'tʃeːna]
  Donizetti [donid'dzetti]

- When *z* begins a word, it is *often* voiced:

  zero ['dzɛːro]   **zelo** ['dzeːlo]   **zefiro** ['dzeːfiro]
  zerbino [dzer'biːno] **zimarra** [dzi'marra]   **zefiro** ['dzeːfiro]
  zanzara [dzan'dzaɾa] **Zerlina** [dzer'liːna]

  but many times unvoiced:

  zitto ['tsitto]   **zio** [tsiːo]   **zucchero** ['tsukkeɾo]   **zingaro** ['tsiŋgaɾo]

The voicing/unvoicing of initial *z* is particularly subject to regional variation, and even dictionaries do not agree on all words.

Consonant Clusters with z

- Apart from double *zz*, the most commonly encountered situation with *z* is after *n*. When this happens the *z* is usually unvoiced. *It is very common to hear such words mispronounced:*

senza ['sɛntsa]	**stanza** ['stantsa]	**danza** ['dantsa]
innanzi [in'nantsi]	**silenzio** [si'lɛntsjo]	**anzi** ['antsi]
costanza [ko'stantsa]	**speranza** [spe'rantsa]	
canzone [kan'tsoːne]	**menzogna** [men'tsoɲɲa]	

In a very few words *z* after *n* is voiced. Be sure that the affricate begins with a /d/ sound, since this does not happen with *-nz-* combinations in English:

pranzo ['prandzo]	**bronzo** ['brondzo]	**gonzo** ['gondzo]
ronzare [ron'dzaːre]	**bonzo** ['bondzo] (*Madama Butterfly*)	
donzella [don'dzɛlla]		

- When *z* follows *l*, it is unvoiced:

  alzare [al'tsaːre]   **calza** ['kaltsa]   **smilzo** ['zmiltso]

- When *z* follows *r*, it is usually unvoiced:

  forza ['fɔrtsa]   **terzo** ['tɛrtso]   **marzo** ['martso]

  but sometimes it is voiced:

  garzone [gar'dzoːne]   **orzo** ['ɔrdzo]   **barzeletta** [bardze'letta]

Double ZZ

Double *zz* can be voiced /ddz/ or unvoiced /tts/. The only helpful guidelines are that certain common suffixes, such as **-ezza** and **-azza** (**-azzo**), are unvoiced and that unvoiced double *zz* is much more common than voiced double *zz*.

Words with unvoiced zz (representative list)

nozze ['nɔttse]	**pezzo** ['pɛttso]	**vezzo** ['vettso]
prezzo ['prɛttso]	**pozzo** ['pottso]	**pazzo** ['pattso]
piazza ['pjattsa]	**razza** ['rattsa]	**palazzo** [pa'lattso]
fazzoletto [fattso'letto]	**terrazza** [ter'rattsa]	**bellezza** [bel'lettsa]
tristezza [tri'stettsa]	**ragazza(-o)** [ra'gattsa(-o)]	
aguzzare [agut'tsaːre]	**pizzicare** [pittsi'kaːre]	
ammazzare [ammat'tsaːre]		

Words with voiced zz (near-complete list)

mezzo ['mɛddzo] and derivatives **mezzogiorno, mezzanotte,
tramezzo, mezzano,** etc.   **lazzo** ['laddzo]

gazza ['gaddza]   **olezzo** [o'leddzo]

gazzetta [gad'dzetta]   **brezza** ['breddza]

bizzarro(-a) [bid'dzarro(-a)]   **azzurro(-a)** [ad'dzurro(-a)]

orizzonte [orid'dzonte]   **dozzina** [dod'dziːna]

azzimato [addzi'maːto]   **bizzeffe** [bid'dzɛffe]

Also all verbs whose infinitives end in **-izzare** have voiced double *zz*, as do their derivatives. This is the equivalent of English verbs ending in *-ize* (British *-ise*).

realizzare [realid'dzaːre]   **scandalizzato** [scandalid'dzaːto]

armonizzazione [armoniddzat'tsjoːne] **agonizzare** [agonid'dzaːre]

C and G

Each of these two consonant-letters has two sounds (excluding *sc*, discussed later), a "hard" sound and a "soft" sound. The hard sound of *c* is /k/. The hard sound of *g* is /g/.

The hard sound of each occurs when the letter is followed by the vowels *a*, *o*, or *u*, or by a consonant (excluding *-gli* and *-gn*, discussed later).

canto ['kanto]   **come** ['koːme]   **sicuro** [si'kuːro]   **credo** ['kreːdo]

che [ke]   **gatto** ['gatto]   **gusto** ['gusto]   **vago** ['vaːgo]

streghe ['streːge]   **negletto** [ne'gletto]

When hard *c* and hard *g* are doubled, the sounds are prolonged as usual:

accanto [ak'kanto]   **fiocco** ['fjɔkko]   **ricche** ['rikke]

aggrada [ag'graːda]   **veggo** ['veggo]   **fuggo** ['fuggo]

The soft sound of each of these consonant-letters is an affricate, or compound sound. Two IPA symbols are required. Soft *c* is /ʧ/ as in English *ch* (chair). Soft *g* is /ʤ/ as in English *j* (jump).

The soft sound of each occurs when followed by *i* or *e*.

città [tʃit'ta]   **duce** ['duːʧe]   **bacio** ['baːʧo]

giro ['ʤiːro]   **gente** ['ʤɛnte]   **giovane** ['ʤoːvane]

In the case of the vowel-letter *i*, it is important to recognize whether it has a vowel function or whether it is silent, serving only to soften the *c* or *g*. Usually if the *i* is followed by another vowel, it will be silent:

cielo [ˈʧɛːlo] **caccia** [ˈkattʃa] **baciare** [baˈʧaːre]
gioco [ˈʤɔːko] **giudizio** [ʤuˈdittsjo]

The exceptions are final, stressed *-ia*, *-ie*, and *-io*:

magia [maˈʤiːa] **bugie** [buˈʤiːe] **leggio** [ledˈʤiːo]

When soft *c* and soft *g* are doubled, the first sound of the compound is prolonged. In the case of soft *cc* the tongue holds the /t/ position, just as for double *tt*.

accidenti [attʃiˈdɛnti] **uccidere** [utˈʧiːdere]
eccellente [ettʃelˈlɛnte] **faccio** [ˈfatˈtʃo]

In the case of soft *gg* the tongue holds the /d/ position, just as for double *dd*.

leggero [ledˈdʒeːro] **passaggio** [pasˈsadʤo]
oggi [ˈɔdʤi] **aggiungere** [adˈʤundʒere]

The following table organizes the sounds and spellings of *c* and *g* in combination with all the vowel sounds (for convenience, *e* and *o* are given only one sound apiece). Note that the letter *i* functions to soften an otherwise hard sound, and that the letter *h* functions to harden an otherwise soft sound:

/ka/	**ca**	/ga/	**ga**	/tʃa/	**cia**	/ʤa/	**gia**
/ke/	**che**	/ge/	**ghe**	/tʃe/	**ce**	/ʤe/	**ge**
/ki/	**chi**	/gi/	**ghi**	/tʃi/	**ci**	/ʤi/	**gi**
/ko/	**co**	/go/	**go**	/tʃo/	**cio**	/ʤo/	**gio**
/ku/	**cu**	/gu/	**gu**	/tʃu/	**ciu**	/ʤu/	**giu**

H

The letter *h* is always silent in Italian. It can occur only in the following contexts:

- After *c* and *g* to indicate the hard sounds of those consonant-letters:

chiacchierare [kjakkjeˈraːre] **ghiaccio** [ˈɡjattʃo]

In interjections such as the following

ahi [aːi]   **ahimè** [aiˈmɛ]   **ohimè** [oiˈmɛ]

At the beginning of a word. Other than foreign words it occurs only in forms of the verb **avere**:

ho [ɔ]   **hai** [aːi]   **ha** [a]   **hanno** [ˈanno] (often apocopated to **han**)

When one of these four words is preceded by another sound in the phrase, the preceding vowel or consonant will connect through the *h* to the next vowel with no lift or break:

non ho [noˈnɔ]   **che hai?** [keˈaːi]   **egli ha** [eʎˈʎa]   **cos'han?** [kɔˈzan]

CONSONANT COMBINATIONS AND THEIR SOUNDS

SC

When s precedes hard *c*, it follows the voicing rules of *s* and is unvoiced.

scuola [ˈskwoːla]   **esco** [ˈɛsko]   **scherzo** [ˈskɛrtso]   **boschi** [ˈboski]

When *s* precedes soft *c* a new combination is formed. The result is the sound /ʃ/ as in English *sh*. When *sci* is followed by a vowel, the *i* is silent, with rare exceptions. Remember that when soft *sc* is intervocalic it is a long sound and doubled in IPA transcription:

scendere [ˈʃendere]   **lasciare** [laˈʃʃaːre]
sciogliere [ˈʃɔʎʎere]   **uscire** [uˈʃʃiːre]

The following table organizes the sounds of *sc* in combination with all the vowel sounds. Compare with the table on p. 29. Once again, *i* is the softening letter and *h* is the hardening letter.

/ska/ *sca*	(**scarpa, tasca**)	/ʃa/ *scia*	(**lascia, sciagurato**)
/ske/ *sche*	(**scherno, tasche**)	/ʃe/ *sce*	(**pesce, scegliere**)
/ski/ *schi*	(**Schicchi, tedeschi**)	/ʃi/ *sci*	(**uscire, scimunito**)
/sko/ *sco*	(**fresco, scoprire**)	/ʃo/ *scio*	(**liscio, sciocco**)
/sku/ *scu*	(**scultura, scudo**)	/ʃu/ *sciu*	(**asciugare, sciupato**)

GN

In Italian, as in French, the combination *gn* always results in the sound /ɲ/. The sound is the same as Spanish *ñ* as in **señor**. It is called a palatalized sound, because the center of the tongue makes contact with the hard palate in a position further back than the tip of the tongue for /n/. It is different from English /nj/ as in **onion**, where the tongue assumes a "normal" /n/ position, then pulls back from that position for /j/. The sound /nj/ is two movements of the tongue, while /ɲ/ is one.

Intervocalically this sound in Italian is always long, indicated in IPA by a doubling of the symbol. The preceding vowel is always short.

> **sogno** ['soɲɲo]   **signore** [siˈɲɲoːre]   **ogni** ['oɲɲi]

GLI

The combination *-gli-* results in the sound /ʎ/. It is a palatalized variant of /l/, just as /ɲ/ is a palatalized variant of /n/. Just as with /ɲ/, the center of the tongue makes contact with the hard palate further back than the tip for /l/. The similar sound in English is /lj/ as in **valiant**, but with the same differences explained above for /nj/.

This sound is long and is rendered in IPA as a double (except when initial). Vowels preceding it are always short.

When *-gli-* is medial in a word and is immediately followed by another vowel-letter, the *i* is silent.

> **meglio** ['mɛʎʎo]   **famiglia** [faˈmiʎʎa]
> **Guglielmo** [guˈʎʎɛlmo]   **orgoglio** [orˈgɔʎʎo]

Sometimes *-gli-* ends a word, in which case the *i* must function as a vowel:

> **gli** [ʎi]   **figli** ['fiʎʎi]   **egli** ['eʎʎi]

The word **gli** is the masculine plural article before words beginning with *s* plus a consonant (**gli studenti**), words beginning with *z* (**gli zii**), and words beginning with a vowel (**gli occhi**). In the latter case the *i* loses all vowel function, and the two words are pronounced as one: ['ʎɔkki]. The spelling **gl'occhi** is often encountered in literary Italian, which more accurately suggests the proper pronunciation. It is absolutely incorrect to pronounce the *i* when **gli** is followed by a vowel, whether in the same word or a different word.

> **gli uomini** ['ʎwoːmini]   **gli astri** ['ʎastri]   **quegli occhi** [kweʎˈʎɔkki]

The word **gli** also functions as the masculine indirect object pronoun (to him, to it). It can be combined with a direct object pronoun to form **glielo** ['ʎeːlo] and **gliela** ['ʎeːla]. The *i* is silent. (**Glielo darò**, I will give it to him).

Very occasionally, -*gli*- is pronounced /gli/. This is most commonly encountered in the word **negligenza** [negli'ʤɛntsa] and derivatives **negligente** [negli'ʤɛnte], **negletto** [ne'glɛtto].

NC NG NQ

In spoken Italian when *n* precedes hard *c*, hard *g*, or *q* within a word, it assumes the sound /ŋ/ as in English **sing** and **sink**. The consonant that follows retains its normal sound.

bianco ['bjaŋko]	**anche** ['aŋke]	**ancora** [aŋ'koːra]
sangue ['saŋgwe]	**inglese** [iŋ'gleːze]	**dunque** ['duŋkwe]

It is common practice among Italian singers sometimes to pronounce *n* with its normal sound /n/ in this context. For example, **dunque** is pronounced ['dunkwe]. This is particularly so in slower, more sustained passages, where the more forward position of /n/ is arguably more conducive than /ŋ/ to the maintaining of the legato line, although the practice is not necessarily recommended. This alternative pronunciation can lead to the insertion of a "shadow" vowel sound between the *n* and the following consonant (**dun-a-que**). This is most emphatically to be avoided, in spite of the fact that it is often heard from Italian singers.

Before soft *c* and soft *g*, *n* retains its normal sound.

incendio [in'tʃendjo]	**lanciare** [lan'tʃaːre]
ingegno [in'ʤeɲɲo]	**ingiuria** [in'ʤuːrja]

PS, QU

The combination *ps* occurs at the beginning of certain Greek-derived words. As in French and German, but not in English, the *p* is lightly pronounced:

psicologia [psikolo'ʤiːa]   **psichiatra** [psi'kjaːtra]

The combination *qu* is pronounced /kw/ as in English. The pronunciation of this combination is often confused with those of French and Spanish, which have no /w/ glide:

dunque ['duŋkwe]   **questione** [kwe'stjoːne]

SINGLE AND DOUBLE CONSONANTS IN ITALIAN

Clear execution of single and double consonants is one of the most important components of good Italian diction, spoken and sung. In no other language is the distinction so crucial.

A single consonant is always articulated as late and as quickly as possible, giving the preceding vowel maximum length. The importance of this point cannot be stressed enough. English-speaking singers often have difficulty in doing this consistently in all situations. Double consonants are always long, making the preceding vowel shorter than it would be before a single consonant.

It is well known that Italian words are often differentiated solely by single and double consonants. Learning such word pairs is perhaps the clearest way to understand this phenomenon:

note ['nɔːte] *notes*	**notte** ['nɔtte] *night*
sono ['soːno] *am, are*	**sonno** ['sonno] *sleep*
Luca ['luːka] *Luke*	**Lucca** ['lukka] city in Tuscany
caro ['kaːɾo] *dear*	**carro** ['karro] *wagon, cart*
fato ['faːto] *fate*	**fatto** ['fatto] *made, done*
casa ['kaːza] *house*	**cassa** ['kassa] *box, cashier*
m'ama ['maːma] *loves me*	**mamma** ['mamma] *mom*
fola ['fɔːla] *fairy tale*	**folla** ['folla] *crowd*
pena ['peːna] *grief*	**penna** ['penna] *feather*
bruto ['bruːto] *brute*	**brutto** ['brutto] *ugly*
ala ['aːla] *wing*	**alla** ['alla] *to the*
dita ['diːta] *fingers*	**ditta** ['ditta] *business, firm*

Many Italian words have various combinations of single and double consonants within them. They must be pronounced with appropriate length for all vowel and consonant patterns:

capello [ka'pɛllo]	**cappello** [kap'pɛllo]
adattare [adat'taːɾe]	**addiritura** [addiɾi'tuːɾa]
affogare [affo'gaːɾe]	**affollare** [affol'laːɾe]
correre ['korreɾe]	**correte** [kor'reːte]
corretto [kor'retto]	**chitarra** [ki'tarra]
barattolo [ba'rattolo]	**barricata** [barri'kaːta]

CHARACTERISTICS OF DOUBLE CONSONANTS

While there are many descriptive categories for consonants (plosive, fricative, etc.), the following is sufficient for understanding proper execution of double consonants:

1. Consonants are either *stop* or *continuing*.
2. Consonants are either *voiced* or *unvoiced*.

The terms "stop" and "continuing" refer to air flow. Stop consonants require a momentary interruption of air flow by the tongue or lips; continuing consonants retain continuous air flow from the preceding vowel.

Stop consonant sounds:

/b/, /d/, /k/, /g/, /p/, /t/

Continuing consonant sounds:

/f/, /l/, /ʎ/, /m/, /n/, /ɲ/, /r/, /s/, /ʃ/, /v/

Certain sounds—/ŋ/, /z/—do not play a role in consonant doubling. /ʤ/ and /dz/ double the /d/ while /tʃ/ and /ts/ double the /t/.

"Voiced" and "unvoiced" refer to whether the vocal folds are vibrating as the consonant is being pronounced. Many consonant sounds can be paired with another as two versions of the same sound, the only difference being that one is voiced and one is unvoiced:

Voiced:	/b/	/d/	/g/	/v/	/z/	/ʤ/	/dz/
Unvoiced:	/p/	/t/	/k/	/f/	/s/	/tʃ/	/ts/

The four unpaired consonants, all voiced, are /l/, /m/, /n/, and /r/ (/ʎ/ is a variation of /l/, and /ɲ/ is a variation of /n/). These are the same four consonants encountered previously as the ones that can end syllables and apocopated words in Italian (the *lemoners*).

Because double consonants are lengthened, the singer must be particularly aware of the appropriate characteristics of the consonant. Some difficulty of execution may at first be encountered. For instance, the singer unused to articulating a double *tt* as in **fatto** is often initially uncomfortable with the length of time the air is not moving and the vocal folds are not vibrating, since these traits seem antithetical to singing. With stop double consonants, moreover, the release must not be accomplished by forcing the air. Double consonants are not more forceful than single consonants, just longer. The student must learn that these characteristics are just as important to good Italian as anything relating to vowels.

Here is a summary of all Italian double consonants grouped by their particular characteristics:

Unvoiced Stop

/kk/	spelled *cc*	**peccato** [pek'kaːto]
	spelled *cq*	**acqua** ['akkwa]
	spelled *qq* (rare)	**soqquadro** [sok'kwaːdro]
/pp/		**troppo** ['trɔppo]
/tt/	spelled *tt*	**letto** ['letto]
	spelled *cc* /tʃ/	**caccia** ['kattʃa]
	spelled *zz* /tts/	**carezza** [ka'rettsa]

Unvoiced Continuing

/ff/	**affanno** [af'fanno]
/ss/	**passato** [pas'saːto]
/ʃʃ/	**uscire** [uʃ'ʃiːre]

Voiced Stop

/bb/		**ubbidire** [ubbi'diːre]
/dd/	spelled *dd*	**freddo** ['freddo]
	spelled *gg* /ddʒ/	**peggio** ['pɛddʒo]
	spelled *zz* /ddz/	**mezzo** ['mɛddzo]
[gg]		**agguato** [ag'gwaːto]

Voiced Continuing

/ll/	**uccello** [ut'tʃello]
/ʎʎ/	**foglio** ['fɔʎʎo]
/mm/	**dimmi** ['dimmi]
/nn/	**sonno** ['sonno]
/ɲɲ/	**sogno** ['soɲɲo]
/rr/	**terra** ['tɛrra]
/vv/	**davvero** [dav'veːro]

MORE ABOUT VOWELS

Open and Closed *e* and *o*, Continued

Because of the complexity of determining whether *e* is to be pronounced /e/ or /ɛ/, and whether *o* is to be pronounced /o/ or /ɔ/ in Italian, diction texts have had to devote a considerable amount of space to this subject. This emphasis can give the impression that it is perhaps the most important aspect of Italian diction. While it is certainly important, other aspects of Italian are more fundamental (for example, the purity of vowel sounds and appropriate articulation of single and double consonants) and should be perfected before a great deal of time is spent learning the intricacies of open and closed *e* and *o*. For this reason, a detailed analysis of when stressed *e* and *o* are open or closed is relegated to the appendix of this chapter.

Stressed versus Unstressed Syllables

In spoken Italian, the open pronunciation of the vowel-letters *e* and *o* occurs in the *stressed* syllable only, and then only sometimes:

> **bene** ['bɛːne] (open *e*) but **bere** ['beːre] (closed *e*)
> **posta** ['pɔsta] (open *o*) but **posto** ['posto] (closed *o*)

All *unstressed* *e*'s and *o*'s are therefore considered closed (/e/ and /o/):

> **ridere** ['riːdere]   **ridono** ['riːdono]

As a result, it is not possible for a simple word to have more than one open *e* or *o*. Compound words (not very common in Italian) could have more than one. It follows that /e/ and /o/ far outnumber /ɛ/ and /ɔ/.

Notice how vowel quality can change with a change of word stress:

> **bella** ['bɛlla]   **bellezza** [bel'lettsa]

The sung language is approached somewhat differently. The Italian tradition of *bel canto* requires the singer to find the vowel position that will yield the most beautiful sound. With *e* and *o*, the singer, in general and within reason, should favor whatever position on the spectrum of open to closed best suits that voice on a given pitch.

Various diction texts have dealt with this phenomenon in various ways. Some adopt the rules of spoken Italian without further explanation, while others recommend singing open /ɛ/ and /ɔ/ in some or all unstressed syllables.

It has been customary for some pedagogues to require every unstressed *e* and *o* to be sung open. This approach is problematic on two counts:

1. Singers often over-open the vowels in a way that distorts the language. For example, the word **vedere** would be transcribed in this approach as [vɛ'deːre]. If this word is sung on a single pitch in the

middle voice with this pronunciation, it sounds very un-Italian. It is more appropriate to form all the vowels the same, the relative openness or closedness of the vowel determined by what sounds best in that voice on a given pitch.

2. The special color of the open vowel in the stressed syllable is lost. The words **vogliono** ['vɔʎʎono], **possono** ['pɔssono], and **muovono** ['mwɔːvono] all have open /ɔ/ in the first, stressed syllable. If one sings these words on a single pitch in the middle voice following the recommendation to open the unstressed o's as well, the vowel color of the stressed syllable loses its special quality.

A suitable approach is to treat IPA transcription of the sung language the same as that of the spoken language. In singing, however, it must be understood that *Italian closed* e *and closed* o *are not as closed as their counterparts in French and German.* The practical application of this difference for the singer is that, while French and German closed *e* and closed *o* are very near to the position of /i/ and /u/ respectively, Italian closed *e* and *o* are not. The open and closed positions of these vowels in Italian are very near to each other. Just as it is incorrect to overly open vowel sounds, it is also incorrect to overly close them. Furthermore, vocal considerations necessarily play a role. With any vowel, the singer may be called upon to make technical adjustments that may seem at odds with the strict application of the IPA symbol.

A further consideration is that the closed quality of a stressed *e* or *o* will subtly differ from that of an unstressed *e* or *o*. This is another fine point that the IPA cannot convey without resorting to a confusing array of symbols. The singer must be reasonably flexible in the vocal approach (though avoiding outright distortion) and not apply the "rules" too rigidly.

Another essential factor in all of this is the style of singing involved. In *recitativo secco* the distinction between open and closed will be greatest, since this style of singing is (or should be) very close to speech. The distinction will be less in *recitativo accompagnato*, and least in arias and other fully concerted music. In art song, one has to take into account the vocal requirements of the specific piece. An intimate, quiet song will likely more closely resemble speech, whereas a song requiring robust singing should be treated like an aria.

The thorny issue of determining when a stressed *e* or *o* is open or closed is one that takes much time to appreciate fully, but even then it is essential to have a reliable dictionary at hand. Basic patterns can (and should) be learned at the outset, but undue time should not be spent trying to memorize all the exceptions until more fundamental skills are perfected.

The appendix to this chapter provides a thorough presentation of open and closed stressed *e* and *o*. It is to be used as a reference source and for continued study as the student becomes more proficient with Italian.

AMBIGUOUS SPELLINGS: IS IT A VOWEL OR A GLIDE?

/iːo/ and /iːa/ vs. /jo/ and /ja/

The syllabification section earlier in this chapter explained that the letters *i* and *u* usually act as glides when followed by another vowel. Common exceptions occur with *i* when it is silent as a result of spelling rules, as in **sbaglio** [ˈzbaʎʎo] **giovane** [ˈʤoːvane], and **lasciare** [laʃˈʃaːre], and when *i* is part of a prefix, as in **riunione** [riuˈnjoːne]. The letter *u* is sometimes considered a vowel rather than a glide in words such as **duetto** [duˈetto] and **tenue** [ˈtɛːnue].

The most problematic situation in this regard is when *a polysyllabic word ends in* i *plus another vowel*. In such cases the *i* is sometimes a vowel, sometimes a glide (or silent), depending on the syllabic stress of the word:

Maria [maˈriːa]	but	**Mario** [ˈmaːrjo]
malia [maˈliːa]	but	**celia** [ˈʧɛːlja]
leggio [ledˈʤiːo]	but	**peggio** [ˈpɛddʒo]
fruscio [fruʃˈʃiːo]	but	**guscio** [ˈguʃʃo]
magia [maˈʤiːa]	but	**magio** [ˈmaːdʒo]
mania [maˈniːa]	but	**smania** [zmaːnja]
profezia [profetˈtsiːa]	but	**propizia** [proˈpittsja]
bugia [buˈʤiːa]	but	**uggia** [ˈuddʒa]
mormorio [mormoˈriːo]	but	**dormitorio** [dormiˈtɔːrjo]
armonia [armoˈniːa]	but	**cerimonia** [ʧeriˈmɔːnja]

When the *i* is a vowel, it sometimes has an accent. This makes matters clear, but the practice is unfortunately not consistent:

Lucìa or **Lucia** [luˈʧiːa]   **follìa** or **follia** [folˈliːa]

When the *i* is a glide, sometimes the vowel in the *preceding* syllable is spelled with an accent, but this situation is encountered even less often:

ària or **aria** [ˈaːrja]   **tragèdia** or **tragedia** [traˈʤeːdja]

Musical settings will usually make the glide/vowel question clear. Nevertheless a reliable dictionary is essential for reference.

A few Italian words have the unusual formation of /w/ plus /j/ plus vowel. All are in the same syllable:

seguiamo [seˈgwjaːmo]   **quieto** [ˈkwjeːto]

Problematic Verb Forms

In this context, it is important to know and recognize certain verb forms, notably the present subjunctive forms **sia** [siːa] and **siano** [ˈsiːano] from the verb **essere**. The second person plural form has the glide, **siate** [ˈsjaːte]. *These forms are commonly encountered* and are generally not found as separate entries in dictionaries. **Siano** may be apocopated to **sian** [siːan], and it may be found in an antiquated literary form **sieno** [ˈsiːeno], sometimes apocopated to **sien** [siːen]. The following are a few examples from the literature:

quali al trono *sian* compagni
Arbace's aria *Se il tuo duol* from *Idomeneo*.

***siate* per me faci ferali**
Giulietta's recitative *Eccomi* from *I Capuleti ed i Montecchi*.

dar speme a tutti, *sien* belli o brutti
Despina's aria *In uomini* from *Così fan tutte*.

***sien* dolci o ruvidi**
Isabella's aria *Cruda sorte* from *L'italiana in Algeri*.

In addition, singers should be familiar with certain literary verb forms that are not used in the modern language, and therefore not found in dictionaries or modern Italian grammar texts, but are frequently encountered in opera libretti and other vocal texts. The most common of these are antiquated forms of the conditional tense. These forms follow the /iːa/ pattern and are alternatives to the more standard conditional forms:

saria [saˈriːa] instead of **sarebbe**
sariano [saˈriːano] (also **sarieno**) instead of **sarebbero**
potria [poˈtriːa] instead of **potrebbe**
potriano [poˈtriːano] instead of **potrebbero**
avria [aˈvriːa] instead of **avrebbe**
avriano [aˈvriːano] instead of **avrebbero**

The longer forms are subject to apocopation:

> **sarian, potrian, avrian**

Examples from the repertoire:

> *saria* **per me sventura**
> Violetta's recitative *È strano* from *La traviata*.

> **verso noi** *sarian* **buffoni**
> the aria *Rivolgete a lui lo sguardo* originally in *Così fan tutte*.

> *potria* **novel rigore**
> Amina's aria *Ah! non credea* from *La sonnambula*.

> **Se men vado, si** *potria* **qualche cosa sospettar**
> Quartet from *Don Giovanni*, act 1.

> **chi creduto l'***avria*?
> Figaro's recitative *Tutto è disposto* from *Le nozze di Figaro*.

> **non** *avria* **più bel contento**
> *Vanne o rosa fortunata,* song by Bellini.

> **tutti colmi** *sarieno* **e traboccanti**
> Orfeo's aria *Rosa del ciel* from *Orfeo* (Monteverdi).

Occasionally this antiquated conditional form is found with other verbs:

> **Non** *volgeria* **il pensier**
> Norina's aria *So anch'io la virtù magica* from *Don Pasquale*.

> **Ei che** *vorria* **dell'anima**
> The Duke's aria *Parmi veder le lagrime* from *Rigoletto*.

Another situation that results in final /iːa/ diphthongs is the literary elimination of the letter *v* in the imperfect tense of **-ire** verbs:

> . . . *colpia* (colpiva) **la fonte un pallido raggio** . . .
> *Regnava nel silenzio* from *Lucia di Lammermoor*.

Ella *sentia* (sentiva), **quell'angelo**
Rigoletto's aria *Deh non parlare al misero.*

Dormia (dormiva) **presso la cuna**
Ferrando, first scene of *Il trovatore.*

. . . e l'onor mio *tradia* (tradiva)
Radamès, *Aïda,* Judgment Scene.

. . . poi mi *sfuggia* (sfuggiva)
Alfredo, *La traviata,* act 3.

Double Vowel-Letters

Occasionally doubled vowel-letters occur in Italian. In musical settings they are usually found on two or more notes, sometimes on one. Normally the result is a continuous single vowel sound:

Non hai tu in Menfi desiderii, speranze?—*Aïda,* act 1

Ti udii! . . . tu menti!—*La Gioconda,* act 1

Sii maledetto—*Rigoletto,* act 1

Sii certa, o cara—*Così fan tutte,* act 1

D'amor sull'ali rosee—Leonora's aria, *Il trovatore*

The word **dee** may either be the shortened form of **deve** ['dɛːve]:

. . . dee volar—*Sempre libera* from *La traviata*

. . . viver dee o morire?—*Rigoletto,* final scene

or the plural of **dea** [dɛːa]:

Queste chiamate dee—Figaro's aria *Aprite un po'*

In these examples, and this one from *Aïda:*

. . . dell'Egizie coorti   [koˈɔrti]—*Ritorna vincitor* from *Aïda*

the adjacent vowels are /ɛe/ and /oɔ/ respectively. The singer should make only the slightest change in differentiating the vowels.

PHRASAL DOUBLING IN ITALIAN

In Italian a consonant at the beginning of a word may be pronounced as if it were a double in certain circumstances when the preceding word ends in a vowel. This phenomenon is commonly pointed out by Italian phoneticians (**raddoppiamento sintattico** in Italian) and is called *syntactic doubling*, or *phrasal doubling*. It is commonly heard in spoken Italian and is an important component of expressive singing of Italian. It can occur in the following situations:

- After most monosyllabic words:
  Interjections—**ah! oh! o! deh!**
  Prepositions—**a, da, fra, su, tra** (but not **di**)
  Conjunctions—**che, e, ma, nè, o, se**
  Adverbs—**che, già, giù, là, lì, più, qua, qui, sì**
  Disjunctive (stressed) pronouns—**chi, che, me, sè, te, tu**
  Monosyllabic verb forms—**dà, do, è, fa, fu, ha, ho, può, sa, so, sta, sto, va, vo**
  Other miscellaneous words—**no, re, tre**
- After a polysyllabic word ending in a final stressed vowel (e.g., **perché, pietà, ahimè**), which includes many verb forms (**sarà, dirò, andrà**).
- After the following two-syllable words: **come, contra, dove** (**ove**), **qualche**, and **sopra** (**sovra**).

Phrasal doubling does *not* occur after articles (**la, le, lo, gli, i**) or conjunctive pronouns (**ci, la, le, lo, li, mi, ti, si, vi, gli, ne**), which are considered unstressed.

The easiest way to understand the difference between stressed and unstressed pronouns is that a stressed pronoun form follows prepositions: **a te, da me**. The unstressed form is used with verbs: **ti vedo, mi vede**. Notice that the pronoun following the preposition takes the stress, whereas the one preceding the verb loses stress. The word **che** has several different functions, but it can also be the object of a preposition, as can **chi**.

Notice that monosyllabic words with diphthongs (**lei, noi, voi, sei, hai**, etc.) or words with stressed final diphthongs (**avrai, sarei**) do not cause phrasal doubling. The syllable causing the doubling may have one vowel only, or an initial silent *i* as in **già** or **giù**, or a glide as in **più, può**, or **qui**. That is why **tu** is the only nominative form pronoun that causes doubling.

Notice also the words that differ in spelling only by an accent mark: **là, lì, sì**, and **nè** can cause doubling, but **la, li, si**, and **ne** cannot. However **dà, è, sè** and **da, e, se** all may cause doubling. Doubling occurs only if the consonant in question is a single consonant. A word beginning with a consonant cluster is not subject to phrasal doubling.

Phrasal doubling can clearly be seen in some words whose spellings have changed to reflect it:

chissà from **chi sa**	**giammai** from **già mai**
sissignore from **sì signore**	**dammi** from **da mi**
davvero from **da vero**	**ebbene** from **e bene**

In older Italian and in some relatively modern poetic Italian, one encounters spellings without the double consonants that are found in modern Italian spelling: **de la** for **della**, **su la** for **sulla**. Because of the phenomenon of phrasal doubling, these combinations should be pronounced as doubles no matter what the spelling.

La serenata—Tosti

E'l	ven-to	**su**	**la**	fron	da
[el	'ven to	'su	lla	'fron	da]

Here are some examples of possible phrasal doubling from the repertoire:

ma poi, Masetto mio . . . [mappɔːi]
Zerlina's recitative before *Batti, batti* (*Don Giovanni*).

Perché mai se in pianti e in pene . . . [per'kemmaːi]
per me tutto si cangiò   [per met'tutto]
Countess's aria *Dove sono* (*Le nozze di Figaro*).

A Londra, è vero? [al'londra ɛv'veːro]
Figaro's recitative before *Se vuol ballare* (*Le nozze di Figaro*).

Voi sapete quel che fa. [keffa]
last line of Leporello's "catalogue" aria (*Don Giovanni*).

piegò il ginocchio e disse [ed'disse]
recitative before Norina's aria (*Don Pasquale*).

è bello [ɛb'bɛllo] . . .
ma per buttarmi [mapper] . . .
o Dio [od'diːo]
all from *O mio babbino caro* (*Gianni Schichhi*)

Rodolfo's aria from *La bohème* has numerous examples of possible phrasal doubling, as well as numerous examples of when it is not allowed. **Che gelida** . . . **che giova** . . . **ma per** . . . **e come** . . . **e per** . . . **ho milionaria** . . . are all situations in which phrasal doubling may be applied. On the other hand, **la luna** . . . **le dirò** . . . **vi piaccia** do not allow for phrasal doubling, because the first word is either an unstressed pronoun or an article.

Although phrasal doubling is potentially a strong expressive device in singing, the moderately experienced singer should treat it with caution. Like vocalic harmonization in French, it may be considered an option rather than a necessity.

It is also possible for a literal phrasal doubling to occur, that is, a word ends in a consonant and the next word begins with the same consonant (this is, of course, possible only with *l*, *m*, *n*, and *r*).

> **del tuo consorte al lato** [alˈlaːto]
> from *Fra poco a me ricovero* (*Lucia di Lammermoor*)

ARTICULATING ITALIAN DOUBLE CONSONANTS IN SINGING

In musical settings, exact vowel length is of course determined largely by the length of the note as well as by what consonants follow it. A long note will always have a long vowel, but if it is followed by a double consonant, the vowel will be shortened at the end of the note. A short note involving a double consonant will be approximately half vowel and half consonant.

The following excerpt from *Don Giovanni* is notated in the score thus:

Bat - ti   bat - ti,o   bel   Ma - set — to

Here is the rhythm rewritten to illustrate how the double *tt*'s should be articulated, stopping the consonants on the tied notes as indicated:

Bat — ti   bat - ti,o bel   Ma - set — to

As an example of a double consonant at the end of a long note, this excerpt from Donaudy's song *Vaghissima sembianza* is notated:

v'ha   ri - trat - - ta

The double *tt* at the end of the long note should be executed like this (occurring on the final tied note):

v'ha ri - tra - t - ta

While there is a certain artificiality in placing the double consonant in a precise rhythm, it is an excellent means by which the inexperienced singer can get a sense of how to execute double consonants. After the skill is developed, the crutch can be abandoned.

SINGING CONSONANT CLUSTERS

When /l/, /m/, /n/, /ŋ/, and /r/ begin a consonant cluster, those sounds are lengthened, rather like double consonants. Use of the colon /:/ or doubling the IPA symbol in these cases would seem logical, but it is not standard. Remember that the preceding vowel is short, and the subsequent consonant (part of the same syllable) is arrived at rather quickly.

colpa [ˈkolpa]	**tempo** [ˈtɛmpo]	**donde** [ˈdonde]
sangue [ˈsaŋgwe]	**porta** [ˈpɔrta]	

Failure to pronounce these sounds with enough vocal resonance, enough forward placement of the tongue, or simply enough energy is very common among singers inexperienced with Italian. The initial sound of the cluster is therefore muffled or lost altogether, compromising clarity of text and expressiveness of singing.

For English speakers this difficulty is particularly problematic when the cluster is preceded by /a/. The tendency to pronounce /a/ too darkly, combined with the tendency to position the tongue too far back for /n/ and especially /l/, often results in serious distortion in such words. The following words, for example, must be pronounced with the /a/ sound bright and the consonants forward:

caldo ['kaldo] **altro** ['altro]   **saltare** [sal'taːre]
santo ['santo] **quanto** ['kwanto]   **campo** ['kampo]

In musical settings, when a vowel followed by a consonant cluster is set to a long note, the first consonant of the cluster may be somewhat anticipated, both to imply a shorter vowel sound and to give expressive length to the consonant sound. This situation is similar to treatment of double consonants previously discussed; placing the sound in a precise rhythm may also be a useful exercise here. The extent to which this is done will vary according to context.

When *r* ends a syllable, it may be rolled or flipped, though in singing it is usually rolled (see the section dealing with *r*, pp. 23). Whether and how long to roll depend on the dramatic/emotional intensity of the moment.

While expressive lingering on the first sound of a consonant cluster is a device that can lend appropriate color to the Italian language, it should be treated with care. It should not be overdone.

MUSICAL SETTINGS OF ITALIAN DIPHTHONGS

In the section "Syllabification" it was explained that diphthongs are considered to be in one syllable. This effect can be seen in innumerable musical settings in which composers set first-vowel syllabic diphthongs on a single note:

Diphthongs can also be set to two or more notes, just as any syllable can be, but the frequent setting of diphthongs on one note is an indication that they are heard as a single syllable.

Composers virtually always separate second-vowel syllabic diphthongs over two notes:

Così fan tutte

So - **a** - ve sia il ven - to

although very occasionally they are set to one note:

Le nozze di Figaro

Don Ba - si - lio, mio **mae** - stro di can - to

Unstressed diphthongs are treated similarly to first-vowel syllabic diphthongs. Single-note setting is very common, but the two vowel sounds are also frequently separated over two notes:

Il trovatore

Oh Leo - no - ra!

Il trovatore

Le - **o** - no - raè mi - a!

Here are some representative examples of diphthongs set by composers to one note:

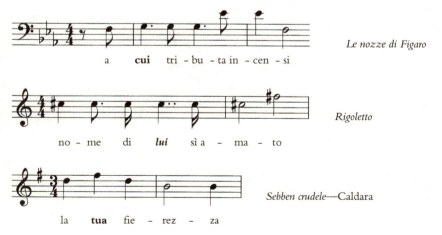

Le nozze di Figaro

a **cui** tri - bu - ta in - cen - si

Rigoletto

no - me di *lui* sì a - ma - to

Sebben crudele—Caldara

la **tua** fie - rez - za

Le nozze di Figaro

al   mio   duo – lo

Falstaff

(e innamo) – ran – do **l'aer** an – te – lu – ca – no

Lucia di Lammermoor

mi   col – pì   di   **sua**   vo – ce!

Il barbiere di Siviglia

Al – l'i – **dea**   di quel   me – tal – lo

Vanne, o rosa fortunate—Bellini

non   a – **vria**   più bel   con – ten – to

ITALIAN DIPHTHONGS: VOWEL DISTRIBUTION IN SINGING

Distribution of vowel sounds in first-vowel syllabic diphthongs set to one note usually results in one of two possibilities:

1. The syllabic vowel receives the majority of the note value, with the nonsyllabic vowel occurring late in the note:

O del mio dolce ardor —Gluck

L'au – ra   che   tu   re – spi – ri

Il trovatore

Il   ba – len   del **suo**   sor – ri – so

2. The two vowel sounds receive approximately equal time (although the syllabic vowel remains stressed). This is often the case in shorter note values:

Il trovatore

Sper - da il so - le d'un **suo** sguar - do

It is often suggested that the note on which the diphthong occurs should be divided into smaller note values to reflect the distribution of the vowel sounds over the note:

Amarilli—Caccini

A - ma - ril - li **è il mio a**-mo- (re)

Although this can be useful at an initial stage, it is extremely important that such a subdivision not be heard as separate notes. If a composer wishes to set a diphthong to more than one note, the composer will do so, and often does. If a composer chooses to set a diphthong to one note, it must sound as one; the transition must be very smooth. In the end, the vowel transition *should have no strongly rhythmic character.*

Slurs

When a first-vowel syllabic diphthong is slurred over two or three notes, the second vowel sound will fall on the final note, unless slur markings indicate otherwise:

Lucia di Lammermoor

La pie - ta - - de in **suo** fa - vo - re

Il trovatore

del **mio** cor

If there are four or more notes in a moderate to fast tempo, changing the vowel on the second to last note is advisable:

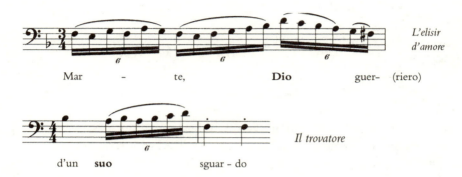

unless the second vowel is weak (*i* or *u*), in which case it should go on the final note:

but the composer may indicate vowel division with specific slur markings:

MUSICAL SETTINGS OF ITALIAN TRIPHTHONGS

Monosyllabic words with triphthongs are often set to one note. The first vowel-letter is a glide and the second is the syllabic vowel. The final vowel is very late and very short:

The final vowel may, of course, be given a separate note:

Lucia di Lammermoor

l'e – co   de'   **mie-i**   la – men – ti

SINGING PHRASAL DIPHTHONGS AND TRIPHTHONGS

Earlier in this chapter it was noted that a characteristic of Italian is the frequent occurrence of adjoining vowels between words, creating "phrasal" diphthongs and triphthongs When words within a phrase meet in this way in musical settings, the vowels connecting the words usually receive one note. To the inexperienced eye, it often looks as if there are not enough notes for the number of syllables:

I puritani

ripiombarlo agli a – bissi in e – terno

Non-Italian scores will sometimes indicate phrasal diphthongs with the symbol ‿ , but the practice is not consistent. Italian scores do not do this, assuming the (presumably Italian) reader will understand how to connect words in this way. The singer must learn to recognize phrasal diphthongs and triphthongs and determine to which note they are applied.

VOWEL DISTRIBUTION IN SINGING PHRASAL DIPHTHONGS

Singers often do not accurately execute the phrasal diphthong set to one note. Improper execution results in the addition of a note.

Don Giovanni

sta – rò   qui   **come a** – gnel – li – na

should be

sta – rò   qui   **come‿a**– gnel – li – na

not

sta – rò   qui   **come a**– gnel – li – na

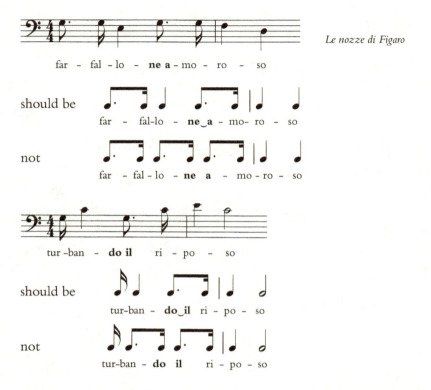

Le nozze di Figaro

far - fal - lo - **ne a** - mo - ro - so

should be

far - fal-lo - **ne_a** - mo- ro - so

not

far - fal - lo - **ne a** - mo - ro - so

tur -ban - **do il**   ri - po - so

should be

tur-ban - **do_il** ri - po - so

not

tur-ban - **do il**   ri - po - so

Once it is determined which note takes the phrasal diphthong, the singer must determine how much of the note value to give to each vowel sound. When the phrasal diphthong occurs on a short note value, the two vowel sounds are given approximately equal time, as with ordinary diphthongs.

Vaga luna
—Bellini

El - **la è** sol, si, el - **la è** sol nell' av - ve - nir.

Care selve—Handel

ven   -   **go in** trac - cia del   mio cor

It is when the note value is longer that it becomes necessary to determine the relative length of vowel sounds. The following guidelines are offered to help this process:

- Two of the same vowel-letter sound as one:

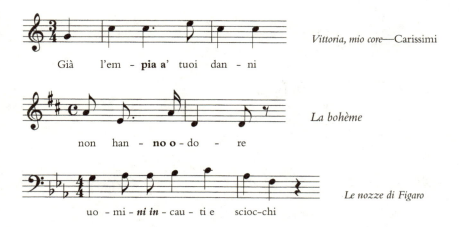

Vittoria, mio core—Carissimi

Già   l'em - **pia a'** tuoi   dan - ni

La bohème

non   han - **no o** - do   -   re

Le nozze di Figaro

uo - mi - **ni in** - cau - ti e   scioc-chi

- The most common phrasal diphthongs consist of two unstressed vowels. When this happens with combinations of the vowel-letters a, e, and o (the so-called strong vowels), the second will usually be longer, as if in anticipation of the stressed syllable of the second word. The phrasal diphthong must be pronounced as its own syllable:

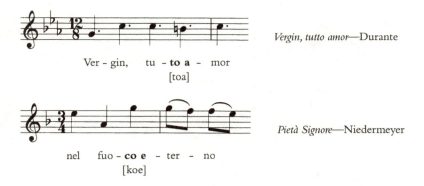

Vergin, tutto amor—Durante

Ver - gin,   tu - **to a** - mor
            [toa]

Pietà Signore—Niedermeyer

nel   fuo - **co e** - ter - no
        [koe]

The frequent elision of some of these unstressed phrasal diphthongs reflects the relatively greater importance of the second vowel:

quest'amplesso   **Donn'Elvira**

- When *i* and *u* are unstressed, they are usually short and weak in the phrasal diphthong, regardless of their position there:

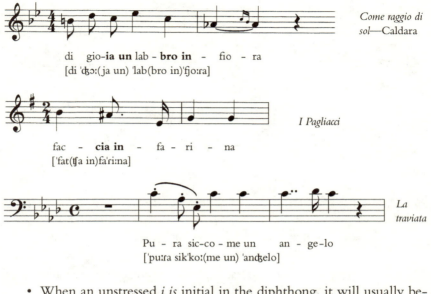

Come raggio di
sol—Caldara

di   gio-**ia un** lab - **bro in** -   fio - ra
[di ˈʤɔː(ja un) ˈlab(bro in)ˈfjoːra]

I Pagliacci

fac - **cia in** -   fa - ri - na
[ˈfat(ʧa in)faˈriːna]

La traviata

Pu - ra sic-co - me un   an - ge-lo
[ˈpuːra sikˈkoː(me un) ˈanʤelo]

- When an unstressed *i is* initial in the diphthong, it will usually become /j/, including before *u:*

Vaga luna— Bellini

Ed   in - spi - **ri, ed** in spi   **ri a**gli ele - men - ti
[edinˈspiː(ɾjed)inˈspiː(ɾj aʎ)ʎeleˈmenti]

Le nozze di Figaro

Vie - **ni o** - ve a - mo   -   re
[ˈvjeːn(j ˈoː)(ve a)ˈmoːɾe]

La bohème

ti   pren-**di un** al - tro a - man - te
[ti ˈpren(dj un) ˈaltr(o a)ˈmante]

- When an unstressed *i* after *c* or *g* is initial in the diphthong, it becomes virtually silent:

Le nozze di Figaro

Por -   **gi, a** - mor
[ˈpor(ʤ a)ˈmoːr]

Il barbiere di Siviglia

e   tu   non sor - **gi an** - co   -   ra
[e tu non 'sor(ʤ aŋ)'koːra]

Così fan tutte

far   che   can- -**gi af**- -fet - **to il**   cor
[faːr ke 'kan(ʤ af)'fɛt(to il) kɔːr]

- When a stressed vowel occurs before an unstressed vowel, the first, stressed vowel will take more of the note value. This situation is usually found with certain (not all) monosyllabic words containing *a*, *e*, or *o*, which are considered stressed in a phrasal diphthong:

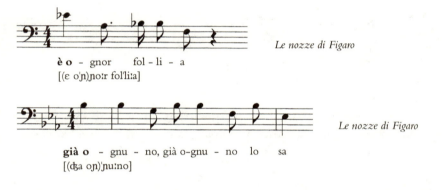

Le nozze di Figaro

è o - gnor   fol - li - a
[(ɛ oˈɲ)ɲoːr folˈliːa]

Le nozze di Figaro

già o - gnu - no, già o-gnu - no   lo   sa
[(ʤa oɲ)ˈɲuːno]

Sometimes special circumstances require exceptions to the above guidelines. In the following example, the word **tu** is stressed within the phrase and therefore the /u/ will be long in the phrasal diphthong:

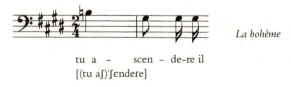

La bohème

tu a -   scen - de-re il
[(tu aʃ)ˈʃendere]

When the singer is executing a tenuto, a fermata, or even just stretching a phrase on a phrasal diphthong, it is often desirable to remain on the first vowel, even if the guidelines suggest otherwise: In the following two examples, remaining longer on the first vowel /a/ may be preferable:

La Bohème

Son   tran - quil - la e   lie - ta
[soːn traŋˈkwil(lae) ˈljeːta]

Il barbiere di Siviglia

a - man - te   che   fi - da e   co - stante
[ˈfiː(dae)koˈstante]

In addition, there are various situations in which the rigid application of the above guidelines does not necessarily yield the best result. For example, although /i/ is usually weak in a phrasal diphthong, in the following example it seems preferable to make /i/ stronger:

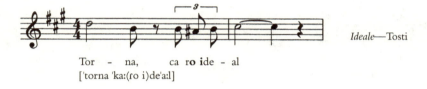

Ideale—Tosti

Tor - na,   ca ro ide - al
[ˈtorna ˈkaː(ɾo i)deˈaːl]

The following long-note phrasal diphthongs seem to work better if the first vowel is longer, instead of yielding quickly to the second vowel as suggested above:

Ombra mai fu—Handel

ca - ra ed   a - ma - bi - le
[ˈkaː(ɾa e)d aˈmaːbile]

Per la gloria d'adorarv, i—Bononcini

vo - glio a   - mar - vi
[ˈvɔʎ(ʎo a)ˈmaːrvi]

I Capuleti ed i Montecchi

O   quan - te vol - te,o   quan   - te
[o ˈkwante ˈvɔl(te o) ˈkwante]

In Donna Elvira's opening scene in *Don Giovanni*, two stressed monophthongs (the word **e** and the word **a**) occur on a single half note. Equal distribution would make the half note sound like two quarter notes. The best solution is to shift vowels fluidly either just before or just after the second beat:

Don Giovanni

e a　me　non tor-　-na an - cor
[(e a) me non 'tornaŋ'koːr]

While the guidelines for vowel distribution in phrasal diphthongs should be studied and understood, these exceptions demonstrate that there is considerable room for variance. Once again, there is often no single correct solution. The most important point to keep in mind is the *fluid change of vowels* so that the single note does not sound like two notes.

PATTERNS OF PHRASAL TRIPHTHONGS IN ITALIAN

When three vowel sounds join together between words, the result is a phrasal triphthong. The most common type of phrasal triphthong involves a stress on the second of the three vowels, resulting either when a diphthong follows an unstressed final vowel:

Aida

Mor - tal,　di - let - **to ai** Nu - mi
[morˈtaːl diˈlet(to aːi) ˈnuːmi]

Otello

Cre-do che Cas si**o ei** fos　se
[ˈkreːdo ke ˈkas(sjo eːi) ˈfosse]

or when the second of the three vowels is one of the stressed monophthongs (the words **a**, **è**, **e**, and **o** meaning *or*):

La forza del destino

La vi　-　**ta è in**- fer　-　no
[la ˈviː(ta ɛ in)ˈfɛrno]

La bohème

A te-**la o a** se - ta ri - ca-mo in ca sa e
[a 'teː(la o a) seːta]

La forza del destino

dan na **to a e** ter no   pian to
[dan'naː(to a e)'tɛrno 'pjanto]

Rarely, phrasal triphthongs can result from three unstressed vowels:

La bohème

fior   ch'io fac - **cio, ahi**-mè
[kiːo 'fat(tʃoai)'mɛ]

In such cases the stressed vowel (or, in the last example, the second vowel) of the phrasal triphthong receives most of the note value, although with short note values it is difficult to define vowel distribution exactly. Even if distribution is approximately equal, the correct stress must still be brought out.

Phrasal triphthongs can also result from first-vowel syllabic diphthongs followed by an unstressed vowel. The first vowel is stressed and, if the note value allows, lengthened:

Madama Butterfly

il **mio a**-mor
[il m(iːo a)'moːr]

La bohème

vo - **lea un** mu - si - ci - sta
[vo'(leːa un) muzi'tʃista]

It is interesting to observe that phrasal triphthongs are often set to very short note values, indicating their unstressed nature within the phrase.

Just as with phrasal diphthongs, there are times when these general guidelines for phrasal triphthongs need to be modified for particular musical settings.

Here is an example:

Le nozze di Figaro

fin - chè l'a-**ria è an**-cor bru - na
[fiŋˈke ˈlaː(rja ɛ aŋ)ˈkoːr]

The three vowels of the phrasal triphthong should probably be distributed equally (and smoothly!) over the eighth note. Attempting to give **è** more time can detract from the smooth transition between vowel sounds and thus the overall legato line.

This famous phrase from a well-known aria is a rare (perhaps unique) example of a phrasal triphthong of three unstressed vowels set to a long note:

Orfeo ed Euridice

Che fa - rò senza **Eu** - ri - di - ce
[ke faˈrɔ sɛn(tsa eu)riˈdiːtʃe]

The best solution here is to artificially lengthen the /a/ in order to set up the most natural pronunciation of the name "Euridice." Certainly lengthening the middle vowel does not yield a satisfactory result here.

Another famous aria has a particular setting of a phrasal triphthong:

Le nozze di Figaro

di **mia in** - fe - li - ci - ta
[di m(iːa in)felitʃiˈta]

Where does one place the /a/ of **mia** and the first /i/ of **infelicità**? One often hears the /a/ placed on the second quarter note beat and the /i/ on the tie into the third beat. If Mozart had intended this he would have written two quarter notes over the first two beats and not written the tie. The notation implies that the /i/ of **mia** should receive the entire duration of the half note plus tied eighth, followed by the /a/ of **mia** and the first /i/ of **infelicità** executed as a phrasal diphthong on the eighth note following the tie.

ITALIAN WORD UNDERLAY IN SCORES

In musical scores the placement of Italian words under notes is often highly misleading in terms of which syllables should be sung on which notes.

Here is an example from a score of *L'elisir d'emore*:

In o - gni   ar - te è pro - fes - sor

This is to be performed (and should be notated):

In   o - gni ar - te è   pro - fes - sor

Another example is from a score of *Le nozze di Figaro:*

non l'ha il Con - te   a - bo - li - to?

The double rhythmic notation is for the Italian original and the English translation. Although the second eighth note of the full measure is for the English translation only, the second syllable of Conte is placed directly beneath it, giving the impression that that syllable should be placed there. The proper notation of the Italian text with Mozart's notes is:

non l'ha il Con - te a - bo - li - to?

A similar example comes from a score of Così fan tutte:

(ma non) voglio a - ver   col-pa   se poi   nasce   un im-bro glio

A more appropriate notation is:

se poi   na - sce un im - bro - glio

The final allegro section of Fiordiligi's aria *Come scoglio* has a text under-lay question that warrants comment in the *Neue Mozart Ausgabe:*

Ri - spet   -   ta - te, a - ni me in - gra - te,
Ri - spet   -   ta - te,   a - ni me ingra - te,

Mozart's notation here is somewhat unclear, since the repeated pattern of two barred eighth notes could be interpreted more than one way. The first underlay indicated above is what is usually heard, but it results in a false word stress on the word **anime**. The second version corrects this problem and is recommended.

Misleading word underlay is common. The text must be spoken to find the proper linking of sounds, which then must be placed in the given rhythm, paying particular attention to slur markings provided by the composer.

OTHER POSSIBLE ASSIMILATIONS OF *n*

Assimilation of *n* means that orthographic (written) *n* assumes a sound dif-ferent from /n/. An example is the situation described previously where orthographic *n* is pronounced /ŋ/ as in **stanco**. Two further assimilations of *n* are possible in Italian:

- When *n* occurs before any of the three bilabial consonants *b*, *m*, and *p* (consonant sounds requiring lip closure), it may be pronounced

/m/. While this change is common in speech, it is much less common in singing, with its greater extension of sound over time. It is more likely to occur in *secco* recitative:

Il barbiere di Siviglia

Don Bar - to - lo,   Don Bar   -   to - lo!   Don Ba - si - lio
[dom'bartolo]   [domba'ziːljo]

though it may occur in lyric singing when note values are short. When singing is more sustained, such assimilation is less likely, though certainly possible. If one singer chooses to do [un bɛl di] another may choose to do [um bɛl di]; both are valid.

• A further possible context for assimilation of *n* is before /f/ and /v/ (labiodental sounds, requiring contact of upper teeth and lower lip). When *n* is assimilated before these sounds, the tongue does not come into contact with the hard palate, but the sound is replaced by a "hum" in the position of the /f/ or /v/ following. The IPA symbol for this situation is /ɱ/:

un fior [un fjoːr] or [uɱfjoːr]
invano [in'vaːno] or [iɱ'vaːno]

This text does not employ /ɱ/ for Italian. Although the singer certainly may use it when it is appropriate, I am of the opinion that this sound is not necessary for idiomatic Italian.

ITALIAN DICTIONARIES

It is essential to acquire an Italian dictionary, but dictionaries vary greatly in the information they provide. The student for whom the pronunciation of the language is a major concern will need more than simple word translation from a dictionary.

In recent years, several Italian–English dictionaries have been published in which standard IPA has been used to indicate pronunciation. Before that, few Italian or Italian–English dictionaries used the IPA, but most of the larger ones used some system to indicate pronunciation. Since Italian is phonetic (that is, spelling and sound are consistent) except for the letters *e*, *o*, *s*, and *z*, one needs only an indication for these letters. With the two vowels, unstressed *e*'s and *o*'s are considered closed and therefore have no special indication. When closed *e*'s and *o*'s fall in the stressed syllable, they usually have an acute accent, and open ones will have a grave accent. Alternative symbols may be employed, such as a dot (.) underneath a stressed closed vowel, and a cedilla (˛) under a stressed open vowel. Words with open vowels may be spelled with the IPA symbols /ɛ/ and /ɔ/.

With *s* and *z* the question is whether they are to be pronounced voiced or unvoiced. Usually the voiced sound is indicated by some symbol such as a dot underneath; otherwise the unvoiced pronunciation is assumed. Some indication of voicing/unvoicing is particularly essential for *z*, which is highly irregular.

Note that, although *n* before hard *c* (/k/) as in **anche** [ˈaŋke], hard *g* (/g/) as in **sangue** [ˈsaŋgwe], and *qu* (/kw/) as in **dunque** [ˈduŋkwe] assimilates to the sound /ŋ/ (as in English **finger**), most Italian dictionaries do not indicate assimilations of *n*, either by using the phonetic symbol /ŋ/ or by using any other symbols.

A good dictionary will also give appropriate verb forms if there is a change in vowel quality from the infinitive, such as in **prèndere (prési, préso)**.

Finally, word stress must be indicated. It may be given for all words, but at the very least the antepenult (third to last) syllable should be indicated (e.g., **u̲mile**, **de̲bole**). If no indication is given, the assumption is the penult (second to last) syllable stress, or, in the case of final accented vowels, final syllable stress.

SAMPLE TEXTS

Below are two sample texts with IPA transcription. The first is a simple song with relatively simple Italian; the second is more difficult. Possible phrasal doublings are given next to the appropriate line, as are a few comments about specific issues. Phrasal diphthongs with initial *i* are transcribed with /j/. Otherwise phrasal diphthongs are not given special treatment in IPA transcriptions but should be executed as discussed on pp. 51–57.

VAGA LUNA

Poem by anonymous
Music by Vincenzo Bellini

Vaga luna che inargenti
['vaːga 'luːna ke inar'dʒenti]

queste rive e questi fiori
['kweste 'riːve e 'kwesti 'fjoːri]

ed inspriri agli elementi
[ed in'spiːrj'aʎʎele'menti]

The musical setting repeats
text: [ed in'spiːrjed . . .]

Il linguaggio dell'amor;
[il liŋ'gwaddʒo della'moːr]

testimonio or sei tu sola
[testi'mɔːnjo ɔːr seːi tu 'soːla]   [tus'soːla]

del mio fervido desir
[del miːo 'fɛrvido de'ziːr]

ed a lei che m'innamora
[ed a leːi ke minna'moːra]   [kemminna'moːra]

conta i palpiti e i sospir.
['konta i 'palpitjeːi so'spiːr]

Phrasal triphthong /jeːi/ on one note.

Dille pur che lontananza
['dille puːr ke lonta'nantsa]   [kellonta'nantsa]

il mio duol non può lenir
[il miːo dwɔːl non pwɔ le'niːr]   [pwɔlle'niːr]

che se nutro una speranza
[ke se 'nuːtro uːna speː'rantsa]

[kessen'nuːtro] is possible but not to be
exaggerated.

ella è sol nell'avvenir.
['ella ɛ soːl nellavve'niːr]

The musical setting inserts **sì**:['ella ɛ ssoːl
si 'ella ɛ ssoːl]

Dille pur che giorno e sera
['dille puːr ke 'dʒorno e 'seːra]   [ked'dʒorno] [es'seːra]

conto l'ore del dolor
['konto 'loːre del do'loːr]

che una speme lusinghiera
[ke 'uːna 'speːme luziŋ'gjeːra]

The musical setting repeats **una speme,
una speme. Una** is often unstressed in
the phrase, so the length of /uː/ is lost.
The phrasal diphthong *eu* has equal
value for each vowel.

mi conforta nell'amor.
[mi kon'forta nell'a'moːr]

I PASTORI

Poem by Gabriele d'Annunzio
Music by Ildebrando Pizzetti

Settembre, andiamo. È tempo di migrare.
[set'tɛmbre an'djaːmo ɛ 'tɛmpo di mi'graːre]   [ɛt'tɛmpo]

Ora in terra d'Abruzzi i miei pastori
['oːra in 'tɛrra da'bruttsi i mjeːi pa'stoːri]

lascian gli stazzi e vanno verso il mare:
['laʃʃan ʎi 'stattsje 'vanno 'vɛrso il 'maːre]   [ev'vanno]

scendono all'Adriatico selvaggio   Note separation of *-ia-* in
['ʃendono alladri'aːtiko sel'vaddʒo]   **Adriatico.**

che verde è come i pascoli dei monti.   Phrasal diphthong *e-è*
[ke 'verde ɛ 'koːme i 'paskoli deːi 'monti]   combined with phrasal
                                                doublings: [kev'verdɛk'koːme]

Han bevuto profondamente ai fonti   Phrasal triphthong [eaːi] on
[an be'vuːto profonda'mente aːi 'fonti]   one note.

alpestri, che sapor d'acqua natìa   **fonti alpestri** set as
[al'pestri ke sa'poːr 'dakkwa na'tiːa]   ['fontjal'pestri]. [kes'sapoːr].
                                                Natìa set to only two notes.

rimanga nei cuori esuli a conforto,   **cuori esuli** not set as phrasal
[ri'maŋga neːi 'kwɔːri 'eːzulja kon'forto]   diphthong. [akkon'forto]

che lungo illuda la lor sete in via.   [kel'luŋgo]
[ke 'luŋgo il'luːda la loːr 'seːte in viːa]

Rinnovato hanno verga d'avellano.
[rinno'vaːto 'anno verga davel'laːno]

E vanno pel tratturo antico al piano,   [ev'vanno]
[e 'vanno pel trat'tuːro an'tiːko al 'pjaːno]

quasi per un erbal fiume silente,
['kwaːzi per un 'ɛrbal 'fjuːme si'lɛnte]

su le vestigia degli antichi padri.   Literary **su le** must be
['sulle ve'stiːdʒa deʎʎan'tiːki 'paːdri]   pronounced as **sulle.**

O voce di colui che primamente
[o 'voːtʃe di koˈluːi ke primaˈmente]   [ovˈvoːtʃe]

conosce il tremolar della marina!
[koˈnoʃʃe il tremoˈlaːr della maˈriːna]

Ora lungh'esso il litoral cammina   literal phrasal double
['oːra luŋˈgesso il litoˈraːl kamˈmiːna]   [illitoˈraːl]

la greggia. Senza mutamento è l'aria.
[la 'greddʒa 'sɛntsa mutaˈmento ɛ 'laːrja]   [ɛlˈlaːrja]

Il sole imbionda sì la viva lana
[il 'soːle imˈbjonda si la 'viːva 'laːna]   [silla]

che quasi dalla sabbia non divaria.
[ke 'kwaːzi 'dalla 'sabbja non diˈvaːrja]   [kekˈkwaːzi]

Isciacquìo, calpestìo, dolci romori.   Notice nouns ending with
[iʃʃakˈkwiːo kalpeˈstiːo 'doltʃi roˈmoːri]   –ìo diphthong. Pizzetti gives
                                                        only one note per diphthong.

Ah perchè non son io co' miei pastori?   [apperˈke]
[a perˈke non soːn iːo ko mjeːi paˈstoːri]   **son io** to be executed
                                              [soˈniːo]

APPENDIX

Guidelines for Determining Open and Closed e and o in the Stressed Syllable

This section is meant to be used as a reference and as an aid in recognizing patterns of Italian spelling and word structure. While every attempt has been made to be thorough, the scope of this appendix is necessarily limited. A reliable dictionary is essential.

Students frequently ask why Italian has open and closed sounds for these two vowel-letters. The answer lies to a large extent in the development of Italian from Latin. Classical Latin has long and short vowels, indicated by signs (‾ ˘) over the vowels, which affect pronunciation. Latin words spelled with ē or i became Italian words with /e/: **lex, lēgis** becomes **legge** ['leddʒe] (meaning *law*). Latin words spelled with ĕ became Italian words with /ɛ/: **lĕgo, lĕgere** becomes **leggo** ['lɛggo], **leggere** ['lɛddʒere] (meaning *read*). Latin words spelled with ō or u became Italian words with /o/: **curro, currere** becomes **corro** ['korro] **correre** ['korrere] (meaning *run*). Latin words spelled with ŏ became Italian words with /ɔ/: **cŏr, cŏrdis** becomes **cuore** ['kwɔːre] or **core** ['kɔːre] (meaning *heart*). Also some Italian words with /ɔ/ are derived from the diphthong -*au*- in Latin words: **oro** ['ɔːro] from **aurum**; **povero** ['pɔːvero] from **pauper**; **poco** ['pɔːko] from **pauci**, and so on.

Remember that spoken Italian assumes all unstressed *e*'s and *o*'s to be closed. See the discussion of these vowels in the main text for application to singing.

- Monosyllables (excluding diphthongs and apocopated words) are generally *closed*. All the following words have /e/ or /o/:

  e, me, te, se, sè, ce, ve, le, ne, nè, re, che, tre, per, o, lo, con, non, do

  also contractions:

  men, ten, sen, ven, del, pel, sel, tel, vel, col, nol, fo (faccio)

  Exceptions (open sound):

  è, tè (tea), **deh, piè** (truncation of **piede**), **est**—all have /ɛ/
  ciò, ho (avere), **oh, no, nord, pro, so** (sapere)—all have /ɔ/

  Usually **vo** (or **vo'**) is a truncation of **voglio** ['vɔʎʎo] and is pronounced [vɔ]. It sometimes is a contraction of **vado** and is pronounced [vo].

- Polysyllabic words, stressed *final* syllables.

  1. Final stressed *e* is usually *closed*.

     All combinations with -*chè*:

     perchè [per'ke], **poichè, finchè, benchè, fuorchè**, others.

     Words resulting from apocopated -*de*:

     mercè [mer'tʃe], **fè** (except **piè** [pjɛ], above)

     Past absolute (*passato remoto*) third person verb tense:

     credè [kre'de], **temè**, etc.

  2. A few words have stressed final *open* /ɛ/:

     caffè [kaf'fɛ], **ahimè, ohimè, Moisè**

3. Final stressed o occurs in two verb tenses and is always *open* /ɔ/.

Future tense, first person singular:

amerò [ame'rɔ], **andrò, sarò**, etc.

Past absolute (*passato remoto*) third person singular:

amò [a'mɔ], **andò, volò**, etc.

• Polysyllabic words, penultimate stressed, open-syllable *e* and *o*. (There are many recurring *endings* of this pattern [penultimate syllable stressed vowel preceding a single consonant] that are consistent in vowel quality. Some of these categories have many examples, others just a few):

1. Closed *e*:

    -*ele*: adjectives

    fedele [fe'deːle], **crudele**

    -*ese*: adjectives

    cortese [kor'teːze], **arnese, palese, inglese, francese**, many others.

    -*esa*: nouns derived from past participles

    attesa, difesa, offesa, presa, resa, sorpresa, spesa, tesa

    -*ere*: usually verb infinitive, but some can be nouns

    vedere [ve'deːre], **bere, temere, tenere, piacere, volere, potere**, many others.

    -*ete*: second person plural form, present tense, of all -*ere* infinitives

    vedete [ve'deːte]

2. Open *e:*

    -*ero*: nouns, adjectives

    mistero [mis'tɛːro], **impero, ministero, altero, sincero, intero, austero, leggero**

-teca: nouns

biblioteca [bibliotteːka], **enoteca, pinacoteca**

3. Closed *o:*

   -ore: nouns, adjectives

   amore [aˈmoːre], **dolore, favore, dottore, ardore, minore, superiore**, many others.

   -oso: adjectives

   amoroso [amoˈroːzo], **doloroso, pauroso, famoso, pericoloso**, many others. (Note: nouns have open *o*: **riposo** [riˈpɔːzo], **sposo** [spɔːzo])

   -one: nouns

   padrone [paˈdroːne], **canzone, farfallone, cannone**, including all words ending *-ione* **nazione** [naˈtsjoːne], **ragione** [raˈdʒoːne], many others.

4. Open *o:*

   -oro: nouns

   coro [ˈkɔːro], **oro, pomodoro, ristoro, tesoro, Lindoro, Alidoro, foro** (*forum*). Exceptions: **lavoro** [laˈvoːro], **foro** (*hole*) [ˈfoːro]

   -olo -ola: nouns

   parola [paˈrɔːla], **piazzola, pinolo, pistola, usignolo, fagiolo, figliolo, nocciolo** (-a) (sometimes this suffix is spelled *-uolo* after *gn* and *gli*).

Discounting *verb forms* (including nouns that are essentialy past participles), words with *adjacent vowel-letters*, words with the doubling combinations *gn, gli, sci,* or *sce* ending the stressed syllable, and words with the patterns listed above, the number of words with penultimate stressed *e* or *o* ending an open syllable is surprisingly limited. The following lists are not exhaustive but are quite extensive. The purpose of the lists is not to memorize each word, but to observe patterns of relative occurrence of open vs. closed (e.g., the frequent occurrence of open /ɔ/), and consistent patterns with certain letter combinations (e.g. two-syllable words beginning with stressed *mo-*, *pro-*, and *ro-* have an open vowel, and two-syllable words beginning with stressed *pe-* and *-ve* have a closed vowel). Other patterns can be gleaned from the lists.

- Simple words of *two syllables*, penultimate stressed open syllable, long *e* or *o*.

    1. Open *e*:

       bene ['bɛːne], breve, crema, eco, gelo, greco, greve, meta, metro, plebe, prego, prete, sede, speme, treno, remo, rene, retro, scena, scheda, schema, sede, speme, stele, teca, tema, tempra, tesi, tetro, treno, veto, zebra, zelo, zero, zeta

    2. Closed *e*:

       cena ['tʃeːna], cera, freno, lega, leva, mela, meno, mese, nero, neve, pelo, pena, pepe, pera, pesa (-o), rena, rete, sega, seme, seno, sera, seta, sete, strega, tela (-o), tesa, vela, velo, vena, vero, vetro

    3. Open *o*:

       brodo ['brɔːdo], cono, cosa, doge, dose, dote, droga, flora, frode, globo, lobo, loco, lode, loto, moda, modo, mola, mole, molo, mora, moro, moto, nodo, nolo, nota, noto, nove, oca, posa, prode, prora, prosa, prova, roba, roco, rogo, rosa, scrofa, soda, sodo, spola, sposa (-o), stola, strofa, toga, tomo, tono, topo, toro, trono, trota, zona

    4. Closed *o*:

       coda ['koːda], come, croce, dono, dopo, dove, foga, gola, loro, noce, nome, ora, otre, pomo, Roma, scolo, scopa, sole, solo, sopra, sprone, voce, voga, volo, voto

Words of *three syllables*, penultimate stressed and long *e* or *o*, discounting the categories named above, are listed below. As above, the lists are not exhaustive but are very thorough. Compounds derived from words above, such as *almeno*, *allora*, *ancora*, and *appena*, are not included. The small number of words points up the importance of the recurring endings in Italian word formation. The fairly even distribution among the four patterns (words with closed *o* are noticeably fewer) indicates that, in the absence of the most common suffixes, assumptions should not be made about whether a stressed *e* or *o* is open or closed. While some smaller patterns may emerge (*ema* yields an open sound), others do not: **profeta** (open) but **moneta** (closed); **completo** (open) but **segreto** (closed); **querela** (open) but **candela** (closed); **arena** (open) but **catena** (closed); **sincero** (open) but **intero** (closed).

1. Open *e*:

   ameno [aˈmɛːno], **arena, atleta, bufera, collega, completo, emblema, estremo, faretra, galera, miscela, osceno, patema, profeta, querela, sincero, sistema, supremo, tutela**

2. Closed *e*:

   aceto [aˈtʃeːto], **arredo, balena, baleno, bottega, candela, canneto, catena, cometa, ginepro, intero, moneta, parete** (wall), **pineta, tappeto, segreto, vigneto**

3. Open *o*:

   addome [adˈdɔːme], **approdo, alloro, aroma, aurora, congedo, custode, decoro, devoto, dimora, manovra, patrono** (-a), **precoce, pilota, rinnovo, riposo**

4. Closed *o*:

   atroce [aˈtroːtʃe], **corona, feroce, perdono, poltrona, veloce** (-*oce* would appear to be a consistent ending, except for **precoce** [preˈkɔːtʃe])

- Polysyllabic words, penultimate stressed, open-syllable *e* and *o*, continued. (When vowels precede the combinations *gn*, *gli*, *sce*, or *sci*, the syllable is technically open but the vowel sounds are short, since those patterns are pronounced as doubled sounds. The number of words with these patterns is not large, but many occur frequently):

  1. Before -*gn*, both stressed *e* and stressed *o* are *closed*:

     degno [ˈdeɲɲo], **legno, pegno, segno, regno, sdegno, convegno, ingegno, sostegno**

     sogno [ˈsoɲɲo], **ogni, bisogna, vergogna, zampogna**

  2. Before -*gli*, stressed *e* is usually *closed*:

     egli [ˈeʎʎi], **veglio, sveglia, teglia**
     Exception (open): **meglio** [ˈmɛʎʎo]

3. Before -*gli*, stressed *o* is usually *open*:

foglio ['fɔʎʎo], **foglia, doglia, soglio, voglio, orgoglio, scoglio**
Exceptions (closed): **moglie** ['moʎʎe], **germoglio**

4. Before -*sce*, -*sci* stressed *e* and *o* are usually *open*:

rovescio [ro'veʃʃo], **coscia, camoscio, angoscia** [aŋ'gɔʃʃa]
Exception: **pesce** ['peʃʃe].

Verb forms from **uscire** and **mescolare** have open /e/, but all forms of
crescere have closed /e/ and all forms of **conoscere** have closed /o/.

- The following three patterns involve *adjacent vowels*. Monosyllables
  with diphthongs are included where applicable. These patterns are
  valid for stressed *e* and *o* in both open and closed syllables, so examples of both are given. The result is usually an *open vowel sound*,
  although there are exceptions. The patterns are as follows:

  1. Stressed *e* or *o* *preceded* by another vowel-letter, usually a glide, is
     normally *open* /ɛ/ or /ɔ/.

     Examples with stressed *e*:

     cavaliere [kava'ljeːre], **dietro, guerra** ['gwɛrra], **ieri, inquieto**
     [iŋ'kwjeːto], **lieto, miei, maniera, mestiere, niente, pensiero,**
     pieno, many others, including verb forms from *venire, tenere, sedere,*
     dare: **viene, tiene, siede, diede**

     Non-glide examples:

     cielo ['tʃeːlo] **maestro** [ma'estro] **poeta** [po'eːta]

     Examples with stressed *o*:

     buono ['bwɔːno] **chiodo, cuoio** [kwɔːjo], **cuoco, cuore, fuoco,**
     fuori, idiota, pioggia, ruota, stuolo, tuono, uomo, viola, vuoto,
     uomo, many others, including the four triphthongs **puoi** ['pwɔːi],
     suoi, tuoi, and **vuoi**

     Special notes: The words **cuore** and **fuoco** are often seen with-
     out the glide, as **core** and **foco**. The *o* remains open. With the
     exception of **cuore**, words ending in a recurring suffix retain the
     vowel quality of the suffix, even if that suffix is preceded by a
     vowel. Therefore **fiore, maggiore; nazione, ragione, leone;**

noioso, **furioso**, and the many words like them have stressed closed *o*.

There are a few exceptions to this adjacent vowel pattern: all forms of **questo** and **quello** have closed *e*, as do **paese** and **saetta**. Words with stressed closed *o* include **biondo**, **giorno**, **piombo**, **trionfo**, and **Giorgio**.

2. Stressed *e* or *o* followed by another vowel-letter usually results in *open* /ɛ/ or /ɔ/.

Examples with stressed *e*:

dea [dɛːa], **ebreo** [eˈbrɛːo], **feudo** [ˈfɛːudo], **idea**, **lei**, **reo**, **sei**, **Orfeo** [orˈfɛːo] **Romeo** [roˈmɛːo], **trofeo**

Examples with stressed *o*:

boa [bɔːa], **boia** [ˈbɔːja], **Boito** [ˈbɔːito], **eroe** [eˈrɔːe], **gioia** [ˈʤɔːja], **noia**, **poi**, **eroico** [eˈrɔːiko]

Special notes: Literary Italian often uses contractions in the imperfect tense, eliminating the *v*: **aveva** becomes **avea**, **taceva** becomes **tacea**, **potevano** becomes **poteano** or **potean**. All retain the stressed closed *e* of the original form.

The contraction of **di** + **i** is **dei** [deːi] with closed sound as in **dei libri**. The word **devi** [ˈdɛːvi] ("you must") can be contracted to **dei**; and the plural of **dio** is **dei** [dɛːi], both with open sound. The *passato remoto* verb ending -*ei* is closed: **potei** [poˈteːi], though the conditional ending -*rei* is open: **potrei** [poˈtrɛːi].

There are few exceptions, but they include two common pronouns: **noi** and **voi** have closed *o*. The contraction of **con** + **i** is **coi** [koːi], retaining the closed *o* of **con**.

3. Stressed *e* or *o* followed by adjacent vowels in the syllable following (usually involving a glide) almost always results in open /ɛ/ or /ɔ/. This pattern is quite common.

Examples with stressed *e*:

commedia [komˈmɛːdja], **criterio** [kriˈtɛːrjo], **etereo**, **ferie**, **genio**,

inebrio, ingenua, medio, privilegio [priviˈlɛːdʒo], **sedia, serie, serio, tedio, tempio, tenue, tragedia,** many others.
Exceptions: **empio** [ˈempjo] **tregua** [ˈtreːgwa]

Examples with stressed *o*:

Antonio [anˈtɔːnjo], **demonio, elogio, gloria, memoria, negozio, odio, ovvio, storia, vittoria, proprio, marmoreo** [marˈmɔːreo], others.

• A large number of Italian words have antepenultimate syllabic stress. Stressed *e* and *o* in the antepenultimate syllable very often have an *open* vowel sound. The pattern applies in both open and closed syllables, therefore examples of both are given below. Because the number of such words is large, the number of exceptions to this pattern is greater. When such a word is encountered, a reliable dictionary must be consulted.

1. Examples with antepenultimate stressed open *e*:

    celebre [ˈtʃeːlebre], **credulo, edera, Elena, esule, fremito, gelido, gemito, immemore, medico, merito, perfido, secolo, tenebro, termine, Venere, veneto, zefiro** [ˈdzɛːfiɾo], many others.

    Some exceptions:

    vedova [ˈveːdova] **femmina** [ˈfemmina] **Cesare** [ˈtʃeːzaɾe] **cembalo** [ˈtʃembalo] **debole** [ˈdeːbole] **semplice** [ˈsemplitʃe]

    Antepenultimate stressed *e* occurs in a number of *-ere* verbs. Most have /ɛ/.

2. Verbal antepenultimate stressed open /ɛ/:

    accendere [atˈtʃɛndere], **cedere, chiedere, difendere, emergere, essere, fremere, leggere, offendere, pendere, perdere, premere, prendere, proteggere, reggere, rendere, riflettere, ripetere, spegnere, spendere, stendere, tendere**

3. Verbal antepenultimate stressed closed /e/:

    adempiere [aˈdempjeɾe], **credere, crescere, mettere, ricevere, scegliere, scendere, vendere**

There are many verbs that are derived from the above by the addition of prefixes: **dipendere, succedere, attendere, permettere, rincrescere,** etc. The patterns of the basic verb are maintained.

Note the large number of verbs with stressed *-en-*. When the infinitive has /ɛ/, so will all forms that retain the stressed *-en-*: **prendo** [ˈprɛndo], **difende** [diˈfɛnde], etc. However, all of these verbs have a past participle in *-eso* with *closed e*: **preso** [ˈpreːzo], **difeso** [diˈfeːzo], etc.

4. Examples with antepenultimate stressed open *o*:

> **anonimo** [aˈnoːnimo], **codice, comico, comodo, complice, docile, mobile, morbido, nobile, opera, ottimo, povero, popolo, solito,** others

Some exceptions (closed *o*):

> **compito** [ˈkompito], **giovane, logoro, ordine, polvere, porpora, ricovero, rondine**

Antepenultimate stressed *o* occurs in a number of *-ere* verbs. The majority have /ɔ/.

5. Verbal antepenultimate stressed open /ɔ/:

> **accorgersi** [akˈkɔrdʒersi], **cogliere, cuocere, mordere, muovere, nuocere, percuotere, piovere, porgere, risolvere, scuotere, togliere, torcere, volgere**

6. Verbal antepenultimate stressed closed /o/:

> **conoscere** [koˈnoʃʃere], **correre, fondere, nascondere (ascondere), rispondere, rodere, rompere, sorgere**

- Closed syllables: stressed *e* and *o* before double consonants. (Stressed *e* or *o* before a double consonant is sometimes open, sometimes closed. There are no reliable spelling patterns to indicate which sound is correct. Words must be learned individually, and a reliable dictionary is essential. There are a great many such words; here are just a few examples which juxtapose similar spellings with different vowel sounds):

bella ['bɛlla] stella ['stella]   donna ['dɔnna] sonno ['sonno]
sesso ['sɛsso] spesso ['spesso]   cotto ['kɔtto] rotto ['rotto]
pezzo ['pɛttso] vezzo ['vettso]   coppia ['kɔppja] doppio ['doppjo]
petto ['pɛtto] tetto ['tetto]   rocca ['rɔkka] bocca ['bokka]
ecco ['ɛkko] secco ['sekko]   folle ['fɔlle] folla ['folla]
Giuseppe [ʤu'zɛppe] ceppi ['ʧeppi]   nozze['nɔttse]pozzo ['pottso]

- Closed syllables: stressed *e* and *o* before consonant clusters with *l*, *m*, *n*, *r*, *s*:

  1. Stressed *el* + *cons* is infrequent:

     /ɛ/   belgo ['bɛlgo], delta, gelso, Guglielmo, pompelmo
     /e/   belva ['belva], felce, feltro, peltro, scelta (-o), selva, svelto

  2. Stressed *em* + *cons* is infrequent. It is always found -*emb*- or -*emp*-:

     /ɛ/   esempio [e'zɛmpjo], grembo, membro, sempre, tempo
     /e/   forms of adempiere [a'dempjere] (adempio etc.) cembalo, empio, forms of sembrare (sembro, etc.)

  3. Stressed *en* + *cons* is common and usually open:

     /ɛ/   accento [at'ʧɛnto], argento, benda, cento, centro, contento, dente, denso, gente, immenso, intenso, lente, lento, senso, senza, tremendo, vento, ventre, others.

  4. This pattern is found in some recurring endings:

     Adjective/noun ending -*ente*:

     cruente [kru'ɛnte], dolente, frequente, niente, parente, patente, presente, recente, tenente, many others.

     Gerund ending -*endo*: all -*ere* and -*ire* verbs:

     avendo [a'vɛndo], venendo, etc.

     Noun ending -*enza*:

     esistenza [ezi'stɛntsa], presenza, partenza, etc.

     Exceptions with /e/:

     dentro ['dentro], entro, mente, mento, mentre, trenta, venti (twenty)

Recurring endings with closed -*en*:

Noun ending –*mento*:

tormento, tradimento, elemento [ele'mento], **lamento**, etc.

Adverb ending -*mente*:

dolcemente [dolʧe'mente], **fieramente, lentamente**, etc.

Note particularly the difference between -*ente*, -*ento* (with /ɛ/) and -*mente*, -*mento* (with /e/). See also verbs listed under "verbal antepenultimate stressed *e*" above.

5. Stressed *er* + *cons* is common and almost always open:

/ɛ/   **aperto** [a'pɛrto], **Berta, certo, cervo, concerto, coperto, erba, eterno, governo, inerme, inferno, interno, lanterna, Minerva, perla, serto, servo, terme, terzo, verba, verso**

/e/   **cerchio** ['tʃerkjo], **fermo, per, verde, Verdi**

6. Stressed *es* + *cons* is common and usually open, with exceptions:

/ɛ/   **destra** ['dɛstra], **festa, finestra, foresta, funesto, gesto, lesto, mesto, orchestra, palestra, pesca** ['pɛska] (*peach*), **peste, presto, sesto, tempesta, testa, veste,** others. Also verb forms with stressed -*est*-: **attesto, detesta,** etc.

/e/   **bestia** ['bestja], **cespo, cesta, esca, fresco, questo, tedesco, pesca** ['peska] (*fishing*), **pesto,** the suffix -*esco* as in **donnesco** [don'nesko]

7. Stressed *ol* + *cons* is usually closed:

/o/   **colmo** ['kolmo], **colpa, colto** (cultured), **dolce, folto, golfo, molto, oltre, polpa, polvere, sepolcro, stolto, volgo, volpe, volto,** forms of **ascoltare** (ascolto, etc.)

/ɔ/   **soldi, volta** verbs: **colto** ['kɔlto], **tolto** (p.p. of *cogliere, togliere*), **risolvere** [ri'sɔlvere], **volgere**

8. Stressed *om* + *cons* is closed:

/o/   **bomba** ['bomba], **colomba, compito, ingombro, ombra, piomba, tomba, tromba, rompere**

9. Stressed *on* + *cons* is almost always closed:

/o/   **Alfonso** [al'fonso], **Alonso, biondo, bonzo, bronzo, con, conte, contro, donde, fondo, fronda, fronte, mondo, non, rondine, secondo, tondo, tronco**

/ɔ/   **conscio** ['kɔnʃo], **console** ['kɔnsole]

10. Stressed *or* + *cons* is about equally divided:

/o/   **bordo** ['bordo] **borgo, borsa, corto, corsa, dintorno, forma, forno, forse, giorno, intorno, ordine, orso, porpora, risorsa, sordo, sorso, torta** verb: **sorgere** (all forms)

/ɔ/   **corda** ['kɔrda], **comporto, consorte, corpo, corvo, forte, forza, morbido, morte, morso, porta, ricordo, scorno, sorte, torto** verbs: **mordere, porgere, torcere** (all forms)

11. Stressed *os* + *cons* is usually open:

/ɔ/   **arrosto** [ar'rɔsto] **bosco, costo** (-a), **nostro, oste, posta, rospo, sosta, Tosca, tosto, vostro**

/o/   **agosto** [a'gosto], **conoscere** (all forms), **fosco, mostro, posto**

Additional Suffixes and Verb Endings

The discussion above presented recurring suffixes and verb endings characterized by penultimate stress preceding a single consonant: *-ele, -esa, -ese, -ere, -ero, -ete, -teca, -olo, -one, ore, -oro, -oso*. A few others were also given. There are many additional recurring suffixes and verb endings characterized by double consonants, consonant clusters, diphthongs, or antepenultimate stress. Those involving stressed *e* or *o* are presented below.

• Suffixes with stressed closed /e/ in closed syllables:

-etta, -etto

These common diminutive suffixes always have closed /e/. They are often used with proper names:

Rigoletto [rigo'letto]   **Violetta** [vjo'letta]
Musetta [mu'zetta]   **Masetto** [ma'zetto]
caminetto [kami'netto]   **cuffietta** [kuf'fjetta]
balletto [bal'letto], many others.

Beware: some words end in nondiminutive -*etto*, with open /ɛ/:

affetto [afˈfɛtto]   **aspetto** [asˈpɛtto]   **diletto** [diˈlɛtto]
letto [ˈlɛtto]   **perfetto** [perˈfɛtto]
although nondiminutive **fretta** has /e/.

-*mente*, -*mento* (/e/) vs. -*ente*, -*ento* (/ɛ/)

lentamente [lentaˈmente]   **dolcemente** [doltʃeˈmente]
leggermente [leddʒerˈmente]   **portamento** [portaˈmento]
tradimento [tradiˈmento]   **tormento** [torˈmento]

But:

dolente [doˈlɛnte]   **sente** [ˈsɛnte]   **contento** [konˈtɛnto]
cento [ˈtʃɛnto]   **lento** [ˈlɛnto]

Other double consonant suffixes, and one *s*-cluster suffix:

-*essa*	**contessa** [konˈtessa]	**baronessa** [baroˈnessa]
-*ezza*	**bellezza** [belˈlettsa]	**fierezza** [fjeˈrettsa]
-*eccia*	**freccia** [ˈfrettʃa]	**breccia** [ˈbrettʃa]
-*eggio*	**pareggio** [paˈreddʒo]	**corteggio** [korˈteddʒo]
-*esco*	**donnesco** [donˈnesko]	**trecentesco** [trecenˈtesko]

Antepenultimate stressed suffixes (open syllable):

-*efice*	**carnefice** [karˈneːfitʃe]	**orefice** [oˈreːfitʃe]
-*evole*	**piacevole** [pjaˈtʃeːvole]	**colpevole** [kolˈpeːvole]

• Suffixes with *stressed open* /ɛ/ in closed syllables:

-*ello(a)*	**gemello** [dʒeˈmɛllo]	**damigella** [damiˈdʒɛlla]
		(but not **ella** [ˈella])
-*estre*	**silvestre** [silˈvɛstre]	**calpestre** [kalˈpɛstre]
-*enza*	**partenza** [parˈtɛntsa]	**confidenza** [konfiˈdɛntsa]

Antepenultimate stress (open syllable):

-*esimo*	**centesimo** [tʃenˈtɛːzimo]	**undicesimo** [undiˈtʃɛːzimo]

Recall that, as was discussed above, -*ele*, -*esa*, -*ese*, -*ere*, and -*ete* have closed /e/; -*ero* and -*teca* have open /ɛ/.

• Suffix with stressed open /ɔ/:

-otto	**vecchiotto** [vekˈkjɔtto]	**giovinotto** [ʤoviˈnɔtto]

Recall that, as was discussed above, *-one*, *-ore*, and *-oso* have closed /o/; *-oro* and *-olo* have open /ɔ/.

Note that the greater issue of verb stems is beyond the scope of this appendix. The stem is usually unstressed in the infinitive but stressed in some conjugated forms. If the stem vowel is an *e* or *o*, it may be open or closed when stressed: **gelare** [dʒeˈlaːre], **gelo** [ˈʤeːlo]; **seguire** [seˈgwiːre], **seguo** [ˈseːgwo]; and there are of course irregular forms: **potere** [poˈteːre], **posso** [ˈpɔsso]. Providing this information is one of the primary advantages of a large dictionary over a smaller one.

- Verb endings with stressed closed /e/:

-ei	**credei** [kreˈdeːi]	
	(*past absolute tense*), however conditional is *-rei* [. . . rɛːi]	
-emmo	**avemmo** [aˈvemmo]	**credemmo** [kreˈdemmo]
	(*past absolute*)	
	avremmo [aˈvremmo]	**crederemmo** [kredeˈremmo]
	(*conditional*)	
-esse	**avesse** [aˈvesse]	**credesse** [kreˈdesse]
	(*imperfect subjunctive*)	
-essi	**avessi** [aˈvessi]	**credessi** [kreˈdessi]
	(*imperfect subjunctive*)	
-esso(a)	**messo** [ˈmesso]	**permessa** [perˈmessa]
	(*past participle*)	
-esti	**avesti** [aˈvesti]	**credesti** [kredeˈresti]
	(*past absolute*)	
	avresti [aˈvresti]	**crederesti** [kredeˈresti]
	(*conditional*)	
-este	**aveste** [aˈveste]	**credeste** [kreˈdeste]
	(*past absolute*)	
	avreste [aˈvreste]	**credereste** [kredeˈreste]
	(*conditional*)	
-evano	**avevano** [aˈveːvano]	**credevano** [kreˈdeːvano]
	(*imperfect*)	
-erono	**crederono** [kreˈdeːrono]	
	(*past absolute*)	
-essero	**avessero** [aˈvessero]	**credessero** [kreˈdessero]
	(*imperf. subjunctive*)	
-essimo	**avessimo** [aˈvessimo]	**credessimo** [kreˈdessimo]
	(*imperf. subjunctive*)	

- Verb endings with stressed *open* /ε/:

-rei	**avrei** [aˈvrɛːi]	**crederei** [kredeˈrɛːi]
	(*conditional tense*)	
-ebbe	**avrebbe** [avˈrɛbbe]	**crederebbe** [kredeˈrɛbbe]
	(*conditional*)	
-ebbero	**avrebbero** [avˈrɛbbero]	**crederebbero** [kredeˈrɛbbero]
	(*conditional*)	
-endo	**avendo** [aˈvɛndo]	**credendo** [kreˈdɛndo]
	(*gerund*)	

Literary Italian has an alternative form for past absolute tense (*passato remoto*), first person singular for a few verbs: **credetti** [kreˈdɛtti] with open /ε/, instead of **credei** [kreˈdeːi] with closed /e/.

GERMAN DICTION

INTRODUCTION

German has a reputation as being a difficult language. This is true of the grammar, which is more complex than that of English and results in many more word inflections. The reputation for difficulty carries over into the pronunciation of the language, which is also often described as "guttural." Mastering certain sounds that do not occur in English may present some difficulty (more so is the sequencing of certain sounds in phrases), but the relationship between spelling and pronunciation is very logical and consistent (German is nearly as phonetic as Italian, and much more so than French and English). Of the two sounds that could be considered guttural, one (the uvular pronunciation of *r*) is not used in singing, and the other (the ach–Laut /x/) is very light and of short duration.

The sound patterns of German are much closer to English than are those of Italian and French. English is, after all, a Germanic language. Once the German sounds that do not occur in English are mastered, phrasal inflection tends to come more easily than for the Romance languages.

In order for one to achieve an intermediate level of proficiency with German diction, the following areas must be mastered:

1. An understanding of German word structure, which significantly affects the pronunciation of German, in particular vowel quality and length.
2. Proper pronunciation of the ich-Laut /ç/ and the ach-Laut /x/ and knowledge of when each is used.
3. Correct and consistent formation of the mixed vowels.
4. Correct and consistent formation of /e/ and /o/.
5. Proper sequencing and articulation of consecutive consonant sounds, within and between words.

This chapter makes reference to the two standard pronunciation books for German, Siebs and Duden. They are described more fully at the end of the chapter.

International Phonetic Alphabet Symbols for German

Vowels
/a/ /aː/ **M_ann, V_ater**
/e/ /eː/ **M_elodie, s_ehr**
/ɛ/ /ɛː/ **d_enn, Tr_äne**
/i/ /iː/ **Univ_ersit_ät, l_ie_gen**
/ɪ/ **b_in, inm_itten**
/o/ /oː/ **w_oran, S_ohn**
/ɔ/ **S_onne, tr_ocken**
/u/ /uː/ **J_uwel, B_uch**
/ʊ/ **M_utter, _Ungeduld**
/yː/ **B_ücher, El_ysium**
/ʏ/ **M_ütter, Gl_ück**
/øː/ **sch_ön, G_oethe**
/œ/ **pl_ötzlich, G_ötter**
/ə/ **geg_eb_en, Lieb_e**
/ɐ/ **Brud_er, nu_r, _Erde**

Diphthongs
/ae/ **m_ein, H_ain**
/ao/ **Fr_au, B_aum**
/ɔø/ **_euch, B_äume**

Glide
/j/ **_ja, _jetzt, Lil_ie**

Plosive Consonants
/b/ **_beben**
/p/ **_Pracht, _pfeife, a_b**
/d/ **_dadurch**
/t/ **_Teil, re_tten, Ba_d**
/g/ **_gegen _Gnade**
/k/ **_Knie, bli_cken, Tag**

Fricative Consonants
/v/ **_Wagen, Kla_vier**
/f/ **_von, _Philosoph**
/s/ **e_ssen, bi_s**
/ʃ/ **_spät, _Stern, ra_sch**
/z/ **_See, gewe_sen**
/h/ **_Hoheit**
/ç/ **i_ch, dur_ch, seli_g**
/x/ **a_ch, au_ch, do_ch**

Affricate Consonants
/ts/ **z**ehn, **C**ä**c**ilie
/tʃ/ **Deutsch**

Nasal Consonants
/n/ **N**acht, **n**e**nn**en
/m/ **m**ehr, i**mm**er
/ŋ/ si**ng**en, da**n**ken

Lateral Consonants
/l/ **L**icht, fü**ll**en

Vibrant Consonants
/r/ **r**ot, i**rr**en

Other Symbols
/ː/ long vowel sound
/'/ primary syllabic stress
/‚/ secondary stress
/ʔ/ glottal separation

THE *UMLAUT*

The *Umlaut* (¨) is the only diacritical mark used in German. The word can be translated roughly as "sound modification" and refers specifically to vowels. It occurs over the vowel-letters *a*, *o*, *u*, and the diphthong *au*, thereby changing their sounds:

- The letter *a* sounds as /a/ or /aː/
  but the letter *ä* sounds as /ɛ/ or /ɛː/.
- The letter *o* sounds as /ɔ/ or /oː/
  but the letter *ö* sounds as /œ/ or /øː/.
- The letter *u* sounds as /ʊ/ or /uː/
  but the letter *ü* sounds as /ʏ/ or /yː/.
- The diphthong *au* sounds as /ao/
  but the diphthong *äu* sounds as /ɔø/.

WORD ORIGIN: GERMANIC AND NON-GERMANIC

Over the centuries the German language has absorbed into its vocabulary a large number of words derived from Latin and Greek. Many such words are very common, such as **privat**, **Musik**, and **Familie**. The casual student of German is not necessarily aware of this fact until encountering a less common word, such as **benedeit**, in which word stress and vowel quality might seem confusing. The student must be aware of these two broad categories of words, Germanic and non-Germanic, and two important points concerning them:

- Patterns of word stress are different in non-Germanic words than they are in Germanic words.
- Patterns of determining vowel quality (open or closed) and vowel length (long or short) are different in non-Germanic words than they are in Germanic words.

The first part of this chapter will deal with patterns in words of Germanic origin. Patterns in non-Germanic words are referenced throughout the chapter but are presented fully beginning on p. 125.

GERMAN VOWELS AND VOWEL LENGTH

Most German vowel sounds are paired, open and closed, with each sound of the pair represented by the same vowel-letter. It is helpful to organize and discuss them this way:

Vowel-Letter	Closed Sound	Open Sound	Alternative Sound
i	/iː/ wider	/ɪ/ Winter	/j/ Nation
(ie)	/iː/ wieder	—	/jə/ Lilie
e	/eː/ sehen	/ɛ/ senden	/ə/ sehen
o	/oː/ Dom	/ɔ/ Dorn	
u	/uː/ rufen	/ʊ/ runden	
ü, y	/yː/ fühlen	/ʏ/ füllen	
ö	/øː/ König	/œ/ können	
a	—	/a/ sangen	
		/aː/ sagen	
ä	—	/ɛ/ Blätter	
		/ɛː/ Bläser	

This chart gives all German single vowel-letters with the IPA representation of their possible sounds. In addition, the combination *ie* is given. All other vowel combinations are normally diphthongs, discussed on p. 100.

In words of *Germanic origin,* there is a consistent relationship between vowel *quality* (whether it is open or closed) and vowel *length* (whether it is long or short in duration):

- *Closed* vowels in the stressed syllable are always *long.*
- Except for /aː/ and /ɛː/, *open* vowels are always *short.*

Long vowel sounds are indicated in IPA by the colon /ː/, as is shown in the chart. Long vowel sounds are about twice as long as short ones. There are some special situations affecting vowel length in certain words, which will be explained further below. Also see the Preface for additional discussion of vowel length.

WORD STEM, WORD STRESS, VOWEL LENGTH

A brief introduction to German word structure is necessary before the individual sounds are presented. More about word structure is presented later in the chapter. The structure of German polysyllabic words is based on *word stems* or *root stems*. The stem of a word is that part to which prefixes, suffixes, and verb endings are added. Normally the primary syllabic stress falls on the stem, though there are consistent exceptions, noted later in this chapter.

In words of Germanic origin, *the number of consonants ending the stem determine the quality and length of the vowel in the stem.*

In German, **leb** is the common stem of **leben**, **lebend**, **lebst**, **gelebt**, **lebendig**, and **lebhaft**. Because the stem ends with just one consonant, the vowel of the stem is *closed and long,* /eː/.

In the words **retten**, **rettest**, **gerettet**, **Rettung**, and **Retter**, the common stem is **rett**. Because the stem ends with two consonants, the vowel of the stem is *open and short,* /ɛ/.

Two additional circumstances affect vowel quality and length in the stem.

1. If the vowel in the stem is immediately followed by the letter *h,* the vowel will be long and/or closed:

   fühlen /yː/   **sehnen** /eː/   **während** /ɛː/   **lohnen** /oː/
   mahnen /aː/   **versöhnen** /øː/   **Buhle** /uː/

2. If the vowel in the stem is doubled the result is one long and/or closed vowel sound:

   Saal /aː/   **Seele** /eː/   **Boot** /oː/

Finally, when *-ie-* occurs in the stem, the result is always /iː/, even if it is followed by two or more consonants in the stem:

   Dienstag [ˈdiːnstaːk]

It is possible for a stem to be polysyllabic: **König, Königin, König-**
reich. In such instances, the first syllable is stressed and functions as the
stem.

SPECIFIC VOWEL SOUNDS IN GERMAN

/a/ /aː/

These two sounds are spelled with the letter *a*. The only difference between them is one of length. If *a* is doubled (**Saal** [zaːl]) or is followed by
h (**wahr** [vaːr]) or by a single consonant in the stem (**sagen** ['zaːgən]), the
sound is long /aː/. (See below for alternative pronunciation for double *aa*,)
If *a* is followed by two or more consonants in the stem (**wallen** ['valən]),
the sound is short (there are some exceptions; see below). See the Preface
for a discussion of the IPA symbols /a/ and /ɑ/.

The bright sound represented by /a/ occurs in American English, but
it is usually *not* spelled by the letter *a*. It is usually spelled by the letter *o* as
in **hot, on, costume**, as pronounced by most Americans (some Americans pronounce these words with /ɑ/; British English pronounces these
words with /ɔ/).

The typical problem with Americans pronouncing /a/ is that it is not
bright enough. It often sounds like /ɔ/. Key words to remember in this
regard are German **all** [al], **alle** [alə], and American English **all** [ɔl]. The
vowels are not the same!

Compare long and short sounds in the following words. /aː/ is about
twice as long as /a/:

/aː/		/a/	
Staat	[ʃtaːt]	**Stadt**	[ʃtat]
ahnen	['aːnən]	**ander**	['andɐ]
aber	['aːbɐ]	**ab**	[ap]
Bad	[baːt]	**Band**	[bant]
Wagen	['vaːgən]	**Wange**	['vaŋə]

Furthermore, English *unstressed a* is usually neutralized to schwa. German
a must remain bright /a/ in all positions. In German, unstressed *a* is most
commonly found in the suffixes *-bar*, *-sal*, and *-sam,* which have a *long*
vowel sound, even though unstressed.

langsam ['laŋzaːm]   **dankbar** ['daŋkbaːr]   **Trübsal** ['tryːpzaːl]

Unstressed *a* is also found in combinations with *all-* and *da-* and in some proper names. It must not be neutralized as it is in English.

Compare:

English		German	
alone	[əˈloʊn]	allein	[aˈlaen]
balsam	[ˈbɔlsəm]	Balsam	[ˈbalzaːm]
Judas	[ˈdʒudəs]	Judas	[ˈjuːdas]
Atlas	[ˈætləs]	Atlas	[ˈatlas]

In a few (non-Germanic) proper names, double *aa* divides into two syllables. The second *a* may be initiated with a light glottal stroke:

> **Kanaan** [ˈkaːnaan]   **Jochanaan** [joˈxaːnaan]

Irregular Long /aː/

In addition to the suffixes *-bar*, *-sal*, and *-sam*, mentioned above, some words with *a* plus two or more consonants have long /aː/ (see list on p. 125):

- Some (not all) words with *-ach-*:

  > **nach** [naːx]   **Schmach** [ʃmaːx]   **Sprache** [ˈʃpraːxə]

- words with *-ar-*+consonant):

  > **Art** [aːrt] **Arzt** [aːrtst] **zart** [tsaːrt]

  including the less common suffix *-artig* (derived from **Art**), which takes a secondary stress (and a glottal separation): **eigenartig** [ˈaegənˌʔaːrtɪç]

- isolated words:

  > **Bratsche** [ˈbraːtʃə]   **Jagd** [jaːkt]
  > **Magd** [maːkt]   **Papst** [paːpst]

Note also that the words **Heimat** [ˈhaemaːt] and **Heirat** [ˈhaeraːt] have long /aː/, but **Monat** [ˈmoːnat] does not.

/iː/   /ɪ/

The sound /iː/ is usually spelled *ie* but can also be spelled with *i*.

When *ie* occurs in the stressed syllable, it is pronounced /iː/ as in the English word **seen**:

    fliegen [ˈfliːgən]   **nieder** [ˈniːdɐ]   **geblieben** [gəˈbliːbən]

When *ie* occurs in an unstressed syllable or is divided over two syllables, the word is of non-Germanic origin and rules of pronunciation are different. See p. 127.

If *i* is the only vowel in the stressed syllable, it will be pronounced /iː/ if followed by a single consonant, as in **wider** [viːdɐ] (exceptions are found in a few common monosyllables, such as **in**, **im**, and **bis**, which have the open sound /ɪ/—see discussion of monosyllables on p. 122). A more common pattern for /iː/ is stressed *i* followed by *h*:

    ihm [iːm]   **ihn** [iːn]   **ihnen** [ˈiːnən]   **ihre** [ˈiːrə]

The sound **/ɪ/** is spelled with the letter *i* only. It is the same as the /ɪ/ of British English, but the American version is rather different. The latter tends to be wider and lower, the former higher and more pointed. Compare the word **bitter**, which is common to both languages. The American pronunciation is different from the British and German pronunciations, but IPA symbols cannot show such differences. Compare these lists of words with /ɪ/:

German	*English*
mit	mitt
ist	is
in, im	in
Bild	built
sich	sick

In German, /ɪ/ occurs in stressed syllables when *i* is followed by more than one consonant in the word stem:

    finden [ˈfɪndən]   **geblickt** [gəˈblɪkt]

/ɪ/ also occurs whenever *i* is the only vowel-letter in an unstressed syllable (in words of Germanic origin):

    endlich [ˈɛntlɪç]   **selig** [ˈzeːlɪç]

In singing, it is often desirable to "cheat" the sound /ɪ/ toward /i/. Particularly in longer note values, the greater focus of /i/ can yield a vocally more satisfying result. Caution is advised, however; this is not license to change every occurrence of /ɪ/ to /i/.

/eː/ /ɛ/

These two sounds are spelled with the letter *e* when it is the only vowel-letter in the stressed syllable. If the *e* is doubled within the word stem (**Seele** [ˈzeːlə]), followed by *h* (**fehlen** [ˈfeːlən]) or followed by only one consonant in the word stem (**beten** [ˈbeːtən]), the result is /eː/. If the *e* is followed by two or more consonants in the stem, it is open /ɛ/ (**Ende** [ˈɛndə], **wecken** [ˈvɛkən]).

The only Germanic word with an unstressed closed and short /e/ is **lebendig** [leˈbɛndɪç].

Five common inseparable, unstressed prefixes traditionally have the sound /ɛ/:

> **er-** as in **ertragen** [ɛɐˈtraːgən]
> (Do not confuse the prefix **er-** with the word **er** [eːɐ].)
> **ver-** as in **verstehen** [fɛɐˈʃteːən]
> **zer-** as in **zerreissen** [tsɛɐˈraesən]
> **emp-** as in **empfehlen** [ɛmpˈfeːlən]
> **ent-** as in **entzücken** [ɛntˈtsʏkən]

The prefix *her* is unique. When stressed or standing alone, it has /eː/:

> **herstellen** [ˈheːɐʃtɛlən]   **Herkunft** [ˈheːɐkʊnft]   **hin und her** [hɪn ʊnt heːɐ]

but unstressed has /ɛ/:

> **heran** [hɛˈran]   **herunter** [hɛˈrʊntɐ]   **herbei** [hɛɐˈbae]

Exception: the words **Herberge** and **herbergen** have [ˈhɛr . . .]

The sound /eː/ does not normally exist in English, although it is approximated in certain diphthong sounds in English. Compare:

German		English	
der	[deːɐ]	**dare**	[deɚ]
geht	[geːt]	**gate**	[geɪt]
Lehm	[leːm]	**lame**	[leɪm]
Seel'	[zeːl]	**sail**	[seɪl]

Not only does the German sound have no diphthong, it is more closed than the first sound of the English diphthongs. In fact, /eː/ is very near to the position of /iː/. Virtually all problems in pronouncing this vowel involve pronouncing it with a diphthong or pronouncing it too open, as /ɛ/.

This is extremely important for singing! The vocal position for /eː/ is nearly the same as, and sometimes identical to, the vocal position for /iː/. If difficulty is encountered with /eː/, substitute /iː/. It will almost always sound right. See p. 162 for the same sound in French.

The sound /ɛ/ does exist in English but it is slightly different from its German counterpart. The situation is identical to that with /ɪ/: the German version is higher and more pointed than it is in American English. Compare:

German		English	
Bett	[bɛt]	**bed**	[bɛd]
denn	[dɛn]	**then**	[ðɛn]
hell	[hɛl]	**hell**	[hɛl]
nett	[nɛt]	**net**	[nɛt]

Refer to the discussion of appropriate vocalization of this sound on p. 7. /ɛ/ can also be spelled with ä. See p. 94.

Some German words have double *ee* which separate into different word elements and syllables. This occurs with the prefixes *ge-* and *be-* preceding a stem beginning with *e*. The first *e* is pronounced as schwa, the second as /e/ or /ɛ/ initiated with a light glottal stroke, indicated by /ʔ/:

      beenden [bəʔɛndən]   **geehrt** [gəʔeːrt]

Also with *be-* and *ge-* preceding *ein-*:

      beeinflüssen [bəʔaenˌflʏsən]   **geeinigt** [gəʔaenɪçt]

A few nouns of non-Germanic origin have plural forms in /-eːən/. There is no glottal separation:

Museum [muˈzeːʊm]		**Museen** [muˈzeːən]	
Idee [iˈdeː]		**Ideen** [iˈdeːən]	
Fee [feː]		**Feen** [ˈfeːən]	
Allee [aˈleː]		**Alleen** [aˈleːən]	

Schwa /ə/

This sound is spelled only with the letter *e* in unstressed syllables.

The sound /ə/ is called *schwa*, and it is a special case. The symbol /ə/ represents a short, unstressed neutral vowel sound. The actual nature of the sound varies from language to language, and even within a given language, depending on context. Compare the versions of schwa in English, French, and German:

pretonic:	**again** [əˈgɛn]	**fenetre** [fənɛtr(ə)]	**geliebt** [gəˈliːpt]
posttonic:	**fireman** [ˈfaːˑmən]	**livre** [liːvr(ə)]	**Liebe** [ˈliːbə]

When the schwa is artificially lengthened, as it regularly is in singing, it is effectively no longer schwa, since by definition schwa is very short and neutral. One must therefore determine an appropriate vowel sound to sustain. (See discussion of French schwa on p. 171.)

Defining the sound of German schwa with precision is difficult. Most authorities describe it as a version of /ɛ/ but not as open as the stressed version, and requiring variation of color according to context—a little higher following a syllable with a narrow vowel, and a little lower following a syllable with a wider vowel. Some suggest the color of /œ/ or /ø/, but this suggestion conflicts with the exhortation from most that there should be no lip-rounding, which is a characteristic of /œ/ and /ø/. It is commonly emphasized that German schwa should not sound like /ʌ/, the vowel sound in English *but*.

These last two points summarize the two common ways in which English-speaking singers sound unidiomatic with German schwa. One is to overly round the lips and sound too French. The other is to pronounce it much too open and far back, as in English. Thus **Liebe** [ˈliːbə] becomes [ˈliːbʌ] ("lee-buh"). It is also pointed out by some that if German final /ə/ is pronounced with the color of either /œ/ or /ʌ/, it can be confused with the sound /ɐ/, which is used for final -er in German words, resulting in **Liebe** sounding like **lieber**. The sound /ɐ/ is discussed below under the letter *r*.

Some sources dealing with German for singers employ alternative phonetic symbols for unstressed *e*. However, it is desirable to use the symbol /ə/ consistently. Most dictionaries and texts use this symbol. It is also helpful in differentiating when the letter *e* is stressed and when it is unstressed.

With the exceptions, then, of words of non-Germanic origin, the prefixes *er-*, *ver-*, *zer-*, *ent-*, and *emp-*, the word / prefix *her* when unstressed, and the isolated word **lebendig** [le'bɛndɪç], all unstressed *e*'s are to be transcribed as /ə/. Often there is more than one in a word:

eine ['aenə]	**beenden** [bə'ɛndən]
Gelegenheit [gə'le:gənhaet]	**gegebenen** [gə'ge:bənən]
folgenden ['fɔlgəndən]	**manches** ['mançəs]
Wanderer ['vandərər] or ['vandərɐ]	

/ɛ/ /ɛː/ (spelled ä)

The letter *ä* results in one of these two sounds, the only difference being one of length. If the *ä* is followed by *h* (**wähnen** ['vɛːnən]) or by one consonant in the word stem (**Väter** ['fɛːtɐ]), it will be long /ɛː/. If it is followed by two consonants in the stem (**Blätter** ['blɛtɐ]), it will be short /ɛ/. The vowel quality is the same as discussed under /ɛ/ on p. 92.

Some German speakers pronounce /ɛː/ in a more closed fashion, near to or identical with /eː/. Some commentators describe this sound as somewhere between /ɛː/ and /eː/. This text will follow the example of Siebs and Duden and use /ɛː/ for the long version of this vowel, while again acknowledging that the IPA is an imperfect tool and urging students to become sensitive to subtle shadings of vowel sounds as they become more familiar with the language.

Compare vowel sounds and lengths in these words:

/ɛː/ *Spelled* ä	/ɛ/ *Spelled* ä	/ɛ/ *Spelled* e
Väter ['fɛːtɐ]	**Blätter** ['blɛtɐ]	**Vetter** ['fɛtɐ]
Tränen ['trɛːnən]	**trällern** ['trɛlɐn]	**trennen** ['trɛnən]
fährt [fɛːrt]	**fälschen** ['fɛlʃən]	**Ferse** ['fɛrzə]
nächst [nɛːçst]	**Nächte** ['nɛçtə]	**necken** ['nɛkən]

In singing, vowel length is determined largely by the composer in the note values chosen for each word. Nevertheless the singer must learn sensitivity to vowel length for those styles of singing that would require it more, such as recitative or parlando.

/oː/ /ɔ/

These two sounds are spelled only with the letter *o*. In the stressed syllable, if the *o* is doubled (**Boot** [boːt]) or immediately followed by *h* (**wohnen** ('voːnən]) or by only one consonant in the word stem (**loben** ['lo:bən]), it will be closed /o:/. If it is followed by two consonants in the word stem (**wollen** ['vɔlən]), it will be open /ɔ/.

Unstressed *o* is unique among German vowels in that it is usually pronounced closed, as will be discussed below.

A few German proper names end in -*ow*, pronounced /o/ with silent *w*:

von Bülow ['by:lo]   **Lützow** ['lʏtso]

Monosyllables are more irregular; see p. 122.

The sound **/o:/** is analogous to /e:/ in that the nearest equivalent in English is always part of a diphthong. Compare:

German		English	
Lohn	[lo:n]	**loan**	[loʊn]
Boot	[bo:t]	**boat**	[boʊt]
Not	[no:t]	**note**	[noʊt]
vor	[fo:ɐ]	**for**	[foɚ]
Kohl	[ko:l]	**coal**	[koʊl]

Just as /e:/ is close to /i:/, so is /o:/ close to /u:/. Whenever a singer has difficulty identifying the position of /o:/, it may be helpful to sing /u:/.

In *unstressed* syllables the letter *o*, in contrast to other vowels, is usually *closed*. Unstressed *o* is not common, but it is found in final position in the words **desto** ['dɛsto], **also** ['alzo], the archaic word **jetzo** ['jɛtso], and a number of non-Germanic proper names from operatic repertoire:

Tamino [ta'mi:no] **Sarastro** [za'rastro]   **Papageno** [papa'ge:no]
Fidelio [fi'de:ljo]

Though it is closed, final *o* is short. However, if the final *o* is followed by another consonant, it is closed and *long*, even though unstressed:

Kleinod ['klaeno:t]   **Herzog** ['hɛrtso:k]   **Doktor** ['dɔkto:r]
Marmor ['marmo:r]   **Amor** ['a:mo:r]

This includes the common suffix -*los* [lo:s]: **endlos** [ɛntlo:s]. One word with unstressed *o* in non-final position (closed, short) is **Forelle** [fo'rɛlə].

The sound **/ɔ/** does have a counterpart in English, although it is not usually spelled with the letter *o*. Moreover, British and American English often use this sound differently:

German	British	American
Topf	top	taught
noch	not	nought
Stock	stock	stalk
von	fog	fawn
offen	often	often

Note that the German sound is consistently short (the English sounds vary in length) and shaped with a high point. Such height is sometimes true of British English but almost never true of standard American English.

Since the letter *o* when stressed is often pronounced /a/ in American English (e.g., **not** [nat]), the American singer must be careful not to open the sound too far. The vowel of **noch** [nɔx] is different from that of **nach** [naːx].

/uː/ /ʊ/

These two sounds are spelled only with the letter *u*. In the stressed syllable the *u* is closed when followed by *h* (**Ruhm** [ruːm]) or by only one consonant in the stem (**Tugend** ['tuːgənt]). The letter *u* is never doubled within a word stem. If the *u* is followed by two or more consonants in the stem, it will be open (**Mutter** ['mʊtɐ]).

Usually unstressed *u* is pronounced open, most frequently in the suffix *-ung*. It is also open in the prefixes *un-* (usually stressed) and *um-* (usually unstressed but sometimes stressed):

unruhig ['ʊnˌruːɪç] **umsonst** [ʊmˈzɔnst]

Unstressed *u* is pronounced closed and long in the suffixes *-mut* and *-tum* and in the stressed prefix *ur-*:

Wehmut ['veːmuːt] **Heiligtum** ['haelɪçtuːm]   **Urwald** ['uːɐvalt]

The sound /uː/ is equivalent in English and German. English speakers, however, often do not pronounce this sound in a pure form but end it with a diphthong glide-off caused by the lips moving further forward while sustaining the /uː/. One often hears tongue tension in this vowel as well, which causes something like the sound /y/. Such problems with this vowel are distressingly common and tend to carry over into other languages as well. It is crucial to identify the correct tongue position for this vowel and end it with no movement of the tongue or lips.

German		English	
zu	[tsuː]	**to**	[tu]
Ruh	[ruː]	**rue**	[ru]
Mut	[muːt]	**moot**	[mut]
Flut	[fluːt]	**flute**	[flut]
Schuh	[ʃuː]	**shoe**	[ʃu]

THE SOUND /ʊ/ is also equivalent in German and English. The spelling of this sound in English is usually *oo*, sometimes *u*. The tongue position is the same as for /uː/ (arched toward the pharynx) but with the mouth more open.

German		English	
Busch	[bʊʃ]	**bush**	[bʊʃ]
Putz	[pʊts]	**book**	[bʊk]
Lust	[lʊst]	**look**	[lʊk]
Fluss	[flʊs]	**foot**	[fʊt]

It was mentioned in the discussion of /ɪ/ that it is often desirable to "cheat" that sound toward its closed counterpart /i/. The same is true for /ʊ/. It is common to hear good singers focus this sound in the direction of /u/ to allow the sound to "sit" better vocally, especially on sustained notes. Once again, caution is urged. Not every /ʊ/ should be sung as /u/.

Very rarely in German the spelling -*uu*- is found, as in the word **Genugtuung** [gəˈnuːkˌtuːʊŋ]. The two vowels fall into different word elements. This word (which means *satisfaction*) is formed from the words **genug** and **tun** and the suffix -*ung*.

Mixed Vowels

A mixed vowel is one that combines elements of two other "pure" vowels. These sounds do not exist in standard English but are found in German, French, and other languages. In formulating mixed vowel sounds, the first, and more important, element is the "inside" or tongue position, and the second is the "outside" or lip position. Always start with the tongue position. If one encounters difficulty in pronouncing a mixed vowel, reduce it to the tongue position only. It is the core of the sound. The lip position simply colors this core. There are four "mixed" vowel sounds in German, consisting of two related pairs.

/yː/ /ʏ/

These two sounds are spelled with the letter *ü*. If the *ü* is followed by *h* (**fühlen** [ˈfyːlən]) or by a single consonant in the stem (**Blüte** [ˈblyːtə]), the sound will be /yː/. If *ü* is followed by more than one consonant in the stem, the result is /ʏ/ as in **füllen** [ˈfʏlən].

In certain words of non-Germanic (Greek) origin the letter *y* is used, a letter not found in Germanic words. It is equivalent to *ü* in pronunciation (**Lyrik** [ˈlyːrɪk]). In Germanic words these sounds are always found in stressed syllables, never unstressed.

The sound **/yː/** is a mixed vowel with the tongue position of /iː/ and the lip position is of /uː/. Compare the following words, in which the vowel of the English word is maintained for the German word as the lips round to /uː/:

English		German	
fear	[fiɚ]	**für**	[fyːɐ] or [fyːr]
mead	[miːd]	**müde**	[ˈmyːdə]
tear	[tɪɚ]	**Tür**	[tyːɐ] or [tyːr]
cease	[sis]	**süss**	[zyːs]
bleat	[blit]	**Blüte**	[ˈblyːtə]

A common problem is that the proper tongue position of /iː/ is abandoned as the lips move to /uː/, so the singer ends up with essentially /uː/. It is true that some English-speaking singers always tend to sing /iː/ for /yː/. This habit is sheer laziness and ought to be easily corrected.

Examples of German words (all of Greek origin) that spell this sound with the letter *y*:

        Lyrik [ˈlyːrɪk]   **lyrisch** [ˈlyːrɪʃ]   **typisch** [ˈtyːpɪʃ]
        Elysium [eˈlyːziʊm]

The sound **/ʏ/** is a mixed vowel with the tongue position of /ɪ/ and the lip position of /ʊ/. It differs from /yː/ in that the mouth (jaw) is more open. Because it is so short in duration, it is a difficult sound to make in isolation.

        müssen [ˈmʏsən]   **fünf** [fʏnf]   **Hülle** [ˈhʏlə]   **Glück** [glʏk]
        Stück [ʃtʏk]

Here is a comparison of the sounds of /yː/ and /ʏ/ as well as similar English words with /iː/ and /ɪ/:

German /yː/		English /iː/		German /ʏ/		English /ɪ/	
fühlen	[ˈfyːlən]	feel	[fiːl]	füllen	[ˈfʏlən]	fill	[fIɪ]
hüte	[ˈhyːtə]	heat	[hiːt]	Hütte	[ˈhʏtə]	hit	[hɪt]
Düne	[ˈdyːnə]	dean	[diːn]	dünn	[dʏn]	din	[dɪn]
grün	[gryːn]	green	[griːn]	Gründe	[ˈgrʏndə]	grin	[grɪn]

/øː/   /œ/

These two sounds, the remaining mixed vowel sounds, are spelled with the letter ö. If this letter is followed by h (**Söhne** [ˈzøːnə]) or only one consonant in the stem (**Töne** [ˈtøːnə]), the sound will be /øː/. If it is followed by two or more consonants in the stem, the sound will be /œ/ (**gönnen** [ˈgœnən]). In Germanic words, these sounds are always found in stressed syllables, never unstressed.

The sound **/øː/** is a mixed vowel formed with the tongue position of /eː/ and the lip position of /oː/. It is the same sound as French **peu**, **feu**, and **deux**, except that the German sound is normally long. Make sure that the core of the sound is /eː/ and that the shaping of the lips to /oː/ simply completes the sound. English near-equivalents are less helpful with this sound, so none is given here.

> **böse** [ˈbøːzə]   **fröhlich** [ˈfrøːlɪç]   **gewöhnlich** [gəˈvøːnlɪç]
>
> **schön** [ʃøːn]   **Flöte** [ˈfløːtə]   **trösten** [ˈtrøːstən] (irregular)

Sometimes Americans pronounce this vowel sound as if it contained an American retroflex r sound [ɚ], as in *purple*. The American sound requires tensing the tongue by pulling it back and down. There is no such tongue tension in /øː/.

The sound **/œ/** is a mixed vowel formed with the tongue position of /ɛ/ and the lip position of /ɔ/. It is the same as French **coeur** and **fleur**, except that the German sound is always short. The mouth (jaw) position opens from /ø/ and the lips are less rounded.

> **Hölle** [ˈhœlə]   **köstlich** [ˈkœstlɪç]   **plötzlich** [ˈplœtslɪç]
>
> **völlig** [ˈfœlɪç]   **können** [ˈkœnən]   **Götter** [ˈgœtɐ] or [ˈgœtər]

The following summary should be helpful for remembering how the mixed vowels are formed. The student must not confuse these sounds:

/yː/   tongue (inside) positioned for /iː/
        lips (outside) positioned for /uː/

/ʏ/   tongue (inside) positioned for /ɪ/
        lips (outside positioned for /ʊ/

/øː/   tongue (inside) positioned for /eː/
        lips (outside) positioned for /oː/

/œ/   tongue (inside) positioned for /ɛ/
        lips (inside) positioned for /ɔ/

The tongue position of the mixed vowel is the more important. If the student has difficulty speaking or singing any mixed vowel, he or she should start with the tongue position of the vowel.

DIPHTHONGS AND ADJACENT VOWELS

German has three diphthongs. Two IPA renderings are commonly found for each:

/ae/ or /ai/ which may be spelled:

>   -ai- as in **Hain** [haen]   **Mai** [mae]
>   -ei- as in **mein** [maen]   **Geist** [gaest]
>   -ay- as in **Bayreuth** [baeˈrɔɔt]
>   -ey- as in **Meyer** [ˈmaeɐ]

/ao/ or /au/ which is spelled only:

>   -au- as in **auf** [aof]   **Frau** [frao]

/ɔø/ or /ɔy/ which may be spelled:

>   -eu- as in **euch** [ɔøç]   **Freude** [ˈfrɔødə]
>   -äu- as in **Säule** [ˈzɔølə]   **Fräulein** [ˈfrɔølaen]

The first is used by Siebs (though using /ae/ and /ao/), the second by Duden and others. The difference in the IPA rendering is in the second, glide-off sound of the diphthong, which reflects the difficulty in precisely defining this very short sound. The English equivalents of these sounds are rendered /aɪ/, /aʊ/, and /ɔɪ/, suggesting a less tense, less pure glide-off sound after the main vowel than in German. Compare **mein** and **mine**, **Haus** and **house**, and **keusch** and **coin**. The second vowel of German diphthongs is always late and short. There is never the possibility of separating the two sounds over two notes, as can happen in Italian.

This text uses the Siebs IPA alternative for German diphthongs. Although it might seem logical to insert a colon between the IPA symbols for German diphthongs (to indicate the much greater length of the first sound), doing so is not usual practice.

Sometimes in German spelling, two successive vowel-letters do *not* result in a diphthong. The most common example is -*ie*-, already discussed. Occasionally alternative spellings of the umlaut vowels are seen: -*ae*- for *ä*, -*oe*- for *ö*, and -*ue*- for *ü*. An example is the name **Goethe** [gøːtə].

Vowel-letters can be adjacent but in different syllables, thus taking their individual sounds. In German words this can happen with a prefix followed by a stem beginning with a vowel; a glottal separation /ʔ/ is required:

> **beobachten** [bəʔˈoːbaxtən] **beantworten** [bəʔˈantvɔrtən]
> **geändert** [gəʔˈɛndɐt]

It can also happen in German words derived from Latin and Greek:

> **Theater** [teˈaːtɐ] **intellektuell** [ɪntɛlɛktuˈɛl]

including words ending -*ion* and -*ient*, in which the *i* functions as a glide:

> **Nation** [naˈtsjoːn] **Aktion** [akˈtsjoːn] **Patient** [paˈtsjɛnt]

THE GLIDE /J/

The only glide, or semiconsonant, in German is /j/. In Germanic words it is spelled with the letter *j*.

At first glance this German sound seems to be equivalent to English /j/ spelled with *y* as in **yes**. Although the IPA symbol is the same, there is an important difference between the sounds. The English version is a rapid /i/. The German version is described by Siebs as a voiced /ç/, a fricative sound. It therefore has a more concentrated airflow than English *y*. (It must not, however, sound like English *j* as in **jump**.)

> **jetzt** [jɛtst] **Jammer** [ˈjamɐ] **ja** [ja]
> **Jüngling** [ˈjʏŋlɪŋ] **Majestät** [majɛsˈtɛːt]

In words of foreign origin that spell this glide with *i*, as in **Familie** [faˈmiːljə] and **Nation** [naˈtsjoːn], Siebs (and others) uses a different IPA symbol, either /i/ or /ĭ/. This difference is logical, since the sound is not the same as the one described above. However, most texts and dictionaries use /j/ in these words; this text does also.

In words of French origin, j is pronounced /ʒ/:

> **Journal** [ʒurnaːl]   **Jalousie** [ʒaluzi]

GERMAN CONSONANTS

The following pages discuss only those consonant sounds that require specific explanations, either because they do not exist in English or because there are differences from English.

CH

This combination has *three* pronunciations in German:

/x/—Germans call this the "ach-Laut." (**Laut** means "sound.")

The tongue is in the position for the vowel /a/. An unvoiced airstream is focused at the back of the hard palate. It occurs when -*ch*- follows "back" vowels: *a*, *o*, *u*, and *au*.

> **Bach** [bax]   **doch** [dɔx]
> **Buch** [buːx]   **auch** [aox]

/ç/—Germans call this the "ich-Laut."

The tongue is in the position for /ɪ/ or /i/. An unvoiced air stream focuses just behind the upper teeth. It occurs when -*ch*- follows all vowels and diphthongs except the above: *i*, *e*, *ä*, *ö*, *ü*, *ie*, *ei*, *eu*, and *äu*.

> **mich** [mɪç]   **Becher** [ˈbɛçɐ]   **rächen** [ˈrɛçən]
> **Reich** [raeç]   **Bücher** [ˈbyːçɐ]   **Köcher** [ˈkœçɐ]
> **euch** [ɔøç]   **räuchern** [ˈrɔøçɐn]

Important: This sound is also used when -*ch*- follows consonants:

> **Milch** [mɪlç]   **manche** [mançə]   **durch** [dʊrç]

including the common diminutive suffix -*chen*:

Liebchen [ˈliːpçən]   **Mädchen** [ˈmɛːtçən]
Häuschen [ˈhɔøsçən]

To ears that are unused to this sound, /ç/ can sound like /ʃ/, but the two are different and distinct sounds.

Both /x/ and /ç/ are light and of short duration. Non-natives often overemphasize them, especially /x/.

/k/—In some words of Greek origin *-ch-* is pronounced /k/:

Chor [koːɐ]   **Orchester** [ɔɐˈkɛstɐ]
Christus [ˈkrɪstʊs]   **Charakter** [kaˈraktɐ]

although in others it is /ç/:

China [ˈçiːna]   **Cherub** [ˈçeːrʊp]   **Chemie** [çeˈmiː]
Echo [ˈɛço]   **Psychologie** [psyçoloˈgiː]

When it begins German proper names, it is /k/:

Chiemsee [ˈkiːmzeː]   **Chemnitz** [ˈkɛmniːts]

However, **Chamisso**, originally a French name, is [ʃaˈmiso]; in other words of French, Italian, Spanish, or English origin, *-ch-* will generally be pronounced as in the original language.

CHS

Occasionally in German the combination *-chs-* occurs as one element within the stem. In this case it is pronounced /ks/:

Fuchs [fʊks]   **Sachs** [zaks]   **wachsen** [ˈvaksən]
Ochs [ɔks]   **Lachs** [laks] **wechseln** [ˈvɛksəln]
The word **sechs** is [zɛks], but **sechzehn** is [ˈzɛçtseːn] and **sechzig** is [ˈzɛçtsɪç].

The combination *chs* as /ks/ occurs in relatively few words, however. Most of the time when the spelling *-chs-* occurs, the *ch* ends the word stem and the *s* is part of a word ending. *In such cases the* ch *and the* s *are to be pronounced separately.* This is often difficult for non-natives to do.

There are four situations in which *ch* and *s* must be pronounced as separate elements:

- *-ch* plus verb ending *-st*:

  du lachst [laxst]   **du brichst** [brɪçst]   **du suchst** [zuːxst]

- *-ch* plus genitive *s*:

  des Bachs [baxs]   **des Reichs** [raeçs]

- *-ch* plus superlative suffix *-st*:

  höchst [høːçst]   **herrlichster** [ˈhɛrlɪçstɐ]

- in compound words:

  nachsuchen [ˈnaːxˌzuːxən]

There is one word that seems to cause particular difficulty for many people: **nichts** [nɪçts]. In some dialects (and in the libretto of *Der Rosen-kavalier*) this word is spelled and pronounced "nix." Except for these special circumstances, the word must be pronounced properly. Some practice may be required to do so.

*Die Ent-
führung
aus dem
Serail—
Mozart*

Nichts, nichts, nichts, nichts   soll mich erschüt-tern
[nɪçts   zɔl mɪç ɛɐˈʃʏtɐn]

*Matthäus-
Passion—Bach*

von   ei - ner Sün-de weiß er nichts, nichts
[fɔn ˈaenɐ ˈzʏndə vaes eːɐ nɪçts]

R

There are two essential ways of pronouncing the letter *r* for the purposes of singing German:

1. Excluding prefixes, *r* should be pronounced with a flip of the tongue whenever it precedes a vowel. The usual IPA symbol for this is /r/ (used by Siebs and Duden), although /ɾ/ (as for Italian) may be encountered:

Türen [ˈtyːrən]   **Trost** [troːst]
lehren [ˈleːrən]   **Regen** [ˈreːgən]

Rolling the *r* is appropriate when heightened emphasis is required, although usually not with intervocalic *r*.

2. In all other situations, that is, when *r* precedes a consonant, ends a word, or ends a prefix, the *r* may be flipped *or* it may become a vowel sound similar to, but distinct from, schwa. Siebs uses the symbol /ɒ/ for this sound. More recent publications, including Duden, use /ɐ/, as does this text. The symbol /ɚ/ is also seen for this sound, though it is usually employed for English vocalic *r* as in *near*. The sound of /ɐ/ is darker than /ə/ and is always short, often extremely short.

der [deːɐ] or [deːr]   **mir** [miːɐ] or [miːr]
nur [nuːɐ] or [nuːr]   **ernst** [ɛɐnst] or [ɛrnst]
vergessen [fɛɐˈgesən] or [fɛrˈgesən]

In the above examples, the vowel before the *r* receives its usual sound, then the *r* is either flipped or pronounced /ɐ/.

When -*er* (or -*er* plus consonant) ends a *polysyllabic* word or word stem, the IPA rendering is either /ər/ or /ɐ/. In the second version, the two letters make one sound only. In German phonetic transcription /ɐ/ can never follow /ə/.

Lieder [ˈliːdɐ] or [ˈliːdər]   **zittern** [ˈtsitɐn] or [ˈtsitərn]
unser [ˈʊnzɐ] or [ˈʊnzər]   **linderst** [ˈlindɐst] or [ˈlindərst]
Biedermeier [ˈbiːdɐˌmaeɐ] or [ˈbiːdərˌmaeər]

It is important to distinguish between /ə/ and /ɐ/ in final positions. The difference in sound is sometimes the only difference between words, as in **bitte** [ˈbitə] and **bitter** [ˈbitɐ], or between different word endings, as in **süsse** [ˈzyːsə] and **süsser** [ˈzyːsɐ]. These examples show that /ə/ is a brighter sound than /ɐ/.

The *r* is sometimes treated as a vowel sound in this way in English, particularly British English, so the concept is not unfamiliar. German singers are not consistent among themselves as to how to treat *r*; often either of the two solutions could be appropriate. The choice will be influenced by context, musical and literary style, as well as individual taste.

The pronunciation of *r* with the uvula (IPA symbol /ʀ/) is used extensively in German speech, but, as with French, it is not considered appropriate for singing.

B, D, G

These three consonants normally take the voiced sounds /b/, /d/, and /g/, familiar from English and other languages:

lieben [ˈliːbən]   **leiden** [ˈlaedən]   **liegen** [ˈliːgən]

When final in a word, part of a final consonant cluster, or final in a word stem followed by a consonant, *these consonants lose their voiced quality and become devoiced* /p/, /t/, and /k/:

Liebchen [ˈliːpçən]   **Leid** [laet]   **liegt** [liːkt]
endlos [ˈɛntloːs]   **klagst** [klaːkst]   **selbst** [zɛlpst]

This is also the case when truncation of a word results in final *b*, *d*, or *g*:

hab' [haːp] from **habe** [haːbə]   **lieg'** [liːk] from **liege** [liːgə]

When such words are connected to a word beginning with a vowel (**hab' ich**), German singers often reduce the devoiced quality of the consonant considerably, so that it may sound nearly voiced.

When the consonant is final in a stem followed by a vowel, voicing is retained:

Mond [moːnt] but **Monde** [ˈmoːndə]
Mondnacht [ˈmoːntˌnaxt] but **Mondeslicht** [ˈmoːndəˌslɪçt]

but not at the end of a prefix followed by a vowel (rare):

abändern [ˈapˌɛndɐn]

Both Siebs and Duden use the IPA symbols /p/, /t/, and /k/, for the devoiced versions of *b*, *d*, and *g*, but others make a distinction between, for example, devoiced *b* and /p/. The devoiced sounds are generally gentler and less plosive than their unvoiced counterparts. To indicate this distinction, a different symbol can be used, namely /b̥/, /d̥/, and /g̊/.

This text will follow the example of Siebs and Duden for IPA, but it is important to devoice these sounds in an unexaggerated manner. Doing so is particularly essential when the devoicing occurs medially: words such as **ewiglich** and **endlich** should connect the devoiced consonant to the following consonant smoothly, with no separation or aspiration.

When devoicing occurs at the end of words with long vowels, the singer must be sure that an exaggerated devoicing does not shorten the vowel: **Tag** must be pronounced [taːk] or [taːǧ] and not [tak].

A certain family of words whose basic forms end in -*el*, -*en*, or -*er* seem to constitute an exception to the above rule. When such words take endings, the *e* is dropped. If the preceding consonant is *b*, *d*, or *g*, they retain their voiced quality, as if the *e* were still there. Another way to view it is that the *l*, *n*, or *r* ends the stem, not the preceding *b*, *d*, or *g*.

übel ['yːbəl]	**edel** ['eːdəl]	**eigen** ['aegən]	**ander** ['andər]
übler ['yːblɐ]	**edler** ['eːdlɐ]	**eigner** ['aegnɐ]	**andrer** ['andrər]
üble ['yːblə]	**edle** ['eːdlə]	**eigne** ['aegnə]	**andre** ['andrə]
übles ['yːbləs]	**edles** ['eːdləs]	**eignes** ['aegnəs]	**andres** ['andrəs]

The noun **Gold** is [gɔlt], but the adjective **golden** ['gɔldən] retains a voiced *d* in all forms (**goldner, goldne, goldnes**). Similarly, **Wagner** (from **Wagen**) is pronounced ['vaːgnɐ], not ['vaːknɐ]. Unrelated to the above are the verb **widmen** ['vɪtmən] and the noun **Widmung** ['vɪtmʊŋ]. Notice the devoicing of the *d*.

The Suffix -IG

In this common suffix, *g* functions differently than usual. When final, this suffix is pronounced /ɪç/:

heilig ['haelɪç] **selig** ['zeːlɪç] **König** ['køːnɪç] **ewig** ['eːvɪç]

When the -*ig* suffix is in turn followed by a consonant (resulting from grammatical inflection), the suffix retains the /ɪç/ pronunciation. This happens with nouns in the genitive case, with adjectives in the superlative degree, and with certain noun suffixes when they are added to an adjective to create a noun:

Königs ['køːnɪçs]   **seligste** ['zeːlɪçstə]   **Ewigkeit** ['eːvɪçkaet]
Traurigkeit ['traorɪçkaet] **Müßiggang** ['myːsɪçgaŋ]

This is also the case with forms of verbs with infinitives in -*igen*, such as **heiligen, seligen, verkündigen:**

> **er heiligt** ['haelɪçt]   **du seligst** ['zeːlɪçst]   **er verkündigt** [fɛrˈkʏndɪçt]

The verb **predigen** (to preach) has a derived noun **Predigt** (sermon): ['preːdɪçt].

When this suffix is followed by a vowel in the same word the *g* returns to its normal voiced sound:

> **heiligen** ['haelɪgən]   **seliger** ['zeːlɪgɐ]   **Königin** ['køːnɪgɪn]

When this suffix is followed in turn by the suffixes -*lich* or -*reich*, the *g* devoices to a light /k/. The reason is one of euphony, so that /ç/ does not occur twice in the same word:

> **ewiglich** ['eːvɪklɪç]   **Königreich** ['køːnɪkraeç]

One hears deviations from the above in *spoken* German in different parts of German-speaking countries. These are the rules for **Bühnendeutsch**, however, and should be observed by singers.

S

Excluding the combinations listed in the next section, *s* has two sounds: voiced /z/ and unvoiced /s/.

- *s* is voiced /z/ in the following situations:

   At the beginning of a word when it is followed immediately by a vowel:

   sein [zaen]   **singen** ['zɪŋən]   **sauber** ['zaobɐ]
   (*Note:* Some German speakers, particularly Austrians, use /s/ for these words; however /z/ is recommended.)

   Intervocalic:

   böse ['bøːzə]   **Esel** ['eːzəl]   **Hause** ['haozə]

   After a voiced consonant and preceding a vowel:

   unser ['ʊnzɐ]   **also** ['alzo]   **Amsel** ['amzəl]

The suffixes **-sam** and **-sal** *always* have voiced /z/ regardless of what precedes them (although not all German speakers observe this rule):

einsam [ˈaenzaːm]   **Schicksal** [ˈʃɪkzaːl]   **Labsal** [ˈlaːpzaːl]

- *s* is unvoiced /s/ in the following situations:

At the end of a word, even if it is preceded by a voiced consonant:

Haus [haos]   **als** [als]   **uns** [ʊns]

including contractions involving *s*:

ans (**an das**) [ans]   **ich hab's** or **ich habs** [ɪç haːps]

Medially after an unvoiced consonant (except for **-sam** and **-sal**; see above):

Rätsel [ˈrɛːtsəl]   **gipsen** [ˈgɪpsən]

Before any consonant (excluding the combinations in the next section):

lispeln [ˈlɪspəln]   **fast** [fast]

Important: When *s* links parts of a compound word (genitive *s*), it is *always* unvoiced, even when following a voiced consonant. Such words are frequently mispronounced:

Lebensreise [ˈleːbənsˌraezə]   *not* [. . . zraezə]
Himmelsblau [ˈhɪməlsˌblao]   *not* [. . . zblao]
Frühlingsblüten [ˈfryːlɪŋsˌblyːtən]   *not* [. . . zblyːtən]

Included is a word such as **insgesamt** [ˈɪnsgəzamt], in which the *s* connects the prefix to the word stem.

SCH, ST, SP

sch   When part of the same syllable, this combination always forms /ʃ/:

Schule [ˈʃuːlə]   **rasch** [raʃ]   **löschen** [ˈlœʃən]
waschen [ˈvaʃən]   **Tasche** [ˈtaʃə]   **Botschaft** [ˈboːtʃaft]

When *s* and *ch* are adjacent, the *s* sometimes ends the stem and the *ch* begins a suffix. The result is /sç/, a difficult combination for English speakers. This problem happens almost exclusively with the diminutive suffix -*chen*:

Häuschen ['hɔøsçən]   **Röschen** ['røːsçən]

When *s* and *h* occur together in German, they are always in different syllables (different word elements) and therefore to be pronounced separately. Do not confuse this situation with English *sh*:

boshaft ['boːshaft]   **deshalb** ['dɛshalp]

st, sp   When these combinations are at the beginning of a word or word-stem, they are pronounced /ʃt/ and /ʃp/:

stellen ['ʃtɛlən]   **Strauß** [ʃtraos]
zerstören ['tsɛɐˌʃtøːrən]   **Auferstehung** ['aofɛɐˌʃteːʊŋ]
Sprache ['ʃpraːxə]   **Gespräch** [gəˈʃpreːç]
spinnen ['ʃpɪnən]   **entsprechen** [ɛntˈʃprɛçən]

When these combinations are *not* at the beginning of a word or stem, they are pronounced /st/ and /sp/. It is a common mistake to assume that all such occurrences are pronounced with /ʃ/. Learn to recognize word elements to determine which pronunciation is correct:

beste ['bɛstə]   **schnellste** ['ʃnɛlstə]
gestern ['gɛstɐn]   **Postamt** ['pɔstˌamt]
Gastspiel ['gastˌʃpiːl]   **austragen** ['aostraːgən]
Wespe ['vɛspə]   **Knospe** ['knɔspə]
lispeln ['lɪspəln]   **Liebestreue** ['liːbəsˌtrɔøə]

H, V, W, X

h   At the beginning of a word or stem, *h* is given its customary sound (familiar from English), produced by a short voiceless air flow:

Hauch [haox]   **holen** ['hoːlən]   **erheben** [ɛɐˈheːbən]

The same sound occurs in the suffixes -*heit* and -*haft*:

Schönheit ['ʃøːnhaet]   **lebhaft** ['leːphaft]

When *h* follows a vowel within a stem, it is *silent* but renders the preceding vowel closed and/or long:

sehen ['zeːən]   **ruhig** ['ruːɪç]   **Höhe** ['høːə]
sehr [zeːɐ]   **ihr** [iːɐ]   **wahr** [vaːr]

v   In words of Germanic origin, *v* is almost always found at the beginning of a word or stem and is pronounced /f/:

Vogel ['foːgəl]   **Veilchen** ['faelçən]   **davon** [da'fɔn]
unvergeßlich ['ʊnfɐɐgeslɪç]

(One example of medial –*v*– is **Frevel** ['freːfəl] and derivatives.)

In most words of foreign origin, *v* is pronounced /v/:

Klavier [kla'viːɐ]   **privat** [pri'vaːt]   **Universität** [univerzi'tɛːt]

although when final it devoices to /f/:

brav [braːf]   **Motiv** [mo'tiːf]   **intensiv** [ɪntɛn'ziːf]

w   The letter *w* is always pronounced /v/:

Wein [vaen]   **zwei** [tsvae]   **schwarz** [ʃvarts]   **weh** [veː]

except in proper names ending in *-ow*, when it is silent:

Bülow ['byːlo]   **Lützow** ['lʏtso]

x   The letter *x* is always pronounced /ks/. It has the effect of two consonants, thus causing the preceding vowel to be open and short:

Nixe ['nɪksə]   **fixieren** [fɪ'ksiːrən]   **Hexe** ['hɛksə]

Pay particular attention to initial **ex-** plus vowel. Notice the difference from French and English. In German this pattern is always pronounced [ɛks]:

Exemplar [ɛksɛm'plaːr]   **exakt** [ɛk'sakt]   **Exil** [ɛk'siːl]

Z, TZ, SZ, C

The letter *z* is always /ts/:

Zug [tsuːk]   **Zigeuner** [tsi'gɔønɐ]   **Lenz** [lɛnts]

There is no difference in pronunciation between *z* and *tz*; both are /ts/. This is true even when *t* and *z* are in different word elements, as in the last

two examples below. Siebs and Duden differ slightly in how they transcribe such cases, but both imply that it is incorrect to give a separate articulation to the *t* (or release the *t*) and then pronounce /ts/:

setzen ['sɛtsən]   **jetzt** [jɛtst]
entzwei [ɛn'tsvae]   **entzücken** [ɛn'tsʏkən]

The combination *sz* (non-Germanic) is rare. Each letter takes its own
sound, /sts/:

Szene ['stseːnə]   **szenisch** ['stseːnɪʃ]   **faszinieren** [fastsiniːrən]

In words of Germanic origin the letter *c* is found only in combination
with other consonant-letters (*ck*, *sch*). In words of foreign origin, however, *c* can stand alone as a single consonant. Initial *c* before *i*, *e*, or *ä* functions like *z* and is pronounced /ts/ (sometimes such words are spelled
with *z*):

Citrone [tsɪ'troːnə]   **Cäsar** ['tsɛːzar]
Ces [tsɛs]   **Cäcilie** [tsɛ'tsiːljə]

Before *a*, *o*, and *u* the pronunciation of *c* is /k/:

Café [ka'fe]

Other Consonant Combinations

gn   is pronounced /gn/ (the *g* is not silent as in English):

Gnade ['gnaːdə]   **gnädig** ['gnɛːdɪç]

ill   in some foreign words is pronounced /iɣ/ or /ilj/:

Pedrillo [pe'driɣo] (from Spanish)
Pavillon ['paviljõ] or [...jõ] (modified from French)

kn   is pronounced /kn/ (the *k* is not silent as in English):

Knie [kniː]   **Knote** ['knoːtə]
Knödel ['knøːdəl]   **knapp** [knap]

ng   is pronounced /ŋ/ as in English *singer*. It is never /ŋg/ as in English
finger:

lang [laŋ]   **Finger** [fɪŋɐ]   **Sänger** ['zɛŋɐ]   **Engel** ['ɛŋəl]

If *n* and *g* are adjacent but in different word elements, they are pronounced separately:

Angesicht ['angəˌzɪçt]   **Mühlengesang** ['myːləngəˌzaŋ]

nk   is pronounced /ŋk/, just as in English:

danken ['daŋkən]   **Frankreich** ['fraŋkraeç]   **Bank** [baŋk]

pf   is pronounced /pf/. When initial, the /p/ sound is very light and quick:

Pferd [pfeːɐt]   **Pforte** ['pfɔrtə]
Pfingsten [pfɪŋstən]   **Kopf** [kɔpf]

ps   is pronounced /ps/. The *p* is never silent as in English:

Psalm [psalm]   **Psychologie** [psyçoloˈgiː]

ph   is pronounced /f/ as in English. It functions as one consonant in determining the length of the preceding vowel:

Philosoph [filoˈzoːf]   **Phrase** ['fraːzə]

qu   is pronounced /kv/. It is never /kw/ as in English:

Qual [kvaːl]   **Quelle** ['kvɛlə]   **Quartier** [kvarˈtiːr]

th   is pronounced /t/ when both letters are part of the same element:

Theater [teˈaːtɐ]   **Apotheke** [apoˈteːkə]

Sometimes old German uses *th* where modern German uses only *t*:

Theil   Teil [tael]   **Rath   Rat** [raːt]

If *t* and *h* belong to different word elements, they are pronounced separately:

Rathaus ['raːthaos]   **Gottheit** ['gɔthaet]

ti   is pronounced /tsj/ in the suffixes –*tion* and –*tient*:

Nation [naˈtsjoːn]   **Aktion** [akˈtsjoːn]   **Patient** [paˈtsjɛnt]

tsch   is pronounced /tʃ/ as in English **church**. This is the only way to spell this sound in German:

Deutsch [dɔøtʃ]   **tschechish** ['tʃɛçɪʃ]

Double Consonants

In spoken German, double consonants are not particularly lengthened as they are in Italian. In *sung* German, however, they often are. This is especially true in slower, more sustained singing, where the lengthened consonant sound helps to imply the short vowel sound preceding it.

IPA transcription for German does not normally use two consonant symbols to indicate a lengthened sound. Nevertheless, the student should listen carefully to native-speaking singers of German and develop a sense of when a subtle lengthening of the double consonant is appropriate.

The following lists compare similarly spelled words that are differentiated by single and double consonants. In the pronounciation of these words, the essential difference is in the vowel quality and length in the stressed syllable.

ihre	[ˈiːrə]	**irre**	[ˈɪrə]
hehren	[ˈheːrən]	**Herren**	[ˈhɛrən]
fühlen	[ˈfyːlən]	**füllen**	[ˈfʏlən]
bieten	[ˈbiːtən]	**bitten**	[ˈbɪtən]
Höhle	[ˈhøːlə]	**Hölle**	[ˈhœlə]

When the combination -*ck*- is divided syllabically, as it often is in musical scores, it is spelled *k-k*: **blicken** becomes **blik-ken**, **Locken** becomes **Lok-ken**. Sometimes students make the mistake of spelling such words with double *kk*, a combination that otherwise exists only rarely, in non-Germanic words such as **Akkord**.

Phrasal Doublings

In German (as in English) the term "phrasal doublings" refers to the lengthening of a consonant sound when it ends one word and begins the next word within a phrase:

> **dein Name**   **dem Meere**   **der Tag kommt**

The same phenomenon may occur between elements of compound words:

> **Nebelland**   **niederrinnen**   **Bettdecke**

In such cases the consonant sound should be prolonged in the manner of Italian double consonants. The amount of prolongation depends on context, primarily the amount of time the word has to be pronounced.

MORE ABOUT SYLLABIC STRESS AND VOWEL LENGTH

As was described above, most simple polysyllabic words have one stressed syllable, on the word stem. However, syllabic stress works somewhat differently in certain kinds of words:

- Compound Words
  Compound words, a common feature of German, have more than one stem. Such words have a primary stress on the first stem (phonetic symbol /ˈ/ preceding) and secondary stresses on subsequent stems (phonetic symbol /ˌ/ preceding). Vowel length and quality in all stems are still determined by the number of consonants ending the stem. Words such as **Liebeslied** [ˈliːbəsˌliːt] and **Totenklage** [ˈtoːtənˌklaːgə] therefore have two long vowels. In the word **Herbst-gefühl** [ˈhɛrpstgəˌfyːl] the syllable of primary stress has a short vowel sound and the secondary stress has a long vowel sound.

- Compound Adverbs
  Compound adverbs and similarly constructed words (i.e., **warum**, **allein**) are very common in German. They are usually two syllables but sometimes three. They take the stress on the *second element*. Unstressed first syllables have a closed but *short* vowel if that syllable is derived from a one-syllable word with a closed vowel. If the second element begins with a vowel, there is no glottal separation; it is wrong to give it one. Some examples:

zu**rück** [tsuˈrʏk]	da**zu** [daˈtsuː]	vor**über** [forˈyːbɐ]
hin**weg** [hɪnˈvɛk]	her**an** [hɛrˈan]	so**fort** [zoˈfɔrt]
wo**her** [voːˈheːɐ]	vor**bei** [forˈbae]	wie**wohl** [viˈvoːl]
ein**an**der [aenˈandɐ]	zu**sam**men [tsuˈzamən]	

  also zu**fried**en [tsuˈfriːdən], an adjective

- Words with Separable Prefixes
  These words have a different stress pattern and are discussed in detail in the next section.

- Monosyllabic Words
  Monosyllabic words are very common, and their vowel quality is more irregular than in polysyllabic words; some have closed vow-

els and some have open vowels (patterns and extensive word lists are found on pp. 122). If such a word has a closed vowel, the vowel is long. According to both Siebs and Duden, this category includes small, usually unstressed words such as **zu** [tsuː], **so** [zoː], and **die** [diː].

There are a few other exceptions to syllabic stress patterns: most words ending in -*ei,* such as Brauer**ei**, Maler**ei**, and Sklaver**ei** (although not **ein**erlei and **man**cherlei, stressed on the first syllable); numerous proper names such as Jo**hann**es; and especially place names: Ber**lin**, Han**no**ver, and Bremer**ha**ven; in some words of temporal reference, such as Kar**frei**tag and Jahr**zehnt**; if the first element is a number or other quantifier / qualifier, such as Drei**grosch**enoper, Alt**weib**ersommer, and Barm**herz**igkeit.

Some words, according to Duden, have an equal double stress. This is rare:

allerdings [ˈalɐˈdɪŋs]   **immerhin** [ˈɪmɐˈhɪn]

MORE ABOUT GERMAN WORD STRUCTURE

Longer German words are formed by adding prefixes and suffixes to word stems. Prefixes fall into two categories, separable and inseparable. They are primarily associated with verbs, but other parts of speech derived from the verbs also use the prefixes. These prefixes are extremely common. It is important to recognize them and understand how they function, not only for meaning but for word stress and vowel quality.

Verbal Separable Prefixes

Separable prefixes (most derived from prepositions) are stressed in the infinitive (*ankommen, eintreten*), in the past participle (*angekommen, eingetreten*), and in other parts of speech derived from the verb (*Ankunft, Eintritt*). The prefix remains stressed in the phrase when separated from the verb: *ich komme an, sie treten ein.* The vowel quality and length of the prefix are retained from the original form of the word. Note which in the list below have open and/or short vowels and which have closed long vowels. Others have diphthongs or are polysyllabic. Polysyllabic prefixes often follow the pattern of compound adverbs with the stress on the second syllable.

German verbal separable prefixes with examples:

ab-	**abholen** [ˈapˌhoːlən]
an-	**anregen** [ˈanˌreːgən]
auf-	**aufmachen** [ˈaofˌmaxən]
aus-	**ausdrücken** [ˈaosˌdrʏkən]
bei-	**beistehen** [ˈbaeˌʃteːən]
da-	(usually as part of compound prefix)
	davonkommen [daˈfɔnˌkɔmən]
dar-	**darstellen** [ˈdarˌʃtɛlən]
durch-	**durchbringen** [ˈdʊrçˌbrɪŋən]
ein-	**einreden** [ˈaenˌreːdən]
empor-	**emporragen** [ɛmˈpoːɐˌraːgən]
entgegen-	**entgegenhalten** [ɛntˈgeːgənˌhaltən]
fort-	**fortsetzen** [ˈfɔrtˌzɛtsən]
heim-	**heimkehren** [ˈhaemˌkeːrən]
her-	**herkommen** [ˈheːɐˌkɔmən]
hin-	**hinsehen** [ˈhɪnˌzeːən]
los-	**losgeben** [ˈloːsˌgeːbən]
mit-	**mitmachen** [ˈmɪtˌmaxən]
nach-	**nachschlagen** [ˈnaːxˌʃlaːgən]
nieder-	**niederlegen** [ˈniːdɐˌleːgən]
um-	**umkehren** [ˈʊmˌkeːrən]
vor-	**vorsingen** [ˈfoːɐˌzɪŋən]
vorbei-	**vorbeigehen** [foɐˈbaeˌgeːən]
weg-	**wegwerfen** [ˈvɛkˌvɛɐfən]
weiter-	**weiterbringen** [ˈvaetɐˌbrɪŋən]
zu-	**zugreifen** [ˈtsuːˌgraefən]
zurück-	**zurückdenken** [tsuˈrʏkˌdɛŋkən]
zusammen-	**zusammenfassen** [tsuˈzamənˌfasən]

Verbal Inseparable Prefixes

Inseparable prefixes, on the other hand, always remain attached to the stem. These are primarily associated with verbs but are frequently found in other parts of speech as well. The following seven inseparable prefixes are very common and are *always* unstressed:

Two with /ə/:

      ge- /gə/   **be-** /bə/

Five with /ɛ/:

      er- /ɛr/ or /ɛɐ/   **ver-** /fɛr/, /fɛɐ/   **zer-** /tsɛr/, /tsɛɐ/   **emp-** /ɛmp/
      ent- /ɛnt/

Although prepositions as prefixes are usually separable, they can become *inseparable* verbal prefixes, most commonly *unter* and *über* and also sometimes *um* and *durch*. They too remain attached to the stem and generally do not take the primary stress; however, nouns derived from such verbs sometimes take the stress on the prefix and sometimes do not:

> unter**rich**ten, ich unter**rich**te, unter**rich**tet, **Un**terricht
> unter**brech**en, ich unter**brech**e,unter**broch**en, Unter**brech**ung.
> über**trag**en, ich über**trag**e, übertragen, **Über**trag
> über**leg**en, ich über**leg**e, über**legt**, **Über**legung

Further examples of unstressed, inseparable prefixes are um**rank**en, um**hüll**en, um**wob**en, durch**stöb**ern, durch**walt**en, voll**bring**en, and voll**end**en, among others.

Stressed Inseparable Prefixes

Two common prefixes that are normally used with *nouns*, *adjectives*, and *adverbs* are **in-** /ɪn/ and **un-** /ʊn/. The vowels are open and the prefixes are generally *stressed*, taking the stress away from the word stem (**In**haber, **In**begriff, **In**brunst, **Un**glück, **Un**fall, **un**gern, **un**erhört), though there are exceptions, and sometimes the stress can vary according to the sense the speaker wishes to convey.

Another prefix used in nouns and adjectives is **ur-**, as in **ur**alt, **Ur**wald, and **Ur**vater. The prefix is stressed and the vowel is long and closed /uːr-/ or /uːɐ-/. The prefix **miss-** (**miß-**) is stressed before nouns: **Miss**verständnis [ˈmɪsfɛɐˌʃtɛntnɪs], but is variable before verbs: **miß**verstehen [ˈmɪsfɛɐˌʃteːən], **miß**billigen [mɪsˈbɪligən].

Summary of Suffixes

Six common German suffixes have closed and/or long vowels resulting in the occurrence of such sounds in unstressed syllables:

-bar	**dankbar** [ˈdaŋkbaːr]	**verwendbar** [fɛɐˈvɛntbaːr]
-sal	**Trübsal** [ˈtryːpzaːl]	**Wirrsal** [ˈvɪrzaːl]
-sam	**langsam** [ˈlaŋzaːm]	**mühsam** [ˈmyːzaːm]
-los	**endlos** [ˈɛntloːs]	**leblos** [ˈleːploːs]
-mut	**Demut** [ˈdeːmuːt]	**Armut** [ˈarmuːt]
-tum	**Altertum** [ˈaltɐtuːm]	**Heiligtum** [ˈhaelɪçtuːm]

Some of these suffixes are subject to extended forms. The syllable in question remains unstressed, closed, and long:

-losigkeit   **Bewegungslosigkeit** [bə've:guŋslo:zɪçkaet]
-tümlich   **eigentümlich** ['aegənty:mlɪç]

In addition, the less common suffix *-artig* has long /aː/ and is pronounced
with a glottal separation: **grossartig** ['grosʔˌaːrtɪç]

All other suffixes have open/short vowels, schwa, or diphthongs. Those
that begin with vowels do not take a glottal separation:

Noun Suffixes

-chen	**Mädchen** ['mɛːtçən]	**Liebchen** [liːpçən]
-heit	**Schönheit** ['ʃøːnhaet]	**Sicherheit** ['zɪçɐhaet]
-keit	**Eitelkeit** ['aetəlkaet]	**Dankbarkeit** ['daŋkbaːrkaet]
-in	**Gräfin** ['grɛːfin]	**Freundin** ['frɔøndɪn]
-lein	**Blümlein** ['blyːmlaen]	**Fräulein** ['frɔølaen]
-ling	**Frühling** ['fryːlɪŋ]	**Fremdling** ['frɛmtlɪŋ]
-nis	**Ergebnis** [ɛɐ'geːpnɪs]	**Bedürfnis** [bə'dʏrfnɪs]
-schaft	**Botschaft** ['boːtʃaft]	**Leidenschaft** ['laedənʃaft]
-ung	**Regung** ['reːguŋ]	**Meinung** ['maenuŋ]

The suffix *-ei* (**Konditorei** [kɔndito'rae], **Lorelei** [lore'lae]) usually has
the stress on the final syllable, with vowels following non-Germanic patterns. Sometimes, however, *-ei* is unstressed: **einerlei** ['aenɐlae].

Adjective Suffixes

-haft	**lebhaft** ['leːphaft]	**boshaft** [boːshaft]
-ig	**selig** ['zeːlɪç]	**wonnig** ['vɔnɪç]
-isch	**komisch** [koːmɪʃ]	**irdisch** ['ɪrdɪʃ]
-lich	**wunderlich** ['vundɐlɪç]	**vergeblich** [fɛɐ'geːplɪç]

Remember that suffixes play no role in determining the quality and
length of the stem vowel: **Bote / Botschaft**.

Verbal Endings

It is imperative to learn the common verbal endings. Like suffixes, they
are not part of the stem and do not influence the stem vowel. In all of

these forms of the verb **hören**, no matter the ending, the stressed vowel is *long and closed* /øː/.

Present Tense		*Simple Past Tense*	
ich höre	wir hören	ich hörte	wir hörten
du hörst	ihr hört	du hörtest	ihr hörtet
er hört	sie hören	er hörte	sie hörten

Past Participle
gehört

Changing Vowels in Verbs

German irregular verbs (so-called strong verbs) change vowels in different forms of the verb. Sometimes the vowel quality and length change with the vowel change, sometimes not. Often the spelling will make matters clear, but not always. One can learn to recognize patterns to help in remembering some of these changes. Here are some common examples:

Long (Closed) Becomes Short (Open)	*Short (Open) Becomes Long (Closed)*
schliessen /iː/, **schloss, geschlossen** /ɔ/	**bitten** /ɪ/, **bat** /aː/, **gebeten** /eː/
giessen /iː/, **goss, gegossen** /ɔ/	**kommen** /ɔ/, **kam** /aː/, **gekommen** /ɔ/
fliessen /iː/, **floss, geflossen** /ɔ/	**treffen** /ɛ/, **traf** /aː/, **getroffen** /ɔ/
mögen /øː/, **mag** /aː/, **mochte, gemocht** /ɔ/	**sitzen** /ɪ/, **sass** /aː/, **gesessen** /ɛ/
stehen /eː/, **stand, gestanden** /a/	**sprechen** /ɛ/, **sprach** /aː/, **gesprochen** /ɔ/
gehen /eː/, **ging** /ɪ/, **gegangen** /a/	**lassen** /a/, **liess** /iː/, **gelassen** /a/
werden /eː/, **wird** /ɪ/, **wurde** /ʊ/, **geworden** /ɔ/	**fallen** /a/, **fiel** /iː/, **gefallen** /a/

Vowel Changes but Length Remains Constant

rufen /uː/, **rief** /iː/	**raten** /aː/, **riet** /iː/
schlafen /aː/, **schlief** /iː/	**tragen** /aː/, **trug** /uː/
schlagen /aː/, **schlug** /uː/	**geben** /eː/, **gibt, gibst** /iː/, **gab** /aː/
wiegen /iː/, **wog** /oː/	**ziehen** /iː/, **zog** /oː/

CERTAIN CONSONANT CLUSTERS AND VOWEL QUALITY

Words with -gn-

A stressed vowel followed by -gn is closed (long), because such words are derived from words spelled with -gen:

regnen ['reːgnən] (from **Regen**)
segnen ['zeːgnən] (from **Segen**)
Lügner ['lyːgnɐ] (from **lügen**)
Wagner ['vaːgnɐ] (from **Wagen**)
begegnen [bəˈgeːgnən], **Begegnung** [bəˈgeːgnʊŋ] (from **gegen**)

Before the following combinations, stressed vowels are sometimes open and sometimes closed.

Words with -ch-

- *i*, *e*, and *o* are open:

  ich [ɪç]   **dich** [dɪç]   **sich** [zɪç]
  Pech [pɛç]   **sprechen** [ˈʃprɛçən]
  noch [nɔx]   **doch** [dɔx]   **kochen** [ˈkɔxən]

  Exception: **hoch** [hoːx] has /oː/, but **Hochzeit** [hɔxtsaet] has /ɔ/.

- *a* is sometimes long, sometimes short:

  nach [naːx]   **Sprache** [ˈʃpraːxə]   **Dach** [dax]   **Bach** [bax]

- *u* and *ü* are usually *closed*:

  Buch [buːx]   **Bücher** [ˈbyːçɐ]   **Fluch** [fluːx]
  suchen [ˈzuːxən]   **gesucht** [gəˈzuːxt]

  but before -*cht* (in the stem), the *u* or *ü* is *open*:

  Bucht [bʊxt]   **Sucht** [zʊxt]   **Flucht** [flʊxt]

Words with -ss-, -ß-

- *i* and *e* are *open*:

  Kisse [ˈkɪsə]   **Gebiß** [gəˈbɪs]   **essen** [ˈɛsən]
  vergessen [fɛɐˈgɛsən]

- *a* is usually short, sometimes long:

    blaß [blas]   **fassen** [ˈfasən]   but **Maß** [maːs]

- *o, ö, u, ü* are sometimes *open*, sometimes *closed*:

    gross [groːs]   **Schloss** [ʃlɔs]
    grösste [ˈgrøːstə]   **Schlösser** [ˈʃlœsɐ]
    Fuß [fuːs]   **Kuß** [kʊs]
    süß [zyːs]   **küssen** [ˈkʏsən]

(N. B. ß, called *Eszett,* is a ligature of the two forms of handwritten *s* or the letters *s* and *z* from older German spelling. It has been officially eliminated from German usage (not without controversy), but it will still be encountered in material printed before the reform. ß and *ss* are interchangeable except that ß cannot occur between vowels if the preceding vowel is short. Thus **Kuß** and **Kuss** are both acceptable spellings, but the plural has to be spelled **Küsse**, and the verb has to be spelled **küssen**. The plural of **Fuß** (or **Fuss**) can be spelled either **Füße** or **Füsse**.)

GERMAN MONOSYLLABIC (SOME POLYSYLLABIC) WORD PATTERNS FOR VOWEL QUALITY AND LENGTH

The following lists are meant to be used for quick reference in helping to determine *vowel quality in monosyllabic words and irregular polysyllabic words.* Some spelling patterns are consistent in the resulting sounds, but others are not. Most vowels in monosyllables ending in one consonant are closed/long and most ending in two or more consonants are open/short, but there are many common exceptions which must be memorized. The lists, while extensive, are not necessarily exhaustive.

Monosyllabic words with *h* following the vowel always have a *closed and/ or long vowel*:

    ihn, ihm, ihr, mehr, Ohr, Rohr, sehr, wahr, Uhr

Monosyllabic words ending in a vowel always have a *closed and/or long vowel*:

    da, du, ja, je, sie, so, wie, wo, zu

Monosyllabic words ending in a vowel + *r* always have a *closed and/or long vowel*:

Bär, der, dir, er, Flur, für, gar, her (standing alone), **mir, nur, quer, schwer, Tor, Tür, vor, war, wer, wir, zur, zwar;** note also **empor** [ɛmˈpoːr]

Monosyllabic words ending in *i* + a consonant (other than *r*) have an *open short vowel* /ɪ/:

bin, bis, hin, in, im, mit

Most monosyllabic words ending in *-u* and *-ü* plus one consonant have a *long closed vowel*:

Blut, Flug, Flut, Glut, grün, gut, Hut, klug, Mut, nun, tun (all forms), **Zug;** note also **genug.** *Exceptions:* **um** and **zum** have /ʊ/ also **durch** [dʊrç] (regular)

Most monosyllabic words ending in *-o* and *-ö* plus one consonant have a *long closed vowel*:

Brot, Dom, Hof, Lob, Los, Not, Rom, rot, schon, schön, Strom, Tod, Ton, tot. *Exceptions:* **ob, von, vom** have /ɔ/

Monosyllabic words ending in *-e* plus one consonant:

Closed: **der, den, dem, gen (*gegen*), her** (standing alone), **quer, Steg, Weg** (noun), **wem, wen, wer;** also **bequem** [bəˈkveːm]

Open: **es, des, wes;** note also **Hexe** [ˈhɛksə]

Other words with *long closed* /eː/:

Ade [aˈdeː]**, begegnen, Dresden** [ˈdreːzdən]**, jeglich, Krebs, regnen, segnen, stets** (see also below, words with stressed *-er-*)

Summary of monosyllabic words ending in a vowel + one consonant that have an *open short vowel*:

bin, bis, des, es, hin, im, in, mit, ob, um, vom, von, weg (adverb), **wes, zum**

Words with *-ost-*:

Closed /oː/: **Kloster, Ostern, Trost**

Open /ɔ/: **Frost, Most, Ost, Rost**

Other irregular monosyllables with *long closed* /oː/:

Mond, Obst, Vogt

Monosyllables ending in *-och*:

>   *Closed* /oː/: **hoch** (note also **höchst** [høːçst])

>   *Open* /ɔ/: **Bloch, doch, Joch, Koch, Loch, noch** (note also **Hochzeit**)

Monosyllables ending in *-oss* (*-oß*):

>   *Closed* /oː/: **bloss, gross, Schoss, Stoss, stoss (stossen)**

>   *Open* /ɔ/: **Schloss, floss (fliessen), goss (giessen)**

Monosyllables ending in *-uss* (*-uß*):

>   *Closed* /uː/: **Buss, Fuss, Gruss, (grüssen, büssen**—all forms have /yː/
>   or /uː/), also **süss** /yː/

>   *Open* /ʊ/: **Fluss, Kuss, Nuss, Schluss, muss (müssen, küssen**—all
>   forms have /ʏ/ or /ʊ/)

Monosyllables ending in *-uch* and polysyllables with stem ending *-uch*
have closed /uː/:

>   **Buch, Fluch, suchen** (all forms, e.g., **sucht**), **Tuch**

Monosyllables ending in *-ucht* (in the stem) have open /ʊ/:

>   **Bucht, Flucht, Sucht** (as a noun and suffix)

If other forms require an umlaut over the vowel in the above categories,
the corresponding mixed vowel retains the closed or open quality of the
basic form of the word; for example, **gross** /oː/, **grösser** /øː/; **Schloss**
/ɔ/, **Schlösser** /œ/.

Monosyllables and polysyllables containing stressed *-er* plus consonant
with *closed long* /eː/:

>   **Berg, erst, Erde, Erz** (noun), **Herd, Pferd, Schwert, werden, wert**

Monosyllables and polysyllables containing stressed *-er* plus consonant
with *short open* /ɛ/:

>   **erben, ernst, Erz-** (as a prefix as in **Erzbischof**), **fern, fertig, gern,
>   Herberge, Herz, Lerche, Schmerz, Werk**

Other irregular polysyllabic words with long closed vowels:

>   **Geburt** /uː/, **Wüste** /yː/, **düster** /yː/

Monosyllables ending *a* plus one consonant:

> *Long* /aː/: **Grab, Gras, Mal, Qual, Schaf, Schlaf, Tal, Tag, Tat, tat (tun), war, mag (mögen), kam (kommen)**

> *Short* /a/: **an, am, ab, man, hat, das**

Monosyllables and some polysyllables with *-ach*:

> *Long* /aː/: **nach, Sprache, sprach (sprechen), brach (brechen), stach (stechen)**

> *Short* /a/: **ach, Bach, Dach, Nacht, Swach**, also **Nachen**

Monosyllables and a few polysyllables with *-ass (-aß)*:

> *Long* /aː/: **Maß (Mass), Straße (Strasse), Spaß (Spass), aß (essen)**

> *Short* /a/: **daß, Gasse, naß (nass)**

Monosyllables ending *-art* and *-agd* have *long* /aː/:

> **Art, Bart, Jagd, Magd, zart**, also **Arzt**

Other words with with *-a* plus two or more consonants having *long* /aː/:

> **Adler, Bratsche, habt** (*haben*)**, Papst, Wagner**

Note that in a verb such as **sagen** the /aː/ is long in all forms, following the infinitive, but **haben** has short /a/ in **hat** and **hast**, and long /aː/ in all other forms. The irregularities of the various forms of **sein** and **werden** must be memorized, since they are very commonly encountered.

Note also, more generally, that a monosyllable with a long vowel is often unstressed within the phrase. The vowel length may not be clearly in evidence in such instances. In singing, this may happen in *parlando* passages, in faster tempi, or when such words are set to short note values. When it is possible and appropriate, however, the proper vowel length should be brought out.

WORDS OF NON-GERMANIC ORIGIN

As was noted on p. 85, German is full of words derived from Latin and Greek. *Word stress* patterns and the rules for determining *vowel quality* in such words are different from those for words of Germanic origin.

Word Stress in Words of Non-Germanic Origin

Word stress in non-Germanic words generally does not conform to the patterns for Germanic words. Perhaps the most common pattern in these words finds the stress on the final syllable:

Two-syllable words:

Mu**sik**	Ak**kord**	Te**nor**	So**pran**	Kri**tik**
Fi**gur**	Per**son**	Na**tion**	Che**mie**	di**rekt**

Three or more syllables:

Melo**die**	Kompo**nist**	interes**sant**	posi**tiv**
Tele**fon**	Psycholo**gie**	Universi**tät**	Redak**tion**

One can learn to recognize certain suffixes (*-tion, -tät, -ist*) as following this pattern.

Some words of this type end in unstressed *e* or *e* plus a consonant. The word stress falls on the preceding syllable:

Inte**res**se	Ar**ti**kel	Ana**ly**se

Many Latin- and Greek-derived words not ending in unstressed *e*, however, particularly two-syllable words, take the stress on the penult:

Amor	**Chi**na	**pur**pur	**Ly**rik	**Tech**nik	**Ba**sis

Vowel Quality in Words of Non-Germanic Origin

Because non-Germanic words do not usually involve word stems, *pretonic vowels* (that is, vowels in syllables preceding the word stress) and *tonic vowels* (those in the stressed syllable) normally determine their quality simply by how many consonants follow:

If only one consonant follows, the vowel is closed:

Melodie [melo'diː] **Telefon** [tele'foːn]

If two or more consonants follow, the vowel is usually open:

effektiv [ɛfɛk'tiːf] **Komponist** [kɔmpo'nɪst]

Because the structure of such words is not based on word stems as with Germanic words, syllabification plays a role (see the syllabification sections in the Italian and French chapters). If the vowel ends the syllable (except

for final unstressed *e*), it will be closed, even if followed by two consonants (which are in the next syllable).

>**Sopran** (So-pran) [zoˈpraːn]
>**Problem** (Pro-blem) [proˈbleːm]
>**Zypresse** (Zy-pres-se) [tsyˈprɛsə]
>**Psychologie** (Psy-cho-lo-gie) [psyçoloˈgiː]
>**Katastrophe** (Ka-ta-stro-phe) [kataˈstroːfə]
>**Petrus** (Pe-trus) [ˈpeːtrʊs]

Post-tonic vowels are open if followed by a consonant, closed if final.
They are always short:

>**Lyrik** [ˈlyːrɪk]   **purpur** [ˈpʊrpʊr]
>**Fidelio** [fiˈdeːljo]   **Alibi** [ˈaːlibi]

Vowel Length in Words of Non-Germanic Origin

Only tonic vowels can be long, and then only if they are closed in quality.
All nontonic vowels are short, even if closed, as in **Musik** [muˈziːk]). Tonic
vowels are short if open in quality. Tonic *ä* and *a* are long when followed
by one consonant.

>**Dirigent** [diriˈgɛnt]   **Telefon** [teleˈfoːn]
>**Requisit** [rekviˈziːt]   **intensiv** [ɪntɛnˈziːf]
>**Orchester** [ɔrˈkɛstɐ]   **Partitur** [partiˈtuːr]
>**Apparat** [appaˈraːt]   **Universität** [univerziˈtɛːt]
>**rekreieren** [rekreˈiːrən]
>(The Latin prefix *re-* always has closed /e/ in German words.)

Post-tonic *e* is usually schwa:

>**Interesse** [ɪnteˈrɛsə]   **Artikel** [arˈtiːkəl]

but occasionally /ɛ/:

>**Sokrates** [ˈzoːkratɛs]   **Josef** [ˈjoːzɛf]

There is a family of Latin-derived words that ends in unstressed *-ie*, pronounced /jə/:

>**Familie** [faˈmiːljə]   **Lilie** [ˈliːljə]   **Komödie** [koˈmøːdjə]
>**Tragödie** [traˈgøːdjə] **Linie** [ˈliːnjə]   **Arie** [ˈaːrjə]

but in the words **Grenadier** and **Quartier**, as in Heine/Schumann *Die* *beiden Grenadiere*, the *-ie-* is stressed and pronounced /iː/: [grenaˈdiːr], [kvarˈtiːr].

A family of geographical names ends in unstressed *-ien*, pronounced /jən/:

> **Italien** [iˈtaːljən]   **Spanien** [ˈʃpaːnjən]   **Belgien** [ˈbɛlgjən]
> **Asien** [ˈaːzjən] (but **Italiener** [italˈjeːnɐ], **Spanier** [ˈʃpaːnjɐ])

Words (derived from Greek) ending in *stressed -ie* (pronounced /iː/) take a plural of *-ien* (pronounced /iːən/):

> **Harmonie** [harmoˈniː]   **Harmonien**[harmoˈniːən]
> **Melodie** [meloˈdiː]   **Melodien** [meloˈdiːən]
> **Symphonie** [zʏmfoˈniː]   **Symphonien** [zʏmfoˈniːən]

Likewise:

> **Melancholie** [melaŋkoˈliː] **Poesie** [poeˈziː]
> **Phantasie** [fantaˈziː]

German also uses many French words and some English words. Such words are pronounced as in the original language:

> **Régie** [reʒi]   **Souffleur** [suflœːr]   **Parfum** [parfœ̃]
> ... **die Goldorangen glühn** ... [ˈgɔltorãʒən]
> (Goethe, *Kennst du das Land*)

GLOTTAL SEPARATION IN GERMAN

A characteristic of German, as of English, is that words that begin with a vowel are usually initiated with a light glottal stroke. The IPA symbol for this sound is /ʔ/, although both Siebs and Duden use /|/. Compare in English:

> **announce** [ʔəˈnaUns]   **an ounce** [ʔænʔaUns]

Say the following German phrases using a gentle glottal attack on each word that begins with a vowel:

> **Er ist ein alter Mann** [ʔeːɐ ʔɪst ʔaen ʔaltɐ man]
> **In einem Augenblick** [ʔɪn ʔaenəm ʔaogənblɪk]
> **Ich unglücksel'ger Atlas** [ʔɪç ʔʊnglʏkˌzeːlgɐ ʔatlas]

Moreover, such glottal separation is required in German when a word stem begins with a vowel; that is, when a prefix immediately precedes a vowel or when an element within a compound word begins with a vowel:

geändert [gəʔˈɛndɐt]	**verantworten** [fɛɐ̯ʔˈantvɔrtən]
beobachten [bəʔˈoːbaxtən]	**Abendessen** [ʔabənt̩ʔˌɛsən]
erinnern [ʔɛɐ̯ʔˈɪnɐn]	**eigenartig** [ʔaegən̩ʔˌartɪç]

An exception to this rule is found in compound adverbs beginning with *her-*, *hin-*, *dar-*, *vor-*, and *wor-*, as well as in the isolated word **warum**. If the second element begins with a vowel, *there is no glottal separation* before the second element:

herein [hɛˈraen]	**hinab** [hɪˈnap]	**daran** [daˈran]
vorüber [foˈryːbɐ]	**worauf** [voˈraof]	

However, similar constructions formed from elements other than the above will employ the glottal stroke:

bergab [bɛrkˈʔap]	**bergan** [bɛrkˈʔan]

Siebs and Duden indicate glottal separation after the prefix *un-* when it is followed by a vowel:

unaufhörlich [ˈʊnʔˌaofhøːrlɪç]	**unendlich** [ʊnʔˈɛntlɪç]

though connection is frequently heard in such words, in speech as well as in singing.

In German speech, and often in singing, if the word beginning with a vowel is unstressed in the phrase, the glottal separation is frequently omitted. With a normal inflection, the question **Muss ich?** would not have such a separation. If the inflection of the question put the stress on **ich**, there would be a separation. English exhibits similar characteristics in this regard.

GLOTTAL SEPARATION VERSUS LEGATO CONNECTION IN SINGING GERMAN

In singing, glottal strokes should be light and quick so as not to detract from the legato line. It is often permissible, even desirable, to eliminate the glottal separation altogether. The singer should also develop the skill of releasing final consonants and articulating a following vowel with a subtle lift that implies a brief glottal separation but is different from a true glottal.

When to employ the glottal and when not to is a complex issue. The singer is constantly faced with a variety of such situations in German. Decisions will be influenced by musical style, tempo, and the relative importance of musical or textual considerations at that particular moment. In listening to native German-speaking singers, one commonly hears elimination of glottals to enhance legato. In *Lieder* performance this is probably the rule rather than the exception, but do not be surprised to hear different solutions to the same phrase, since there is no absolute uniformity on this point, just as there is no absolute uniformity on pronouncing *r* with a flip of the tongue or as /ɐ/.

Until the singer develops a sense of when to use or omit glottal strokes, two rules of thumb are helpful to remember:

1. Important words in stressed positions, if they begin with a vowel, will likely take a glottal attack (there certainly are exceptions to this rule).
2. If omitting a glottal stroke alters the meaning of a word, or if it unduly compromises the clarity of the text, the glottal stroke should be done.

It cannot be stressed enough that any glottal usage should be light.

Important words can be any part of speech, but here are some examples of nouns in stressed positions that would require a glottal separation:

Kriegers Ahnung—Schubert

lag   sie   in   mei - nem   **Arm**
[laːk ziː ɪn ˈmaenəm ʔarm]

Wie Melodien—
Brahms

und   führt   es   vor   das   **Aug**
[ʊnt fyːrt ɛs foːr das ʔaok]

Vier Ernste Gesänge
—Brahms

so wär ich ein tön - end **Erz**
[zo veːr ɪç aen 'tøːnənt ʔeːrts]

Verbal separable prefixes are usually important and are stressed within a phrase. If the prefix begins with a vowel, it probably will require a glottal separation:

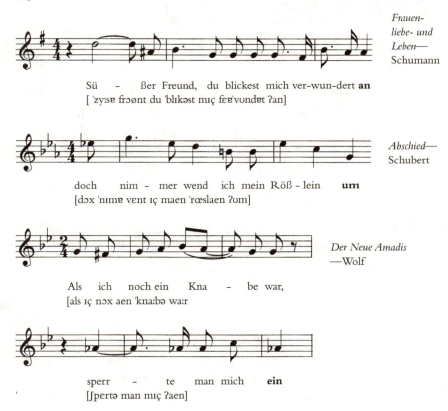

Frauen-liebe- und Leben—
Schumann

Sü - ßer Freund, du blickest mich ver-wun-dert **an**
['zyːsɐ frɔønt du 'blɪkəst mɪç fɐ'vʊndɐt ʔan]

Abschied—
Schubert

doch nim - mer wend ich mein Röß - lein **um**
[dɔx 'nɪmɐ vɛnt ɪç maen 'rœslaen ʔʊm]

Der Neue Amadis
—Wolf

Als ich noch ein Kna - be war,
[als ɪç nɔx aen 'knaːbə waːr

sperr - te man mich **ein**
[ʃpertə man mɪç ʔaen]

In this last example, notice that **ein** occurs twice, once as an unstressed article and once as a stressed verbal prefix (**einsperren**). The first would not require a glottal separation, whereas the second would.

The examples below present some other instances where the singer must decide whether a glottal separation is to be done or not. They are offered to raise awareness of the issue.

When *r* immediately precedes a word beginning with a vowel, a light flip into the subsequent vowel is often heard:

und zu dir ei - lig zieht
[ʊnt tsu diːr‿ˈaelɪç tsiːt] **or** [ʊnt tsu diːɐʔaelɪç tsiːt]

Ich wünscht, ich wär ein Vög - lein
[ɪç vʏnʃt ɪç veːr‿aen ˈføːklaen] **or** [ɪç vʏnʃt ʔɪç veːɐ ʔaen ˈføːklaen]

In a comparison of these two examples, the first is more likely to employ a light glottal separation after the *r*, because the next word (**eilig**) is stressed and emphasized in the musical setting. However, omission of the glottal and a flip of the *r* are still options here. The second example shows the word following the *r* (**ein**) as short and unstressed and therefore unlikely to warrant a glottal stroke.

Was ist Sylvia?
—Schubert

ih - rem Aug' eilt A - mor zu
[ˈiːrəm ʔaok aelt ˈaːmoːɐ tsu]

Here are four successive words beginning with vowels, two of which occur after rests. At the beginning of a phrase, or after a rest within a phrase, glottal attacks should be used very judiciously if at all. Concerning the other two words, it seems clear that **Aug'** should receive a light glottal separation, but **Amor** is less clear. The best solution is probably not a true glottal, but a release of the *t* of **eilt** that distinctly defines it as belonging to the preceding word rather than the following word. Certainly employing a glottal on all four words yields a very unmusical result.

Nur wer die Sehnsucht kennt
—Schubert

weiß was ich lei - de
[vaes vas ɪç ˈlaedə]

In this example, connection from **was** to **ich** is desirable since a glottal separation would emphasize **ich** too much and also detract from legato. As long as the *s* is not exaggerated, the intelligibility of **ich** is not compromised by connecting of the words (though too much time on the *s* might convey **sich**).

Here are two examples in a faster tempo:

Verge-
bliches
Ständ-
chen—
Brahms

Gu-ten   A-bend, mein Schatz, gu-ten   A - bend mein   Kind
['guːtən 'aːbənt maen ʃats 'guːtən 'aːbənt maen kınt]

Der Musensohn—Schubert

So   geht's   von Ort   zu   Ort
[zo geːts vɔn ʔ ɔrt tsu ɔrt]

In the first example, a clear glottal separation before **Abend** sounds unsatisfactory, probably because the note value is short. A connection of the preceding *n* is desirable, as long as it is light and unexaggerated. In the second example, by contrast, the glottal separation before the first occurrence of **Ort** is called for. Even a light connection of the preceding sound compromises the clarity of the text. The second occurrence, following a vowel, probably does not need a separation.

PHRASAL CONSONANT CLUSTERS IN GERMAN

It was mentioned in the Italian section of this text that most Italian words end in vowels and many begin with vowels, the result being the frequent occurrence of phrasal diphthongs and triphthongs. The opposite is true of German (and English). Most words begin with consonants and many end in consonants; the result is frequent juxtaposition of consonant sounds. In many cases this simply requires the singer to clearly articulate adjoining sounds with no separation between them:

all mein   **ich gehe**   **von dir**   **mit Kraft**

If the first sound is a stop consonant (as with **mit** above), there may be a slight separation before the next sound, particularly if the note values are long enough.

Sometimes the phrasal clusters are more difficult because they are not familiar to English speakers. The following example from Schubert's *Winterreise* requires the clear articulation of /sts/ for **es zieht.**

Gute Nacht—
Schubert

Es zieht ein Mon‑den ‑ schat ‑ ten

Here the combination /nftb/ is unusual. Students often have trouble with the word **sanft**:

*O wüsst ich doch—*Brahms

von Lie – be sanft be – deckt

A fairly common phrasal cluster is /çʃ/:

*Das verlassene Mägdlein—*Wolf

ich **sch**aue so da‑rein

*Ach Gol‑
gatha—
Matt‑
häus‑
Passion
—Bach*

Die Un – schuld muß hier schul‑di**g** **sch**ter – ben

Am Feierabend—
Schubert

Was **ich** **sch**nei – de, was **ich** **sch**la ‑ ge

Without separating the sounds, the singer must pronounce /ç/ and move smoothly to /ʃ/. In the first two examples, the relatively leisurely tempo allows for easier execution than the third, at a considerably faster tempo.

These examples (or similar ones) spoken slowly are an excellent means of getting students to hear clearly the difference between /ç/ and /ʃ/. Still another case is /sʃ/:

Des Müllers Blumen—Schubert

Wenn   al - les schweigt

Am Abend da es kühle war-
Matthäuspassion—Bach

Der   Frie - dens - schluß

In the second example, the first *s* is a "genitive s" connecting two parts of a compound word. In all such occurrences, the /s/ must be clear, even if very short, and must yield smoothly to /ʃ/. The lazy singer will omit /s/ and pronounce /ʃ/ only.

It must be said that sometimes consonant juxtapositions in German are particularly difficult to execute fully while musical quality is maintained within a particular musical setting. From the same Brahms song mentioned above:

O wüsst ich
doch—Brahms

Und nichts zu   for - schen,   nichts   zu   späh'n

The words **nichts zu** contain the phrasal consonant cluster /çtsts/. One commonly hears /çts/ only. With a light approach, it is possible to do the entire cluster.

Irrlicht—Schubert

Al - les ein - es   Irr - lichts Spiel

Similarly, this phrase contains /çtsʃp/ (on a very short note value!). In performance the /s/ tends to elide into the /ʃ/.

The singer must learn to articulate consonant juxtapositions clearly, and the proper approach is to do them lightly. Such an approach will prevent the tongue from getting tied up in knots while maintaining musical line. Since German patterns are frequently different from English patterns, some practice may be required.

POSSIBLE ASSIMILATION OF CONSONANT SOUNDS IN GERMAN

In situations involving the adjoining sounds /p/ and /b/; /k/ and /g/; /t/ and /d/; and /s/ and /z/, another, more common possibility of consonant elision arises: **und der** is [ʊnt deːɐ], but should the /t/ be fully released before articulating the /d/? In speech this would not happen unless there was a pause between the words. In normal speech the tongue makes contact with the palate in one motion simultaneously for both sounds, initially devoiced for /t/ but with voiced quality added as the tongue releases for /d/. The phrase **der Tag ging** would call for a similar simultaneous articulation of /k/ and /g/.

In singing, the tempo and style of the music will often determine whether such adjoining sounds should be articulated separately or simultaneously. The "heightened speech" nature of singing, which requires that words clearly project into a large space, results in far more separate articulations than does normal speech in such situations. Nevertheless, true legato singing often requires connection. The student should be aware of the possibilities and should try out the alternatives to determine what yields the most satisfactory result in a given situation, initially in the presence of a teacher or a coach.

A common occurrence of phrasal /td/ is in inversions of the **du** forms of verbs: **bist du, meinst du, lachst du**, and so on. Certainly if the note values are short, it is not necessary or desirable to separate the sounds:

*Ach, ich fühls—
Die Zauber-
flöte—Mozart*

fühl**st d**u nicht   der Liebe Sehnen
[fyːlst‿du nɪçt‿deːɐ (or [nɪçt deːɐ]) 'liːbə 'zeːnən]

When the note values are longer, either solution is possible. Intelligibility is rarely an issue, so the singer must decide whether or not separation otherwise enhances the phrase:

Kennst du das Land—Wolf

Kennst   du   das Land

Die Götter Griechenlands
—Schubert

Schö-ne Welt,   wo   bist   du?

Heimliche Auf-
forderung—
R. Strauss

Doch   hast   du   das Mahl   ge - nos - sen

Und
willst du
deinen—
Wolf

Und willst du deinen Liebsten ster - ben se - hen

Here are some further examples to consider:

Nacht—R. Strauss

Aus dem Wal   -   de **tritt die** Nacht

In this case a separate articulation of the *t* before the *d* seems the best solution. Connection could compromise text intelligibility and does not
particularly enhance legato line. The dotted rhythm also encourages placing the *t* distinctly on the second half of the second beat.

A bit later in the same song, however, connection seems the better
choice:

Nacht—
R. Strauss

und **stiehlt die** Gar   -   ben weg vom Feld

The lack of a dotted rhythm gives less time, causing separation to sound
fussy. The presence of the *l* before the *td* combination helps allow the
word **stiehlt** to be understood clearly.

The tempo of this song makes separation undesirable as well as virtually impossible:

An Schwager Kronos
—Schubert

Fort **den** rass - eln- den   Trott!

Here are two examples of phrasal /kg/:

Gute Nacht—Schubert

der   **We**g **g**e - hüllt   in   Schnee

Although the tempo here is moderate, and separation is possible, nothing is gained by it. Connection certainly enhances legato, and textual clarity is not compromised.

Kinder-
toten-
lieder—
Mahler

Das   Unglü**ck ge** - schah   nur   mir   al - lein

Here the slow tempo allows for the slight separation of the /k/ and /g/ sounds. The clarity of the text is also enhanced. The release of the /k/ should not overwhelm the /g/, however.

Separation is rarely done with phrasal /s/ and /z/, because they are continuing sounds. Furthermore it is very common to hear assimilation so that only a prolonged /s/ is heard:

An die ferne Geliebte
—Beethoven

Was   ge - schie - den   **uns**   **so**   weit

When time allows and the affected words are important, the release should have voicing so that /z/ is heard, however briefly:

An die Leier
—Schubert

Ich will von A - treus' Söhn en

An eine
Aeolsharfe
—Wolf

ge-heim - nis- vol - les Sai - ten- spiel

GERMAN DICTIONARIES AND PRONUNCIATION REFERENCE BOOKS

Most recently published German/English dictionaries employ the IPA, although small dictionaries may not. It is recommended that the student acquire a dictionary using IPA, but be advised that some dictionaries use a nonstandard IPA system for German vowels. While this text employs the standard IPA system that is used by Siebs and Duden (see below), the alternative system has only one IPA symbol for the open and closed vowel pairs. If the symbol has no colon, it is considered the open version of the vowel; if the symbol is followed by a colon, it is considered the closed version. In this system, German **wer** would be transcribed as [veːr] while **wenn** would be transcribed as [ven]. The more standard transcription of **wenn** is [ven].

The problem with the alternative approach is that there is no way to indicate those cases in which a closed vowel is short in duration, which is often the case with words of non-Germanic origin. Thus **Melodie** would be transcribed [meloˈdiː] and one would incorrectly assume that the first two syllables have open vowels. The system used by Siebs, Duden, and most diction texts would transcribe this word the same way, but since /e/ and /o/ represent closed vowels only, the reader would know that all vowels in this word are closed.

The two standard reference books for German pronunciation are *Siebs Deutsche Aussprache* and *Duden—Das Aussprachewörterbuch*. They are available in German editions only. Siebs was originally published in 1898 by Theodor Siebs and has since been revised and reprinted numerous times. The Duden was published in 1990 and is volume 6 of the Duden series on the German language.

Both books have the same general format: introductory sections discussing various aspects of German pronunciation, followed by an alphabetical listing of German and non–German words and proper names with IPA transcriptions. While these books are written with the spoken language in mind, they are invaluable resources for the singer as well, especially for proper names and for foreign and other unusual words. There are minor differences in their applications of IPA, most notably diphthongs and /a/ versus /ɑ/.

SAMPLE TEXTS

Below are two sample texts with IPA transcription. The first employs vocabulary fairly typical of the standard *Lieder* repertoire, with a few unusual words. The brief excerpt from Bach's *Matthäuspassion* provides some examples of antiquated vocabulary found in eighteenth-century German sacred texts, as well as biblical proper names.

Only the most essential glottal separations are indicated, using /ʔ/, since use of glottal separation is highly individual. In many instances one singer may lightly separate and another may not, with equal validity. The use of /ɐ/ as opposed to /r/ is somewhat arbitrary, since the choice is also individual. Note also that monosyllabic words ending in vowels (**zu, da,** etc.) are given by both Siebs and Duden as long sounds, though in context they are usually unstressed and lose length.

ABENDEMPFINDUNG [ˈaːbəntʔempˌfindʊŋ]

Poem by Joachim Campe
Music by W.A. Mozart

Abend ist's, die Sonne ist verschwunden,
[ˈaːbənt ʔɪsts diː zɔnə ɪst fɛɐˈʃvʊndən]

Und der Mond strahlt Silberglanz;
[ʊnt deːɐ moːnt ʃtraːlt ˈzɪlbɐglants]

So entfliehn des Lebens schönste Stunden,
[zoː entˈfliːn dɛs ˈleːbəns ˈʃøːnstə ˈʃtʊndən]

Fliehn vorüber wie im Tanz.
[fliːn forˈyːbɐ viː im tants]

Bald entflieht des Lebens bunte Szene,
[balt ɛnt'fliːt dɛs 'leːbəns 'bʊntə 'stseːnə]

Note the pronunciation of the rare combination *sz*. Each consonant takes its own pronunciation.

Und der Vorhang rollt herab;
[ʊnt deːɐ 'foːɐhaŋ rɔlt hɛr'ap]

Aus ist unser Spiel, des Freundes Träne
[aos ɪst ʊ́nzɐ ʃpiːl dɛs 'frɔøndəs 'trɛːnə]

Fließet schon auf unser Grab.
['fliːsət ʃoːn aof 'ʊnzɐ graːp]

Bald vielleicht (mir weht, wie Westwind leise,
[balt fiː'laeçt miːɐ veːt viː 'vɛstvɪnt 'laezə]

Eine stille Ahnung zu),
['aenə 'ʃtɪlə ʔaːnʊŋ tsuː]

Schließ ich dieses Lebens Pilgerreise,
[ʃliːs ɪç 'diːzəs 'leːbəns 'pɪlgɐˌraezə]

Fliege in das Land der Ruh.
['fliːgə ɪn das lant deːɐ ruː]

Werd't ihr dann an meinem Grabe weinen,
[veːrt iːɐ dan an 'maenəm 'graːbə 'vaenən]

werd't is a contraction of **werdet**.

Trauernd meine Asche sehn,
['traoɐnt 'maenə ʔaʃə zeːn]

Dann, o Freunde, will ich euch erscheinen
[dan o 'frɔøndə vɪl ɪç ɔøç ɛɐ'ʃaenən]

Possible glottals here, but light!

Und will himmelauf euch wehn.
[ʊnt vɪl hɪməlʔaof ɔøç veːn]

The word **himmelauf** is a rarely encountered compound adverb meaning "heavenward." The text in the Peters edition incorrectly has **Himmel auf**. Glottal separation should be very light.

Schenk auch du ein Tränchen mir
[ʃɛŋk aox duː aen 'trɛːnçən miːɐ]

Und pflücke mir ein Veilchen auf mein Grab,
[ʊnt 'pflʏkə miːr aen 'faelçən ʔaof maen graːp]

Und mit deinem seelenvollen Blicke
[ʊnt mɪt 'daenəm 'zeːlənˌfɔlən 'blɪkə]

Sieh dann sanft auf mich herab.

[ziː dan zanft aof mɪç hɛrˈap]

Clearly pronounce all consonants in **sanft**, with particular attention to *n*.

Weih mir eine Träne, und ach! schäme

[vae miːr ˈaenə ˈtrɛːnə ʊnt ʔax ʃɛːmə]

dich nur nicht, sie mir zu weihn;

[dɪç nuːɐ nɪçt ziː miːɐ tsuː vaen]

Oh, sie wird in meinem Diademe

[oː ziː vɪrt ɪn maenəm diaˈdeːmə]

Diadem, inflected form **Diademe**: a non-Germanic word with separation of the adjacent vowels.

Dann die schönste Perle sein!

[dan diː ˈʃøːnstə ˈpɛrlə zaen]

Matthäuspassion (excerpt) [maˈtɛːʊspasˌjoːn]

Text by Martin Luther, translation of the Bible
Music by J. S. Bach

Evangelist [evaŋgeˈlɪst]
Da kam Jesus mit ihnen zu einem Hofe,
[da kaːm ˈjeːzʊs mɪt ʔiːnən tsuː ʔaenəm ˈhoːfə]

/ŋg/ not normally found in German words.

der hieß Gethsemane,
[deːɐ hiːs getˈseːmane] (*Siebs*—[getˈzeːmane])

Note unusual final /e/ sound.

und sprach zu seinen Jüngern:
[ʔʊnt ʃpraːx tsuː ˈzaenəm ˈjyŋɐn]

Jesus [ˈjeːzʊs]
Setzet euch hie, bis dass ich dort hingehe und bete.
[ˈzɛtsət ɔøç hiː bɪs das ʔɪç dɔrt ˈhɪngeːə ʔʊnt ˈbeːtə]

Evangelist
Und nahm zu sich Petrum
[ʔʊnt naːm tsuː zɪç ˈpeːtrʊm]

und die zween Söhne Zebedäi
[ʔʊnt diː tsveːn ˈzøːnə tsebeˈdɛːi]

Note antiquated word **zween**—one syllable.

und fing an zu trauern und zu zagen.
[ʔʊnt fɪŋ ʔan tsuː traoɐn ʔʊnt tsuː tsaːgən]

Da sprach Jesus zu ihnen:
[daː ʃpraːx ˈjeːzʊs tsuː ʔiːnən]

Jesus

Meine Seele ist betrübt bis an den Tod,

[ˈmaenə ˈzeːlə ʔɪst bəˈtryːpt bɪs ʔan deːn toːt]

bleibet hie und wachet mit mir.

[ˈblaebət hiː ʔʊnt ˈvaxət mɪt miːɐ]

FRENCH DICTION

INTRODUCTION

Of the three languages presented in this book, French is by far the least phonetic. A phonetic language, such as Italian or German, is one whose pronunciation follows logically and consistently from its spelling. Italian and German are not entirely phonetic, of course, but they are much more so than either French or English. Unfortunately, the unphonetic nature of French is very different from that of English. This fact is one of the greatest hurdles that an English-speaking singer must overcome in mastering French pronunciation.

In order to achieve an intermediate level of proficiency with French diction, at least the following points must be mastered:

1. A thorough understanding of French spelling and the sounds resulting from those spellings.
2. Purity of vowels (no diphthongs).
3. Appropriate "lift" or brightness to /a/ and /ɛ/.
4. The sounds of the four nasal vowels (including not sounding the *n* or *m*) and keeping the sounds distinct one from another.

5. The proper formation of the mixed vowels.
6. Forward articulation and nonaspiration of consonants.
7. A basic understanding of liaison.

It is up to the teacher to decide to what extent some of the fine points in this chapter should be applied to the class or individual being taught. For those inexperienced with French, it is doubtless too much. Also, many teachers and coaches prefer to dispense with the fine points represented by distinctions between, for example, bright and dark *a*, vocalic harmonization, and vowel length. Many teachers and coaches do make these distinctions, however, and so for the sake of thoroughness, this text presents these points.

International Phonetic Alphabet Symbols for French

"Pure" Vowels
/a/ m<u>a</u>d<u>a</u>me, f<u>e</u>mme
/ɑ/ b<u>a</u>s, <u>â</u>me
/ɛ/ b<u>e</u>lle, cl<u>ai</u>r
/e/ j'<u>ai</u>, <u>é</u>t<u>é</u>, pi<u>e</u>d
/ɔ/ h<u>o</u>mme, F<u>au</u>ré
/o/ tr<u>o</u>p, b<u>eau</u>, ch<u>au</u>d
/i/ v<u>i</u>e, <u>i</u>l d<u>i</u>t, Gu<u>y</u>
/u/ t<u>ou</u>j<u>ou</u>rs, am<u>ou</u>r

"Mixed" Vowels
/y/ t<u>u</u>, d<u>u</u>, r<u>ue</u>
/œ/ c<u>oeu</u>r, s<u>eu</u>l
/ø/ d<u>eu</u>x, f<u>eu</u>
/ə/ l<u>e</u>, s<u>e</u>cret, parl<u>e</u>rai, dis<u>e</u>nt

Nasal Vowels
/ɑ̃/ v<u>en</u>t, ch<u>an</u>ter, <u>Jean</u>
/ɛ̃/ v<u>in</u>, pl<u>ein</u>, b<u>ien</u>, p<u>ain</u>
/ɔ̃/ v<u>on</u>t, t<u>om</u>ber
/œ̃/ h<u>um</u>ble, parf<u>um</u>

Glides
/j/ c<u>i</u>el, trava<u>ill</u>er, ro<u>y</u>al
/w/ <u>ou</u>i, cr<u>oi</u>re
/ɥ/ p<u>ui</u>s, enn<u>ui</u>

Plosive Consonants
/b/ <u>b</u>eau
/p/ <u>p</u>eau
/d/ <u>d</u>e
/t/ <u>t</u>e
/g/ <u>g</u>oût
/k/ <u>c</u>oût

Fricative Consonants
/f/ <u>f</u>aim
/s/ <u>s</u>on, <u>c</u>e, le<u>ç</u>on
/v/ <u>v</u>ain
/z/ ga<u>z</u>on, cho<u>s</u>e
/ʃ/ <u>ch</u>ez, crè<u>ch</u>e
/ʒ/ <u>j</u>'ai, nei<u>g</u>e

Lateral Consonants
/l/ /ll/ <u>l</u>eque<u>l</u>, i<u>ll</u>usion

Vibrant Consonants
/r/ /rr/ <u>r</u>i<u>r</u>e, i<u>rr</u>éel

Nasal Consonants
/m/ /mm/ <u>m</u>ê<u>m</u>e, i<u>mm</u>édiat
/n/ /nn/ <u>n</u>o<u>nn</u>e, i<u>nn</u>ocent
/ɲ/ cy<u>gn</u>e, a<u>gn</u>eau

Additional Symbol
/ː/ long vowel sound

FRENCH DIACRITICAL MARKS

A distinguishing characteristic of written French is the presence of the four diacritical marks. They contribute greatly to the "look" of the language. It is important to have a clear understanding of these signs and in what ways they affect pronunciation.

- **Accent grave** (grave accent): *è, à, où*
  The grave accent occurring over *e* renders it open /ɛ/:

  lèvre [lɛːvr(ə)]   **légère** [leʒɛːr(ə)]

  When it occurs over other vowels, it has no affect on pronunciation.

- **Accent aigu** (acute accent): *é*
  The acute accent occurs only over *e* and renders it closed /e/:

  été [ete]   **passé** [pase]

  Be aware that capital letters often omit diacriticals:

  Nuits d'Etoiles (étoiles)

- **Accent circonflexe** (circumflex): *î, ê, â, ô, û, aî, oî, oû, aû*
  The circumflexe affects pronunciation only with *ê, â,* and *ô*.

ê is always open /ɛ/:	**rêve** [rɛːv(ə)]	**tête** [tɛːt(ə)]
ô is always closed /o/:	**drôle** [droːl(ə)]	**le nôtre** [lə noːtr(ə)]
â is usually dark /ɑ/:	**âme** [ɑːm(ə)]	**pâle** [pɑːl(ə)]

- **Diérèse** (dieresis) or tréma: *ï, ë, ÿ*
  The dieresis occurs over one of the above vowel-letters only when the letter follows another vowel-letter. It indicates hiatus, or separation of the vowel sounds. For example, in the word **naïf** [naif] the dieresis requires the two vowel-letters to be pronounced separately, whereas in the word **maître** [mɛːtr(ə)] the same two letters combine to make the sound /ɛ/.

  Other examples:

  haïr [aiːr]   **foëne** [fɔɛn(ə)]   **Boïeldieu** [bɔjɛldjø]

Rarely, the dieresis indicates that a vowel-letter is silent or has no phonetic function in the vowel group.

Saint-Saëns [sɛ̃sɑ̃ːs]   **ciguë** [sigy]   **Staël** [stal]

The spelling of the name of the composer **Hüe** [y] is a variation of this usage of the dieresis.

In addition to the above diacriticals, there is also the **cédille** (cedilla), which is the small mark found under a *c* when it is to be pronounced as /s/ before *a, o,* or *u.*

     ça [sa]   **garçon** [garsõ]   **reçu** [rəsy]

DEFINITIONS OF TERMS RELATING TO FRENCH DICTION

Mute *e*

In spoken French, when the letter *e* with no accent is the only vowel-letter in a syllable and ends the syllable or word, it is usually silent:

     mouv<u>e</u>ment [muvmɑ̃]   **méd<u>e</u>cin** [medsɛ̃]   **vill<u>e</u>** [vil]

It is also silent in the verb ending *-ent* (but not *-aient*) and in final *-es* (except in monosyllables):

     aim<u>ent</u> [ɛm]   **aim<u>es</u>** [ɛm]   **bell<u>es</u>** [bɛl]

This silent vowel-letter is called mute *e*. In singing, it is generally pronounced, transcribed as /ə/ (schwa), and sounded as /œ/ (see discussion of this sound on p. 171). Except where schwa clearly must be pronounced (such as in monosyllables **le, me,** etc.), this text will indicate mute *e* in parentheses: /(ə)/.

Elision

When a mute *e* ends a word and the next word begins with a vowel or *h,* the *e* is never sounded in speech or in singing. The consonant sound before the mute *e* connects directly to the vowel sound beginning the next word. This is different from liaison.

     elle est [ɛlɛ]   **comme à** [kɔma]
     fatigue amoureuse [fatig amurøːz(ə)]

In the cases of mute *e* spelled *-ent* or *-es*, speech will elide as above, but singing will usually pronounce the *e* (as schwa) and sound the otherwise silent *t* or *s* in liaison to the next word.

Liaison

Liaison is the sounding of a normally silent final consonant before a word beginning with a vowel or a so-called unaspirated *h* (see below). It is very common in French and more common in singing than in speech. However, it does not happen in every instance where it might seem to be called for. See p. 197 for a complete explanation.

vous avez [vu zave]	**mon amour** [mõ namuːr]
deux heures [dø zœːr]	**mes amis** [mɛ zami]

Aspirated *h*, Unaspirated *h*

The letter *h* is always silent in French. When *h* begins a word, it is silent but it sometimes prevents liaison from the previous word. When an initial *h* prevents liaison, it is called an aspirated *h* (*h* **aspiré**). When initial *h* allows liaison, it is called unaspirated *h* (*h* **inaspiré**). There is no way to determine which one applies. Each word must be checked in a dictionary. (*Note*: Do not make the mistake of thinking that aspirated *h* makes an aspirated sound as in English or German. It does not.) The aspirated *h* may result in a light glottal attack, though connecting the vowel sounds is usually more appropriate in singing.

Unaspirated *h*:	**les hommes** [lɛ zɔm]	**en hiver** [ã niveːr]
Aspirated *h*:	**les haricots** [lɛ ariko]	**des haies** [dɛ ɛ]

Vocalic Harmonization

Vocalic harmonization is the rhyming of vowel sounds in adjoining syllables. In French this happens only with two pairs of vowels: /ɛ/ and /e/; /œ/ (or /ə/) and /ø/.

The context for vocalic harmonization is very specific. When one of the above open vowels is followed by its closed counterpart, the open vowel will close to rhyme with it. The opposite situation (closed followed by open) does *not* result in vocalic harmonization.

With /ɛ/ and /e/ the usual patterns are two:

1. When -ai- is followed by -er-, -ez-, or -é-:

   baiser [bɛze] becomes [beze]
   aimez [ɛme] becomes [eme]
   laissé [lɛse] becomes [lese]

2. When monosyllables such as **les, mes, tes, and ces** are followed by a word with /e/ in the first syllable:

   les étoiles [lɛ zetwaːl(ə)] becomes [le zetwaːl(ə)]
   ces études [sɛ zetyd(ə)] becomes [se zetyd(ə)]
   tes baisers [tɛ bɛze] becomes [te beze]
   (Note that in the last example vocalic harmonization can extend over three consecutive syllables.)

With /œ/ or /ə/ and /ø/, vocalic harmonization falls within one word:

   heureux [œrø] becomes [ørø]
   cheveux [ʃəvø] becomes [ʃøvø]

In patterns over two words such as **je veux** [ʒə vø] and **tu ne peux** [ty nə pø], vocalic harmonization does not apply.

Vocalic harmonization occurs in French speech but is not assumed and it is not reflected in French dictionaries' pronunciation transcription (whether IPA or some other system). Although it is common practice in singing, it should be considered not an absolute requirement but rather a recommendation to facilitate vocalism and enhance vocal line. There are those, however, who prefer to dispense with vocalic harmonization, choosing to bring out the distinction between the open and closed vowel sounds.

FRENCH SYLLABIFICATION

Syllabification is presented early in the discussion of French because it will be repeatedly referred to as the chapter progresses. Since the topic is rather complex, the teacher may wish to cover the specific sounds first and then return to syllabification. In any case, it should be consulted regularly until mastered.

Understanding syllabification is crucial for determining the pronunciation of French words. Two adjacent letters may be pronounced one way

if they are in the same syllable and another way if they are in different syllables. French shares with Italian the important trait of being characterized by *open syllabification*, that is, syllables that end in vowels.

A complicating element in French syllabification is the mute *e*. In
speech it is usully nonsyllabic, but in singing it usually is syllabic. Since
this is a textbook for singers, the following discussion will consider mute
e syllabic but put it in parentheses in IPA.

Vowel–Consonant–Vowel

In this common pattern, the syllable will divide before the consonant:

a-mour   **mai-son**   **du-rer**   **pa-ro-le**   **mé-de-cin**

Adjacent Vowels

When adjacent vowel-letters form a single vowel sound, as frequently
happens in French, they all belong to the same syllable:

deux [dø]   **beau-té** [bo-te]   **coeur** [kœːr]   **tou-jours** [tu-ʒuːr]

Sometimes a vowel-letter will represent a glide. French has three glides:
/j/, /w/, and /ɥ/. The glide is part of the syllable of the vowel following
it. If initial or intervocalic, a glide begins a syllable:

aïeux [a-jø]   **vieux** [vjø]   **depuis** [də-pɥi]
alouette [a-lwɛt(ə)]   **oi-seau** [wa-zo]

When *y* occurs between vowels, it has a duel function, essentially that of
a double *ii* with the syllables dividing between the *ii*'s. The function of the
first *i* varies according to the vowel preceding it, but the second *i* always
becomes the /j/ glide:

voyage (voi-ia-ge) [vwa-jaːʒ(ə)]   **payer** (pai-ier) [pe-je]
fuyez (fui-ier) [fɥi-je]   **royal** (roi-ial) [rwa-jal]

In the word **pays** and words derived from it, *y* functions similarly, except
the second *i* has a vowel function (note closed /e/):

pays (**pai-is**) [pe-i]   **paysage** (pai-i-sa-ge) [pe-i-zaː-ʒ(ə)]

A frequent spelling of the /j/ glide in French is *-ill* following another
vowel. This can be particularly confusing for newcomers to French:

travailler (tra-va-iller) [tra-va-je]
cueillir (cue-illir) [kœ-jiːr]   **mouillé** (mou-ille) [mu-je]

When -*ill* does not follow a vowel, it is /ij/:

fille (fi-lle) [fiːj(ə)]   **billet** (bi-llet) [bi-jɛ]

See the section on *l* for pronunciation exceptions.

There are a number of situations involving adjacent vowels in which it is not always clear whether a vowel or a glide is involved. Musical settings usually prefer the vowel and therefore the extra syllable. (See p. 208 for musical examples.)

1. When the noun/adjective ending -*et* follows a vowel:

    rouet [rwɛ]   **muet** [mɥɛ]
    (Dictionaries give these words with glides; musical settings usually set them as vowels: [ru-e], [my-e].)

2. When the infinitive verb endings -*er* and -*ir* follow *i*, *u*, or *ou* in some words:

    lier [lje]   **tuer** [tɥe]   **é-pan-ouir** [e-pan-wiːr]
    (Dictionaries give these words with glides; musical settings usually set them with vowels, creating an extra syllable.)

    Words of this pattern after a consonant plus *l* or *r* have no glide:

    trou-er [tru-e]   **pri-er** [pri-e]   **ou-bli-er** [u-bli-e]
    (Some dictionaries give /ije/ for these last two words.)

    Similarly, when -*io*- or -*ia*- follows a consonant plus *l* or *r*, syllables divide between the vowels:

    bi-bli-o-tèque [bibliotɛk(ə)]   **tri-omphe** [triɔ̃ːf(ə)]
    tri-angle [triɑ̃ːgl(ə)]
    (Some dictionaries insert /j/ between the vowels in these words.)

    Also -*ue*- or -*ua*- following a consonant plus *l* or *r* divides between vowels:

    cru-el [cryɛl]   **tru-and** [tryɑ̃]   **cru-au-té** [kryote]

However, -*ui*- following a consonant plus l or r usually has the glide:

pluie [plɥi]   **bruit** [brɥi]   **bruire** [brɥir(ə)]
but **flu-ide** [flyid(ə)] has vowel-vowel.

But in patterns *gu* plus vowel and *qu* plus vowel, the *u* is silent, therefore there is no syllabic division:

guerre [gɛr(ə)]   **guet** [gɛ]   **Guy** [gi]
quand [kɑ̃]   **quitter** [ki-te]

Adjacent vowel-letters forming different vowel sounds are in different syllables. In addition to the situations described above, there are two ways this can happen:

1. There is a dieresis:

   Thaïs [ta-is]   **Noël** [nɔ-ɛl]

2. One of the adjacent vowels is *é* or *è*:

   poète [pɔ-ɛt(ə)]   **ré-u-ssi** [re-y-si]

Adjacent Consonants

French can have two or three adjacent consonant-letters. Sometimes one or two of these are silent and are therefore not a factor in syllabification. For example, when an *n* or an *m* indicates a nasal vowel, it obviously remains in the syllable of the nasal vowel but is not sounded:

en-fant [ɑ̃fɑ̃]   **loin-tain** [lwɛ̃tɛ̃]   **hum-ble** [œ̃bl(ə)]

Similarly, *h* is always either silent or part of the combinations *ch* and *ph*. Except when initial, it cannot begin a syllable:

bo-nheur [bɔnœːr]   **i-nhu-main** [inymɛ̃]   **go-thi-que** [gɔtik(ə)]

Sometimes consonant clusters will be in one syllable and sometimes they will separate syllabically. The general rule of thumb is *whether the cluster could begin a word*. If the answer is yes, the cluster remains together in the same syllable. This is true of combinations that represent one sound, such as *ch*, *ph*, and *sc* (before *i* or *e*), as well as of blended sounds that can begin a word:

pé-cheur   pro-phè-te   de-scen-dre   pa-tri(e)   vien-dra

If two adjacent consonants could not begin a word, they divide into separate syllables:

par-tir   ob-jet   al-tier

Three adjacent consonants is a situation that occurs rarely, except in combinations involving double consonants (**aggraver, appliquer**; see below) or *n* or *m* creating a nasal vowel (**entre, combler**). Notice that in such combinations the final letter in the cluster is always *l* or *r*. In other combinations the usual pattern is that the three consonants will divide one plus two:

cher-cher   ob-scur

Double consonants present some special situations. Normally they do not divide, nor are they lengthened as in Italian:

do-nner [dɔ-ne]   **pa-sser** [pɑ-se]   **a-ller** [a-le]
(Printed French will divide between double consonants.)

However, they *do* divide in initial *ill*, *imm*, *inn*, and *irr*, and the sounds are lengthened (remember: only when initial!):

il-lu-sion [illyzjõ]   **im-men-se** [immãːs(ə)]
in-no-cent [innɔsã]   **ir-ré-gu-lier** [irregylje]

Initial *emm* and *enn* also divide between the double consonants, but because the first (irregularly) indicates a nasal vowel and the second functions as a consonant. There is no lengthening:

em-me-ner [ãməne]   **en-nui** [ãnɥi]

There is also syllabic division in *cc* and *gg* after *e* or *i*, because two different consonant sounds result:

sug-gé-rer [sygʒere]   **ac-cident** [aksidã]

A special case is also presented by the letter *x*. Since it normally represents two consonant sounds (either /ks/ or /gz/), the two sounds divide between the syllables:

exister (ex-i-ster) [ɛg-zi-ste]
extrème (ex-trè-me) [ɛk-strɛ-m(ə)]

When *x* is sounded in numerical words, it is /s/ or /z/ and therefore functions syllabically as a single consonant:

sixième [sizjɛm(ə)]   **soixante** [swasɑ̃ːt(ə)]

WORD STRESS IN FRENCH

In French words of two or more syllables, the final syllable always takes a light stress, not including final mute *e*. This stress is called *l'accent d'intensité*. All other syllables are equally unstressed. It must be emphasized that the stress on the final syllable is light. Italian, German, and English all have much more emphatic stress patterns, and the lack of such emphasis in French is a special characteristic of the language. This characteristic has influenced composers setting French texts to music, particularly those since Debussy.

When individual words combine to form phrases and breath groups, the light stress falls on the final syllable of the final word (excluding mute *e*), and thus the words preceding the final word lose their stress, although secondary stresses may occur. Just as in any language, a change of inflection, and therefore stress, may occur according to the meaning the speaker wishes to convey. When this happens in French, it is called *l'accent d'insistance*.

Because of the regularity of stress in French words, French dictionaries do not indicate stress. This text follows that precedent.

VOWEL LENGTH IN FRENCH

Although books on French phonetics do discuss vowel length, it has not been customary for singers' diction texts to do so. While it is perhaps not as crucial to the flavor of the language as it is for Italian and German, in some contexts it certainly plays a role. Subtle differences in articulating vowel-to-consonant relationships are crucial to the authentic sound of any language. Just as in Italian and German, such subtleties are particularly exposed in French vocal music that more closely approximates speech, as exemplified in Debussy's *Pelléas et Mélisande* and much twentieth-century art song repertoire, as well as recitative from any period.

There is not absolute unanimity among phoneticians in defining all cases of long vowels in French. All, however, agree on the patterns described below.

All vowels in syllables other than the final one are short.

Vowels in final syllables (including monosyllabic words but excluding mute *e*) may be long if one of the following applies:

- Nasal vowels are lengthened when followed by a pronounced consonant:

  dans [dɑ̃] versus **danse** [dɑ̃ːs(ə)]
  fond [fɔ̃] versus **fondre** [fɔ̃ːdr(ə)
  vin [vɛ̃] versus **timbre** [tɛ̃ːbr(ə)]
  défunt [defœ̃] versus **défunte** [defœ̃ːt(ə)]

- /a/, /o/, /ø/ are lengthened when followed by a pronounced consonant:

  pas [pɑ] versus **passe** [pɑːs(ə)]
  chaud [ʃo] versus **chaude** [ʃoːd(ə)]

  This *always* applies to the common feminine ending *-euse*:

  heureux [ørø] versus **heureuse** [ørøːz(ə)]

- Vowel-letters with the circumflex are lengthened when followed by a pronounced consonant:

  tel [tɛl] versus **tête** [tɛːt(ə)]
  faites [fɛt(ə)] versus **fête** [fɛːt(ə)]
  il [il] versus **île** [iːl(ə)]
  mettre [mɛtr(ə)] versus **maître** [mɛːtr(ə)]
  (Exceptions with verb forms: **êtes** [ɛt(ə)])

- All vowels are lengthened when followed by /z/, /ʒ/, /v/, /r/, or /vr/ as the final sound of the word:

  douce [dus(ə)] versus **douze** [duːz(ə)]
  furtif [fyrtif] versus **furtive** [fyrtiːv(ə)]
  baisse [bɛs(ə)] versus **beige** [bɛːʒ(ə)]
  accorte [akɔrt(ə)] versus **accord** [akɔːr(ə)]
  libre [libr(ə)] versus **livre** [liːvr(ə)]
  régal [regal] versus **regard** [rəgaːr]

- Some phoneticians consider final /j/ or /jə/ to lengthen the preceding vowel sound:

  soleil [sɔlɛːj]   **travail** [travaːj]   **feuille** [fœːj(ə)]

The IPA transcriptions throughout this text indicate long vowels in the situations listed above.

FRENCH VOWEL SOUNDS AND HOW THEY ARE SPELLED

French has fifteen vowel sounds and, counting schwa, sixteen IPA symbols which represent them. One of the greatest problems in learning French pronunciation is learning all of the possible spellings of the vowel sounds. The following sections will examine each vowel sound and present the possible spellings.

/a/

This sound is equivalent to /a/ in Italian and other Romance languages. The bright /a/ occurs much more frequently than the dark /ɑ/. Since native speakers of English tend to pronounce this sound too darkly, it is necessary to make sure that it has enough brightness and "lift."

The sound /a/ is spelled as follows:

- *a* when it is not nasalized and is the only vowel-letter in the syllable:

  apparat [apara]
  (Except situations calling for dark /ɑ/. See next section.)

  This includes *a* before *-ill*, as in **ailleurs** [ajœːr], because of syllabification between *a* and *-ill*.

- *à* when it is the only vowel-letter in the syllable:

  là [la]

- *oi* results in /wa/ (except when nasalized):

  oiseau [wazo]   **moi** [mwa]   **fois** [fwa]
  (Spelled *eoi* in the word **s'asseoir** [saswaːr].)

- *oy* results in /waj/ (except when nasalized):

  royal [rwajal]   **foyer** [fwaje]   **voyons** [vwajõ]

- *e* in medial *-emm* and *-enn*:

  femme [fam(ə)]   **solennel** [sɔlanɛl]   **fréquemment** [frekamã]

However there are exceptions:

flemme [flɛm(ə)]   **gemme** [ʒɛm(ə)]

In addition, there are some irregular spellings of /a/:

ao	**paonne** [pan]	**paonner** [pane]
oe	**moelle** [mwal(ə)] (normally *oe* is part of *oeill* or *oeu* and sounds
	as /œ/)	

/ɑ/

The dark /ɑ/ sound is the same as that found in the English word "father." It is pronounced with a lower, more "back" orientation than bright /a/. It occurs much less often than bright /a/. Some pedagogues prefer to dispense with this sound altogether for singing. In any case, beginners should perfect the bright /a/ before concerning themselves much with the dark /ɑ/.

There are four common situations resulting in dark /ɑ/:

- *â* in all common words:

  âme [ɑːm(ə)]   **château** [ʃato]   **grâce** [grɑːs(ə)]
  (Some subjunctive verb forms use bright /a/ though spelled with *â*: **aimât**.)

- *a* when it is followed by silent final *s* (except in verb forms):

  pas [pɑ]   **bas** [bɑ]   **lilas** [lilɑ]
  (Verbs ending in -*as* use bright /a/: **tu diras** [ty dira].)

- *a* when it is immediately followed by /s/ (numerous exceptions):

  passer [pɑse]   **classe** [klɑːs(ə)]   **basse** [bɑːs(ə)]
  hélas[elɑːs]   **espace** [ɛspɑːs(ə)]
  (Some exceptions: **chasser, harasser, bassin**, and **facile** use bright /a/.)

- *a* when it is followed by /z/ (spelled with -*s*- or -*z*-):

  extase [ɛkstɑːz(ə)]   **gazon** [gɑzõ]   **occasion** [ɔkɑzjõ]
  emphase [ãfɑːz(ə)]

In addition, there are several isolated words that have dark /ɑ/. Dictionaries are not always in agreement about such words, but some of them are the following:

diable [djɑːbl(ə)]	**damner** [dɑne]	**cadavre** [kadɑːvr(ə)]
fable [fɑːbl(ə)]	**paille** [pɑːj]	**trois** [trwɑ]
gagner [gɑɲe]	**effroi** [efrwɑ]	**gars** [gɑ]

/ɛ/

This symbol is used in English for the vowel in such words as *bed* and *get*. In the three languages discussed in this book, this sound is pronounced with a "higher" placement than in English. See the discussion of this sound on p. 7.

The many possible spellings of this sound in French are as follows:

- *è* (always):

  mère [mɛːr(ə)]   **arène** [arɛn(ə)]   **paupière** [popjɛːr(ə)]

- *ê* (always):

  tête [tɛːt(ə)]   **être** [ɛtr(ə)]   **arrête** [arɛːt(ə)]   **mêler** [mɛle]

- *ë*:

  Noël [nɔɛl]   **Israël** [israɛl]
  (Except when silent in rare instances: **Saint-Saëns** [sɛ̃sɑ̃ːs].)

- *é* only when followed by mute *e* in the next syllable (a rare occurrence):

  médecin [mɛd(ə)sɛ̃]   **élever** [ɛl(ə)ve]

  Normally, of course, *é* is pronounced /e/.

- Medial *e* when followed by a consonant in the same syllable (except when nasalized) or a consonant cluster beginning with *s*:

  perdu [pɛrdy]   **infernal** [ɛ̃fɛrnal]   **bestiaire** [bɛstjɛːr(ə)]

- e when followed by a double consonant:

elle [ɛl(ə)]	**terre** [tɛːr(ə)]	**guerre** [gɛːr(ə)]
cette [sɛt]	**tristesse** [tristɛs(ə)]	

- *e* when followed by a final sounded consonant:

  mer [mɛːr]   **avec** [avɛk]   **bref** [brɛf]   **quel** [kɛl]

- *e* followed by final silent *t*:

  jet [ʒɛ]   **secret** [səkrɛ]   **est** [ɛ]   **cet** [sɛ]
  effet [efɛ] (exception: **et** [e])

- *e* in the following words:

  les [lɛ]   **des** [dɛ]   **ces** [sɛ]   **mes** [mɛ]   **ses** [sɛ]   **tes** [tɛ]
  (Spoken French uses /e/ in these words, but sung French traditionally
  uses /ɛ/.)

- *ei* (except when nasalized):

  neige [nɛːʒ(ə)]   **Seine** [sɛn(ə)]   **pleine** [plɛn(ə)]

  including *e* before *-il* and *-ill*:

  soleil [sɔlɛːj]   **abeille** [abɛːj(ə)]   **veiller** [vɛje]

  and, rarely, *ey*:

  Leguerney [ləgɛrnɛ]   **pleyon** [plɛjõ]   **Pleyel** [plɛjɛl]

- ai (except when nasalized):

  mais [mɛ]   **plaire** [plɛːr(ə)]   **aime** [ɛm(ə)]   **vrai** [vrɛ]

  including spelling variations *aie(s)*:

  haie [ɛ] **essaies** [esɛ]

  and verb endings *-ais, -ait, -aient*:

  parlais [parlɛ]   **parlait** [parlɛ]   **parlaient** [parlɛ]

- Medial *ay* results in /ɛj/ unless vocalic harmonization is applied:

  payer [pɛje] or [peje]   **crayon** [krɛjõ]

- Final *-aye(s)* results in /ɛ/:

  payes [pɛ]

Exceptions to the above include the following:

- *e* followed by *n* or *m* in the same syllable results in the nasal vowel /ɑ̃/, including initial *emm* or *enn*:

  emmener [ɑ̃məne]   **ennui** [ɑ̃nɥi]
  (**ennemi** however is [ɛnəmi])

- Medial *emm* and *enn* often have /a/:

  femme [fam(ə)]   **solennel** [sɔlanɛl]
  (but **gemme** [ʒɛm(ə)]   **flemme** [flɛm(ə)])

- Initial *dess, desc, eff,* and *ess* have /e/:

  dessein [desɛ̃]   **dessert**   [desɛːr]
  descriptif [deskriptif]   **descendre** [desɑ̃ːdr(ə)]
  effort [efɔːr]   **effacer** [efase]
  essaim [esɛ̃]   **essence** [esɑ̃s(ə)]

  but two *dess* words have /ə/:

  dessous [dəsu]   **dessus** [dəsy]

- Initial *ress* usually has /ə/:

  ressembler [rəsɑ̃ble]   **ressort** [rəsɔːr]
  ressource [rəsuːrs(ə)] but **ressusciter** [resysite] has /e/.

Other patterns with -*ess*:

  pressentiment, pressentir, presser have [pre . . .],
  but **presse, pressant,** have [prɛ . . .].

  tress- has /e/: **tresser, tressaillir, tressauter.**

  mess- has /e/ in **message** and **messieurs** [mesjø],
  but **messe** has /ɛ/.

  isolated words **lessiver** and **tesson** have /e/.

- -*ail* and -*aill* result in /aj/:

  corail [kɔraːj]   **travailler** [travaje]

- -*ai* is closed /e/ when final in verb forms, which is usually first person singular of the future tense and *passé simple* (past historic tense):

  parlerai [parl(ə)re]   **dirai** [dire]   **verrai** [vɛre]
  aimai [eme] but also includes **j'ai** [ʒe]

- Some isolated words have -ai sounding as closed /e/:

  je vais [ʒə ve]   **je sais** [ʒə se]   **il sait** [il se]
  quai [ke]   **gai** [ge]

- When *ai* is followed by a syllable with a closed vowel, it may be /e/ in some words (dictionaries do not always agree on such words):

  aigu [egy]   **maison** [mezõ]   **plaisir** [pleziːr]

- In the verb **faire** (to do, to make) the *-ai* is the normal open /ɛ/ sound in most forms, but it is irregularly pronounced as schwa /ə/ in two syllable-forms such as the following:

  faisons [fəzõ]   **faisant** [fəzɑ̃]   **faisait** [fəzɛ]

In situations calling for vocalic harmonization, *-ai* may be /e/:

  aimer [eme]   **baiser** [beze]

/e/

The closed sound /e/ does not exist in standard English. The French and German versions of this sound are essentially identical (see p. 91). It is very closed and is almost in the position of /i/. English-speaking singers unused to this sound tend to pronounce and sing it closer to the position of /ɛ/. It is recommended that the novice substitute /i/ in situations calling for /e/ in the presence of a coach or teacher, who can guide the singer in finding the appropriate shape.

The spelling of this sound in French is as follows:

- *é* (generally, except when the next syllable has /ə/; see above)

  étoile [etwal(ə)]   **volupté** [vɔlypte]   **légère** [leʒɛːr(ə)]

- *e* (when not nasalized) before final silent consonants, except *s* and *t*:

  pied [pje]   **clef** [kle]   **chez** [ʃe]   **nez** [ne]

  including all verb forms ending in *-er* and *-ez*:

  parler [parle]   **parlez** [parle]   **aimer** [eme]
  aimez [eme]   **disiez** [dizje]

as well as polysyllabic nouns/adjectives ending in *-er*:

février [fevrje]   **léger** [leʒe]   **baiser** [beze]
boulanger [bulɑ̃ʒe]   **charpentier** [ʃarpɑ̃tje]
(Monosyllables and a few polysyllables ending in *-er* have /ɛr/ as in **cher,
mer, hiver, enfer, amer.**)

- *e* in initial *dess-* and *desc-*:

  dessein [desɛ̃]   **dessécher** [deseʃe]   **descendre** [desɑ̃:drə)]
  except for two words: **dessous** [dəsu] and **dessus** [dəsy]

- *e* in initial *eff-* and *ess-*:

  effet [efɛ]   **effort** [efɔ:r]   **effaroucher** [efaruʃe]
  effroi [efrwa]   **essor** [esɔ:r]   **essuyer** [esɥije]

  and in a number of words with initial consonant plus *ess-*:

  ressusciter [resysite]   **pressentir** [presɑ̃ti:r]
  tresser [trese]   **lessiver** [lesive]   **tesson** [tesõ]
  tressaillir [tresaji:r]   **tressauter** [tresote]
  message [mesa:ʒ(ə)]   **messieurs** [mesjø]

- *ai* when final in verb forms, usually first person singular of the future tense and *passé simple* (past historic tense):

  serai [səre]   **j'irai** [ʒire]   **ferai** [fəre]   **donnai** [dɔne]
  also **j'ai** [ʒe] and, irregularly: **je vais** [ʒə ve]
  je sais [ʒə se]   **il sait** [il se]

- *ai* may be pronounced /e/ when the syllable following it has a closed vowel (dictionaries vary on these words):

  plaisir [plezi:r]   **maison** [mezõ]   **aigu** [egy]

- *ai* in some isolated words:

  quai [ke]   **gai** [ge]

- *ay* in **pays** [pei] and derivatives:

  paysage [peiza:ʒ(ə)]   **paysan** [peizɑ̃], etc.

and in vocalic harmonization:

payer [pɛje] or [peje]   **baiser** [bɛze] or [beze]

/ɔ/

The open sound /ɔ/ is the same sound encountered in Italian (**cosa**), German (**Sonne**), British English (**hot**), and American English (**awe**). In some French words, the shortness of the vowel sound results in a quality almost approaching that of English /ʌ/ as in **but**, though rounder: **comme, bonne, donner.**

The spelling of /ɔ/ in French is as follows:

- *o* when followed by a sounded consonant or *h* in the same word (except the sound /z/):

  dormir [dɔrmiːr]   **frivole** [frivɔl(ə)]   **soleil** [sɔlɛːj]
  donner [dɔne]   **bohème** [bɔɛm(ə)]

  Exceptions: when *o* is followed by /z/, and when it is followed by *-tion*, it is /o/:

  rose [roːz(ə)]   **motion** [mosjõ]

- *o* followed by another vowel-letter sounding as a separate vowel sound in the same word:

  poète [pɔɛt(ə)]   **Noël** [nɔɛl]

Most of the time, therefore, the letter ǫ will result in open /ɔ/ when it is the only vowel-letter in the syllable and not nasalized (see next section for individual exceptions).

- *au only* when followed by *r*:

  Fauré [fɔre]   **aurore** [ɔrɔːr(ə)]   **saurais** [sɔrɛ]

  and in two isolated words:

  mauvais [mɔvɛ]   **Paul** [pɔl]

Otherwise *au* results in /o/. See next section.

- in some words, the spelling -*um* is pronounced /ɔm/, but this is rare.

  album [albɔm]   **référendum** [referɛ̃dɔm]

/o/

The closed sound /o/ is equivalent to German /o/ (**Sohn**). It is not normally used in English. It is analogous to /e/ in that it is very closed, close to the position of /u/.

The spelling of /o/ in French is as follows:

- *o* when final in a word:

  écho [eko]   **Roméo** [rɔmeo]

- *o* followed by a final silent consonant:

  mot [mo]   **trop** [tro]

- *o* followed by the sound /z/ (spelled *s* or *z*):

  rose [roːz(ə)]   **chose** [ʃoːz(ə)]

- *o* followed by -*tion* suffix:

  motion [mosjõ]   **potion** [posjõ]   **émotion** [emosjõ]

- *ô* always:

  hôtel [otɛl]   **hôpital** [opital]   **geôlier** [ʒolje]

- *au* usually (except before *r*):

  automne [otɔn(ə)]   **faux** [fo]   **autre** [otr(ə)]

- *eau* always:

  l'eau [lo]   **beau** [bo]   **anneau** [ano]   **oiseau** [wazo]

Some words with -*oss* have /o/: **grosse** [groːs(ə)] **fosse** [foːs(ə)], although others do not: **gosse** [gɔs(ə)] **bosse** [bɔs(ə)], and in a few words, either sound is accepted: **odeur** /ɔ/ or /o/.

/i/

The sound /i/ is the same as in English *see*.

In French /i/ is spelled as follows:

- *i, î,* or *ï,* when it is the only vowel-letter in the syllable and is not nasalized.

    ici [isi]   **île** [iːl(ə)]   **haïr** [aiːr]

- *y* or *ÿ* when it is the only vowel-letter in the syllable and is not nasalized:

    lys [lis]   **cygne** [siɲ(ə)]   **Louÿs** [lwis]

In spoken French, final *-ie* is /i/, although musical settings sometimes have /iə/:

    vie [vi] or [viə]   **mélancolie** [melãkɔli] or [melãkɔliə]

Verb infinitives in *-ier* have /ie/:

    oublier [ublie]   **prier** [prie]
    (Some dictionaries give /ije/ for these words.)

or /je/:

    dédier [dedje]   **lier** [lje]

but other forms of these verbs have medial *-ie,* which is always just /i/:

    j'oublierai [ʒublire]   **prieras** [prira]
    dédiera [dedira]   **liera** [lira]

See p. 209 for musical examples with some of these situations.

When *-ie* is followed by another letter in the syllable, however, it will be /ije/, as in verb infinitives discussed above, or /jɛ/:

    hier [jɛːr]   **miel** [mjɛl]

The name **Siebel**, a character in Gounod's *Faust*, is irregularly pronounced [sjebɛl]. The glide is followed by /e/, although there is no diacritical.

/u/

The sound /u/ is the same as English **do**, but without the diphthong glide-off. It is the same as Italian **tu** and German **du**. See p. 6 for a discussion of this sound.

In French /u/ is spelled as follows:

• *ou* and variations *où, oû, aou, aoû*

toujours [tuʒuːr]	**coût** [ku]	**doux** [du]
retour [rətuːr]	**août** [u]	**saoul** [su]

When *ou* is followed by another vowel in the same syllable, it usually acts as the glide /w/:

ouest [wɛst]   **oui** [wi]   **rouage** [rwaːʒ(ə)]

Musical settings of polysyllabic words with *ou* plus vowel usually turn the glide into a vowel.

rouet [rwe] becomes [rue]   **jouer** [ʒwe] becomes [ʒue]

When the combination *oue* is followed by a pronounced consonant plus vowel, it is always just /u/, in speech and singing (no pronunciation of /ə/):

rouerie [ruri]   **jouerai** [ʒure]

ou followed by *ill* results in /uj/:

mouiller [muje]   **brouillard** [brujaːr]

MIXED VOWELS

As was described in the German chapter, a mixed vowel is one that combines elements of two other "pure" vowels. The more important element is the "inside" or tongue position, which forms the core of the vowel sound. The "outside" or lip position simply colors the core sound. While German has four "mixed" vowel sounds, French has only three.

/y/

This "mixed" vowel sound is the same as the German closed sound spelled with *ü* as in **müde**. The key to this sound is the arched tongue position of /i/. Students unfamiliar with French see the vowel-letter *u* and instinctively want to pronounce /u/. The lips round to an /u/ position, but the tongue must remain arched as for /i/.

In French this sound is spelled as follows:

- *u, û,* when it is the only vowel-letter in the syllable and is not nasalized:

  une [yn(ə)]   **sur** [syːr]   **brûle** [bryːl(ə)]
  rendu [rãdy]   **dessus** [dəsy]

  (For the rare irregular pronunciation of *u* as in **album**, see under /ɔ/.)

As above with *-ie*, final *-ue(s)* is spoken as just /y/ but is usually set musically with two notes as [yə]:

  vue [vy] or [vyə]   **inconnues** [ɛ̃kɔny] or [ɛ̃kɔnyə]

But when medial in the phrase, *-ue* is normally set on one note as /y/.

Within one word, medial *ue* divides /yɛ/ after consonant plus *l* or *r*:

  cruel [kryɛl]   **fluet** [flyɛ]

but *u* following *g* or *q* is usually silent:

  guerre [gɛːr(ə)]   **que** [kə]

Exception: Some words with **qua** have /kwa/.

  quatuor [kwatɥɔːr]   **équation** [ekwasjõ]
  équateur [ekwatœːr]   but **quasi** [kazi]

Verb infinitives in *-uer* have /ye/:

  muer [mye]   **tuer** [tye]

but other forms of these verbs use only /y/:

  muera [myra]   **tuera** [tyra]

See p. 211 for musical examples with some of these situations.

When *u* precedes other vowel-letters, it usually functions as the glide /ɥ/: **nuit** [nɥi] (See "Glides").

- *eu , eû*, only in forms of the verb **avoir** (normally *eu* is /œ/ or /ø/):

j'ai eu [je y]   **il eut** [il y]   **nous eûmes** [nu zym(ə)]

La Damnation de Faust

que   s'il   **eût   eu**   l'a - mour au   corps
[kə sil y ty lamuːr o kɔːr]

/œ/

This mixed vowel sound is the same as the German open sound spelled with *ö* as in **Götter**. The tongue and jaw are positioned for /ɛ/ and the lips round to /ɔ/.

In French this sound is spelled as follows:

- *eu* and variations *oeu* and *ueu*, when followed by a pronounced consonant-letter or by *-il* or *-ill*:

fleur [flœːr]	**seul** [sœl]	**neuf** [nœf]
coeur [kœːr]	**oeuf** [œf]	**soeur** [sœːr]
langueur [lãgœːr]	**vainqueur** [vɛ̃kœːr]	
feuille [fœːj(ə)]	**deuil** [dœːj]	

  Note that *ueu* happens only after *g* and *q*, and the first *u* is silent.
  (*Exceptions:* Words ending in *-euse* take /ø/, as do the few words ending in *-eutre* and *-eute*. See next section.)

- *ue* in forms *cueil* and *gueil*:

  cueillir [kœjiːr]   **orgueil** [ɔrgœːj]

- *oe* in forms *oeil*:

  oeil [œːj]   **oeillet** [œjɛ]

Remember that this sound is subject to vocalic harmonization:

  heureux [œrø] or [ørø]

/ø/

The sound /ø/ is the same as the German closed sound spelled with *ö* as in **böse**. The tongue and jaw are positioned for /e/ and the lips round to

/o/. As always with mixed vowels, the tongue position is of primary importance.

The French spelling of this sound is as follows:

- *eu* and variations *oeu, ueu*, when final in a word or followed by a final silent consonant:

  feu [fø]   **peu** [pø]   **dieu** [djø]   **pleut** [plø]
  voeu [vø]   **oeufs** [ø]   **queue** [kø]   **fougueux** [fugø]

  The common feminine ending -*euse* is pronounced /øːz(ə)/:

  radieuse [radjøːs(ə)]   **amoureuse** [amurøːz(ə)]   **chanteuse** [ʃɑ̃tøːz(ə)]

  The rare forms with -*eutre* and -*eute* also use /ø/:

  neutre [nøtr(ə)]   **meute** [møt(ə)]

and also the isolated word **jeûne** [ʒøːn(ə)] (not **jeune**).

Breakdown of Mixed Vowels

The following chart is useful for remembering how the mixed vowels are formulated. This information is essential for the singer and should be memorized.

Tongue / Jaw Position of /i/	plus	Lip Position of /u/	=	/y/
Tongue / Jaw Position of /e/	plus	Lip Position of /o/	=	/ø/
Tongue / Jaw Position of /ɛ/	plus	Lip Position of /ɔ/	=	/œ/

Remember that the core of the mixed vowel sound is the tongue position. If any problem is encountered with a mixed vowel, reduce it to the vowel of the tongue position only. See p. 100 for a somewhat different version of this chart.

/ə/

The symbol /ə/ is called schwa. It represents a short, unstressed, neutral vowel sound. It is used in IPA for any language that employs such a sound, including German and English. When such a sound is lengthened for singing, the vowel quality varies from language to language. In French the schwa symbol is used for mute *e*, and the sound is generally considered to be the same as /œ/ when it is sustained for singing, although depending on context (e.g., whether before or after a closed vowel), it may close somewhat. It will definitely close to /ø/ in vocalic harmonization.

In French the schwa /ə/ is used in IPA transcriptions *whenever the vowel-letter e, without accent, is the only vowel-letter in an open syllable.* Recall that an open syllable ends in a vowel, in this case *e* without an accent. This happens most often at the end of words, but it can also happen medially in a word if syllabification so indicates: **demain, de-main** [d(ə)mɛ̃].

When unaccented *e* ends a syllable following *gu* and *qu*, it is also schwa, since the *u* is silent: **bague** [bag(ə)] **pique** [pik(ə)].

The one exception to this pattern is *e* before –*ill*, where *e* is /ɛ/ or part of a combination creating /œ/, as in **meilleur (me-illeur)** [mɛjœːr] and **cueillir (cue-illir)** [kœjiːr].

Parentheses around the schwa /(ə)/ indicate that this sound is generally silent in speech but pronounced in singing. Examples:

- Final in monosyllables:

  de [də] **le** [lə] **me** [mə] **te** [tə] **ne** [nə] **que** [kə] **se** [sə]

- Final in polysyllabic words (silent in spoken French):

  aime [ɛm(ə)] **fille** [fiːj(ə)] **mystère** [mistɛːr(ə)]

- Medial in polysyllabic words (silent in spoken French):

reviens [rəvjɛ̃]	**cheval** [ʃ(ə)val]	**querelle** [kərɛl(ə)]
médecin [mɛd(ə)sɛ̃]	**parlerai** [parl(ə)re]	
souvenir [suv(ə)nːir]	**Marguerite** [marg(ə)rit(ə)]	

Other situations resulting in schwa /ə/ are as follows:

- Final –*es* in plural forms of nouns and adjectives (but not monosyllables such as **les**) and in verb endings. These also are silent in spoken French:

  courtes vestes [kurt(ə) vɛst(ə)]
  jeunes filles [ʒœn(ə) fiːj(ə)]   **tu parles** [ty parl(ə)]

- Final *-ent* in verb endings of the third person plural, present tense (silent in spoken French):

  ils aiment [il zɛm(ə)]   **ils viennent** [il vjɛn(ə)]
  ils parlent [il parl(ə)]

BUT remember that the *-aient* ending (imperfect tense) is /ɛ/ only:

  ils aimaient [il zɛmɛ]   **ils accouraient** [il zakurɛ]
  ils disaient [il dizɛ]

AND remember that when *-ent* is not a verb ending, it is /ɑ̃/:

  souvent [suvɑ̃]   **comment** [kɔmɑ̃]   **maintenent** [mɛ̃t(ə)nɑ̃]

- Initial *ress-* usually has irregular /ə/:

  ressembler [r(ə)sɑ̃ble]   **ressentiment** [r(ə)sɑ̃timɑ̃]
  resserrer [r(ə)sere]   **ressource** [r(ə)surs(ə)]
  ressort [r(ə)sɔr]
  with the exception of **ressusciter** [resysite].

- Two *dess* words have /ə/:

  dessous [dəsu]   **dessus** [dəsy]

- *ai* in forms of the verb **faire**, when *ai* precedes *s* sounding as /z/ (see p. 162):

  faisons [fəzɔ̃] **faisant** [fəzɑ̃] **faisait** [fəzɛ]

See p. 202 for a complete discussion of musical settings of schwa.

NASAL VOWELS

French has four nasal vowels: /ɑ̃/, /ɛ̃/, /ɔ̃/, and /œ̃/. All four sounds occur in the phrase **un bon vin blanc** [œ̃ bɔ̃ vɛ̃ blɑ̃]. The nasal quality of the vowels should be light, unexaggerated.

Alternative phonetic symbols are sometimes used, but the four symbols above are the most commonly accepted.

The pattern for determining nasalization of a vowel is consistent for all of them:

A vowel will be nasalized if it is followed by **n** *or* **m** *in the same syllable. The* **n** *or* **m** *is not in the same syllable if it is immediately followed by a vowel or by,* **m, n,** *or* **h** *in the same word.*

Another way to express this rule is this: if *n* or *m* ends a closed syllable, or if the syllable ends with a cluster beginning *n* or *m*, the preceding vowel will be nasal. Double *mm* and *nn* do not normally result in a nasal vowel (except initial *emm, enn*—see below).

Here are some examples of words with nasal vowels (*n* or *m* part of the same syllable as the preceding vowel):

vain [vɛ̃]	**enfant** [ɑ̃fɑ̃]	**ingrat** [ɛ̃gra]
humble [œ̃:bl(ə)]	**dompter** [dõte]	**champ** [ʃɑ̃]
ombrage [õbra:ʒ(ə)]	**banc** [bɑ̃]	**bientôt** [bjɛ̃to]
printemps [prɛ̃tɑ̃]	**un** [œ̃]	

Here are examples of words without nasal vowels (*n* or *m* in a different syllable from the preceding vowel):

vaine [vɛn(ə)]	**bonheur** [bɔnœ:r]	**automne** [otɔn(ə)]
tenir [təni:r]	**anneau** [ano]	**une** [yn(ə)]
inégal [inegal]	**immémoriale** [imemɔrjal(ə)]	

The *n* or *m* in the syllable of the nasal vowel is *not pronounced* except when final *n* is in liaison. The letter *m* is never in liaison. (See "Liaison").

Exceptions to the nasalization rule are limited to words beginning with *en, enn,* and (*r*)*emm*:

enamourer [ɑ̃namure]	**enivrer** [ɑ̃nivre]
enorgueiller [ɑ̃nɔrgœje]	**ennui** [ɑ̃nɥi]
ennoblir [ɑ̃nɔbli:r]	**emmener** [ɑ̃m(ə)ne]
emmeler [ɑ̃m(ə)le]	**remmener** [rɑ̃m(ə)ne]

A single *enn*- word is *not* nasalized: **ennemi** [enəmi]

Incorrect Sounding of *n* and *m* in Nasal Vowels

As is stated above, when indicating a nasal vowel, the letters *n* and *m* are not pronounced. They become part of the vowel itself.

There are three specific situations in which English cognates to French words with nasal vowels are likely to cause the English-speaking student to pronounce the *n* or *m* because that is what happens in the English words.

- When *n* precedes *d* or *t*, there is a tendency for English speakers to
pronounce the *n*, because the tongue is in the same position for all
three sounds:

onde [õːd(ə)]   **intime** [ɛ̃tim(ə)]
monter [mõte]   **lamente** [lamɑ̃ːt(ə)]
plainte dormante [plɛ̃t(ə) dɔrmɑ̃ːt(ə)]

Similarly, when *m* precedes *b* or *p*, there is a greater tendency to
pronounce the *m*, because the lips are closed for all three sounds:

ombre [õːbr(ə)]   **tombe** [tõːb(ə)]
impossible [ɛ̃pɔsibl(ə)]   **embarquer** [ɑ̃barke]

When a nasal vowel precedes the sounds /k/ or /g/, there is a tendency for English speakers to pronounce /ŋ/, since that is what
happens in English. The sound /ŋ/ does not exist in standard
French:

anglais [ɑ̃glɛ]   <u>not</u>   [ɑ̃ŋglɛ]
encore   [ɑ̃kɔːr(ə)] <u>not</u>   [ɑ̃ŋkɔːr(ə)]
oncle   [õːkl(ə)]   <u>not</u>   [õːŋkl(ə)]

/ɑ̃/

As the IPA symbol implies, it is the dark version of the vowel that is nasalized. Though it is dark, it is open; otherwise it could be confused with /õ/.

The spelling of this sound in French is as follows:

- *an*   **chant** [ʃɑ̃]   **antan** [ɑ̃tɑ̃]   **danser** [dɑ̃se]
  am   **champ** [ʃɑ̃]   **flambeau**[flɑ̃bo]   **Samson** [sɑ̃sõ]
  en   **enfer** [ɑ̃fɛːr]   **serment** [sɛrmɑ̃]   **splendeur** [splɑ̃dœːr]
  em   **temps** [tɑ̃]   **semble** [sɑ̃ːbl(ə)]   **emplir** [ɑ̃pliːr]

Less common variations of the principal spellings are as follows:

- *aen*   **Messiaen** [mesjɑ̃]   **Caen** [kɑ̃]
  aën   **Saint-Saëns** [sɛ̃ sɑ̃ːs]
  ean   **Jean** [ʒɑ̃]
  aon   **paon** [pɑ̃]

Exceptions: -*ien* is pronounced /jɛ̃/:

bien [bjɛ̃]   **chien** [ʃjɛ̃]   **chrétien** [kretjɛ̃]
viens [vjɛ̃]   **tient** [tjɛ̃]

including final -*yen*:

Troyen [trwajɛ̃]   **moyen** [mwajɛ̃]

but these words have /jã/:

patient [pasjã]   **patience** [pasjãːs(ə)]

The following are isolated exceptions (proper names):

Poulenc [pulɛ̃ːk]   **Jonathan** [ʒɔnatan]

/ɛ̃/

This is the one nasal vowel in which the original vowel shape changes slightly in the nasal version. When nasalized, the original open /ɛ/ position is "tilted" forward. This can be accomplished by gently shaping the vowel *in the direction of* /æ/ as in English **hat**. Do not exaggerate, however! It should not have the tight nasal quality characteristic of some American pronunciations of /æ/.

The spelling of this sound in French is as follows:

in	**vin** [vɛ̃]	**Marin** [marɛ̃]	**insensé** [ɛ̃sãse]
im	**timbre** [tɛ̃ːbr(ə)]	**important** [ɛ̃pɔrtã]	
yn	**lynx** [lɛ̃ːks]	**syncope** [sɛ̃kɔp(ə)]	
ym	**thym** [tɛ̃]	**symphonie** [sɛ̃fɔni]	

and variations of the above:

ain	**pain** [pɛ̃]	**certain** [sɛrtɛ̃]	**ainsi** [ɛ̃si]
aim	**faim** [fɛ̃]	**daim** [dɛ̃]	
ein	**plein** [plɛ̃]	**ceinture** [sɛ̃tyːr(ə)]	
eim	**Reims** [rɛ̃ːs]		

- *ien* is /jɛ̃/ **ancien** [ãsjɛ̃] **rien** [rjɛ̃] **mien** [mjɛ̃] **tiens** [tjɛ̃] **vient** [vjɛ̃] **viendra** [vjɛ̃dra]
- *oin* is /wɛ̃/ **loin** [lwɛ̃] **besoin** [bəzwɛ̃] **point** [pwɛ̃] **poing** [pwɛ̃]

- final *yen* **moyen** [mwajɛ̃] **Troyen** [trwajɛ̃] **doyen** [dwajɛ̃]
- Some proper names such as **Poulenc** [pulɛ̃ːk], and the word **examen** [ɛgzamɛ̃].

/õ/

The sound /õ/ was originally rendered as /ɔ̃/ in IPA, but in recent years the accepted symbol has become /õ/. This is more appropriate, since it is the closed version of the vowel that is nasalized. Of the four nasal vowels, this is the only one that is closed.

The spelling of this sound in French is as follows:

- *on* **bon** [bõ] **fontaine** [fõtɛn(ə)] **vont** [võ] **voyons** [vwajõ]
- *om* **nom** [nõ] **tomber** [tõbe] **rompre** [rõːpr(ə)]

/œ̃/

The sound /œ̃/ is the most difficult for students to get right. There are two ways to find it:

1. The usual way is to isolate the vowel /œ/ and then to add nasal quality. Unfortunately, students tend to change the /œ/ sound when nasality is added.
2. An alternative is to isolate the nasal vowel /ɛ̃/, which is usually not a difficult sound for students to make, then round the lips while keeping the jaw open.

Students who have trouble with this sound tend to substitute /ã/. In such cases it is advisable to substitute /ɛ̃/ as the nearest sound. If this habit can be trained, rounding of the lips for the true /œ̃/ is not difficult.

The spelling of this sound in French is as follows:

- *un* **un** [œ̃] **lundi** [lœ̃di] **brun** [brœ̃] **Verdun** [vɛrdœ̃] **opportun** [ɔpɔrtœ̃]
- *um* **parfum** [parfœ̃] **humble** [œ̃ːbl(ə)]

GLIDES IN FRENCH

A glide is a very short vowel sound that gives way immediately to the primary vowel sound of the syllable. French has three glides: /j/, /w/, and /ɥ/. See p. 208 for musical settings of glides.

/j/

/j/ is a short, rapid /i/. *This glide can be spelled as follows:*

- *i* when followed by a vowel other than /ə/:

  ciel [sjel]   **précieux** [presjø]   **science** [sjɑ̃ːs(ə)]

  Exceptions: words with -*ie*-, -*ia*-, or -*io*- after a consonant plus *l* or *r* have no glide:

  prier [prie]   **oublier** [ublie]
  bibliotèque [bibliotɛk(ə)]   **triangle** [triɑ̃gl(ə)]
  (Some dictionaries indicate a /j/ between vowels in these words, i.e., [prije].)

- ï and *y* when intervocalic, and *y* when initial:

  aïeux [ajø]   **payer** [peje]   **royal** [rwajal]   **yeux** [jø]

- *ill* following a vowel. The *i* has no separate function:

  abeille [abeːj(ə)]   **feuillage** [fœjaːʒ(ə)]
  travailler [travaje]   **cuellir** [kœjiːr]
  ailleurs [ajœːr]   **cailloux** [kaju]
  oeillet [œjɛ]   **mouiller** [muje]

- *ill* and *ilh* following a consonant. Here the *i* functions as /i/:

  fille [fiːj(ə)]   **Milhaud** [mijo]   **famille** [famiːj(ə)]
  Paladilhe [paladiːj(ə)]

  Exceptions: Three words and their derivatives have /il/:

  mille [mil(ə)]   **ville** [vil(ə)]   **tranquille** [trɑ̃kil(ə)]
  million [miljõ]   **village** [vilaːʒ(ə)]   **tranquillité** [trɑ̃kilite]

  and initial *ill*- (the *l* sound is doubled):

  illusion [illysjõ]   **illumination** [illyminasjõ]

- Final -*il* and -*ilh* after a vowel, though technically not glides, are given the /j/ symbol in most diction texts:

  soleil [sɔleːj]   **corail** [kɔraːj]   **cercueil** [sɛrkœːj]
  deuil [dœːj]   **Anouilh** [anuːj]

- The combination *-ti-* is pronounced /sj/ in certain suffixes:

  -tion: **addition** [adisjõ]   **motion** [mɔsjõ]

  but not after *s*: **question** [kɛstjõ] or in verbs: **sortions** [sɔrtjõ]

-tience:	**patience** [pasjɑ̃ːs(ə)]	
-tient(e):	**patient** [pasjɑ̃]	**patiente** [pasjɑ̃ːt(ə)]
-tien(ne):	**vénitien** [venisjẽ]	**vénitienne** [venisjɛn(ə)]
-tiel(le):	**confidentiel** [kõfidɑ̃sjɛl]	**essentielle** [ɛsɑ̃sjɛl(ə)]
-tieux(se):	**ambitieux** [ɑ̃bisjø]	**minutieuse** [minysjøːz(ə)]
-tiable:	**insatiable** [ẽsasjabl(ə)]	

  Some words with *ti*, however, have /tj/, including some *-tien(ne)* words:

  chrétien [kretjẽ]   **antienne** [ɑ̃tjɛn(ə)]   **entretien** [ɑ̃tr(ə)tjẽ]

/w/

/w/ is a short, rapid /u/. *This glide can be spelled as follows:*

- *ou* followed by a vowel other than mute *e*:

  oui [wi]   **ouest** [wɛst]   **jouer** [ʒwe]

  Exception: *ou* followed by *ill* is /uj/:

  mouillé [muje]   **brouillé** [bruje]

- *oi* results in /wa/ or /wɑ/:

foi [fwa]	**roi** [rwa]	**vois** [vwa]
soif [swaf]	**noir** [nwaːr]	**oiseau** [wazo]
effroi [efrwɑ]	**croire** [krwɑːr(ə)]	

- Final *oie* is /wa/:

  soie [swa]   **joie** [ʒwa]

  or /waə/ if the *e* is given its own note, but medial *oie* is always /wa/:

  soient [swa]

- *oin* results in /wẽ/:

  besoin [bəzwẽ]   **loin** [lwẽ]   **moindre** [mwẽːdr(ə)]

- *oy* followed by another vowel results in /waj/:

voyage [vwaja:ʒ(ə)] **voyez** [vwaje] **loyal** [lwajal]
moyen [mwajɛ̃] **foyer** [fwaje]

The common verb **s'asseoir** [saswa:r] has an unpronounced mute *e* before the *oi*.

Rarely, *qua* is pronounced /kwa/. Normally *u* is silent after *q*.

quatuor [kwatɥɔ:r] **adéquat** [adekwa]
aquarelle [akwarɛl(ə)]

/ɥ/

Unlike /w/ and /j/, the glide /ɥ/ does not occur in English. For this reason it is often a difficult sound for the student to acquire. It is a short, rapid /y/. When it is incorrect, it sounds like /w/; **nuit** is pronounced [nwi]. For such a word the student should shape the lips for /y/ *as the preceding consonant is being articulated*. If the shaping of the lips happens after the consonant, it is too late and /w/ will result.

The spellings of this sound in French are as follows:

- *u* followed by a vowel other than mute *e*:

nuit [nɥi] **lui** [lɥi] **suis** [sɥi] **fui** [fɥi] **fruit** [frɥi]
Juif [ʒɥif] **cuisine** [kɥizin(ə)] **suave** [sɥa:v(ə)]
nuage [nɥa:ʒ(ə)] **muet** [mɥɛ]

- *uy* results in /ɥij/:

fuyez [fɥije] **essuyage** [esɥija:ʒ(ə)] **ennuyer** [ɑ̃nɥije]

Exceptions: when *u* follows *g* or *q*, it is usually silent:

languir [lɑ̃gi:r] **guetter** [gɛte] **Guy** [gi] **qui** [ki]
quatre [katr(ə)] **muguet** [mygɛ] **quasi** [kazi] **que** [kə]
but the word **aiguille** and derivatives have /gɥi/ [egɥi:j(ə)]).

A few words have *qua* as /kwa/:

quatuor [kwatɥɔ:r] **adéquat** [adekwa] **aquarelle** [akwarɛl(ə)]

When a consonant cluster ending in *l* or *r* precedes *ue* or *ua*, the result is a vowel instead of a glide:

cruel [kryɛl]   **cruauté** [kryote]

This is also true of *-ui-* in the word **fluide** [flyide(ə)] but not in **bruit** [brɥi] or **bruire** [brɥiːr(ə)]. The word **bruyère**, having consonant plus *r*, has no /ɥ/ glide: [bryjɛːr(ə)], but **bruyant**, derived from **bruit** (see above), does have /ɥ/: [brɥijã].

FRENCH CONSONANTS

Any discussion of French consonants must make a distinction between consonant sounds and consonant-letters, since the letters are often silent. Individual consonant-letters as well as combinations are presented here in alphabetical order, with an explanation of their sounds and when they are silent. To facilitate this presentation, the discussion of each letter is in two general parts:

1. When the letter ends a word
2. When the letter is initial or medial in a word

The reason for this two-part discussion is that final consonant-letters are usually silent, whereas consonant-letters elsewhere in a word are usually sounded.

Knowing when final consonants are sounded and when they are silent is one of the more difficult aspects of French pronunciation. A helpful device is the so-called rule of "careful." The four consonant-letters in this English word are usually *sounded* when found at the end of a French word, whereas all other consonant-letters are usually *silent* when at the end of a word. Useful as this crutch is, there are numerous exceptions.

Any consonant before final mute e is pronounced. Many French words have masculine forms ending in a silent letter and feminine forms that add a mute *e*, causing the preceding consonant to be pronounced:

froid [frwa]   **froide** [frwad(ə)]   **Jean** [ʒã]   **Jeanne** [ʒɑn(ə)]
berger [bɛrʒe]   **bergère** [bɛrʒɛːrə]   **vain** [vɛ̃]   **vaine** [vɛn(ə)])

Remember that double consonants in French are not lengthened as they are in Italian, except for initial *ill-*, *imm-*, *inn-*, and *irr-*.

B, BB

When Final

Final *b* is rare in French. If it follows a nasal vowel, it is silent:

plomb [plõ]

At the end of proper names it is sounded and retains voicing,

Mab [mab]   **Jacob** [ʒakɔb]

Initial/Medial

b and *bb* sound as /b/:

bouche [buʃ(ə)] **abbé** [abe]

Exception: When it precedes an unvoiced consonant, it is /p/:

obtenir [ɔpt(ə)niːr]   **absence** [apsɑ̃s(ə)]
obscur [ɔpskyːr]   **observer** [ɔpsɛrve]

C, CC, Ç

When Final

As one of the "careful" consonants, *c* is usually sounded as /k/ when final in French words:

arc [ark]   **parc** [park]   **turc** [tyrk]   **lac** [lak]   **sec** [sɛk]

including in proper names:

Duparc [dypark]   **Bernac** [bɛrnak]   **Poulenc** [pulɛ̃ːk]

In spite of "Poulenc," *c* is usually silent when preceded by a nasal vowel:

banc [bɑ̃]   **jonc** [ʒõ]   **franc** [frɑ̃]

and silent in a few individual words:

estomac [ɛstɔma]   **tabac** [taba]   **croc** [kro]

The word **donc** is somewhat confusing. Most dictionaries give [dõːk], but in practice it is often pronounced [dõ]. French pronunciation books are not in total agreement, but the majority consensus is that it is pronounced [dõːk] in the following cases:

1. At the beginning of a sentence or clause when its meaning is "therefore":

Je pense, donc [dõːk] **je suis.**
Donc, ce sera par un clair jour d'été. [dõːk sə səra . . .]

2. In liaison:

Il est donc [dõːk] **entendu que** . . .
Mais où donc est l'amour? [mɛ u dõ kɛ lamuːr]

3. When standing alone as an interjection:

Donc! [dõːk]

Otherwise it is pronounced [dõ]:

Qu'as tu donc? [ka ty dõ]   **Il est donc venu.** [il ɛ dõ vəny]

Initial/Medial

As in other languages, the letter *c* has two sounds in French:

- "Hard" *c* is pronounced /k/ and occurs when *it* is followed by *a*, *o*, *u*, or a consonant:

carte [kart(ə)] **comme** [kɔm(ə)] **vaincu** [vɛ̃ky]

The word **second** and derivatives irregularly have /g/: [səgõ].

Final -*ct* is silent in **aspect** [aspɛ]. Otherwise it is sounded:

direct [dirɛkt]   **exact** [egzakt]

- "Soft" *c* is pronounced /s/ and occurs when *it* is followed by *e*, *i*, or *y*:

facile [fasil(ə)]   **cette** [sɛt(ə)]   **ciel** [sjɛl]   **cygne** [siɲ(ə)]

including in the combinations *sce* and *sci*:

ascenseur [asɑ̃sœːr]   **scintiller** [sɛ̃tije]

The letter *ç* is always pronounced /s/. It is used in a few words to create /s/ before *a*, *o*, or *u*:

ça [sa]   leçon [ləsõ]   garçon [garsõ]   aperçu [apɛrsy]

Double *cc* is /k/ when followed by *a*, *o*, *u*, or a consonant:

acclamer [aklame]   occuper [ɔkype]   raccord [rakɔːr]

Double *cc* is /ks/ when followed by e or *i*:

accident [aksidã]   accepter [aksɛpte]
(Note that this is similar to English but different from Italian.)

CH

The combination *ch* is never silent and is usually pronounced /ʃ/. This is the only way to spell this sound in French. The French version is pronounced with more lip rounding than the English version.

chercher [ʃɛrʃe]   achever [aʃ(ə)ve]   boucher [buʃe]

In words of Greek origin, *ch* is pronounced /k/:

choeur [kœːr]   orchestre [orkɛstr(ə)]   chrétien [kretjẽ]

D, DD

As in Italian, the sound /d/ is never aspirated (released with a puff of air) in French, as it is in English and German. It must be pronounced dentally, that is, with the tongue making contact with the back of the upper front teeth.

When Final

Usually final *d* is silent:

froid [frwa]   pied [pje]   quand [kã]   canard [kanaːr]

In proper names it is sounded:

le Cid [sid]   Alfred [alfrɛd]   Yniold [injɔld]

It is also sounded in the word **sud** [syd].

In liaison, *d* sounds as /t/ (see "Liaison"):

quand‿il [kã til]

Initial/Medial

d and *dd* sound as /d/:

dans [dã]   fidèle [fidɛl(ə)]   addition [adisjõ]

F, FF

When Final

As one of the "careful" consonants, *f* is usually pronounced as /f/ when it is final in French words:

  chef [ʃɛf]   **soif** [swaf]   **if** [if]   **bref** [brɛf]   **furtif** [fyrtif]

A few words have silent final *f*:

  clef [kle]   **nerf** [nɛːr]   **cerf** [sɛːr]   **chef-d'oeuvres** [ʃɛ dœːvr(ə)]

The words **oeuf** [œf] and **boeuf** [bœf] are irregular in the pronunciation of their plurals: **oeufs** [ø] and **boeufs** [bø].

There are two phrases in which *f* sounds as /v/: **neuf heures** [nœvœːr(ə)] and **neuf ans** [nœvɑ̃]. This is not liaison, since *f* is already pronounced in **neuf** [nœf].

Initial/Medial

f and *ff* always sound as /f/:

  fin [fɛ̃]   **affaire** [afɛːr(ə)]

G, GG

When Final

When *g* ends a French word, it normally follows a nasal vowel and is silent:

  sang [sɑ̃]   **poing** [pwɛ̃]   **long** [lɔ̃]   also **bourg** [buːr]

Final *g* in liaison sounds as /k/ (see "Liaison"):

  long‿hiver [lɔ̃kivɛːr]

Initial/Medial

As in other languages, *g* has two sounds:

- "Hard" *g* is pronounced /g/ and occurs when followed by *a, o, u,* or a consonant:

  gauche [goːʃ(ə)]   **goûter** [gute]   **figure** [figyːr(ə)]

- "Soft" *g* is /ʒ/ and occurs when *g* is followed by *e*, *i*, or *y*:

    givre [ʒiːvr(ə)]   **rouge** [ruːʒ(ə)]   **gymnaste** [ʒimnast(ə)]

Note: Whenever *gu* is followed by a vowel, the *u* has no phonetic value of its own (that is, it is not /y/ or /ɥ/). Its only purpose is to render the *g* hard:

    guerre [geːr(ə)]   **languir** [lɑ̃giːr]
    guide [gid(ə)]   **baguette** [bagɛt(ə)]

Similarly, whenever *ge* is followed by another vowel, the *e* is unphonetic, serving only to render the *g* soft:

    nageais [naʒɛ]   **songeait** [sõʒɛ]
    changea [ʃɑ̃ʒa]   **Georges** [ʒɔːrʒ(ə)]

Double *gg* is /g/ when followed by *a*, *o*, *u*, or a consonant:

    aggraver [agrave]

Double *gg* is /gʒ/ when followed by *e* or *é*:

    suggérer [sygʒere]   **suggestion** [sygʒɛstjõ]

GN

As in Italian, the combination *gn* is normally pronounced /ɲ/:

    ignoble [iɲɔbl(ə)]   **baigner** [beɲe]   **agneau** [aɲo]
    cygne [siɲ(ə)]   **rogner** [rɔɲe]
    (This sound is described in the Italian chapter.)

Exception: **stagnant, stagnante** [stagnɑ̃] [stagnɑ̃ːt(ə)]

There is no /ʎ/ sound in French, so *gl* is always /gl/:

    glisser [glise] **église** [egliːz(ə)]

H

The letter *h* is always silent in French. It may be sounded in foreign words such as "Nahandove" [nahandoːvə] from Ravel's *Chansons Madécasses*. It is true that French singers sometimes pronounce *h* in situations of strong emotional content (**haine, honte**), but this practice is not advisable for non-French singers until they are very proficient with the language. (For a discussion of aspirate and nonaspirate *h*, see Definition of Terms, p. 149.)

J

The letter *j* is never silent and is always pronounced /ʒ/. It is always initial or medial, never final:

juge [ʒyːʒ(ə)]   **jouir** [ʒwiːr]
projet [prɔʒɛ]   **conjoindre** [kõʒwɛ̃ːdr(ə)]

L

When Final

As one of the "careful" consonants, final *l* is usually sounded:

ciel [sjɛl]   **idéal** [ideal]   **avril** [avril]
seul [sœl]   **nul** [nyl]   **cil** [sil]

but words ending in vowel plus *il* end in /j/:

travail [travaːj]   **soleil** [sɔlɛːj]   **pareil** [parɛːj]
deuil [dœːj]   **cerceuil** [sɛrkœːj]   **oeil** [œːj]
vermeil [vɛrmɛːj]   **orgueil** [ɔrgœːj]

A few words ending in consonant plus *il* have silent *l*:

gentil [ʒɑ̃ti]   **fusil** [fyzi]   **sourcil** [sursi]

Initial/Medial

As in Italian, /l/ must be pronounced forward, with the front of the tongue near or at the upper front teeth:

livre [liːvr(ə)]   **galant** [galɑ̃]   **fidèle** [fidɛl(ə)]

The word **fils** [fis], meaning *son* or *sons*, has silent *l*. The word **fil** [fil], meaning *thread*, has a plural form **fils**, also pronounced [fil].

Double *ll* also sounds as /l/:

aller [ale]   **belle** [bɛl(ə)]   **follement** [fɔl(ə)mɑ̃]

although usually -*ill* is /j/ or /iːj/:

fille [fiːj(ə)]   **vieillard** [vjejaːr]   **ailleurs** [ajœːr] with the three common exceptions:

mille [mil(ə)]   **tranquille** [trãkil(ə)]   **ville** [vil(ə)]

and their derivatives.

–ilh– is also /j/:

Milhaud [mijo]   **Anouilh** [anuːj]   **Paladilhe** [paladiːj]

and initial *–ill* has lengthened double /ll/:

illusion [illyzjõ]   **illuminer** [illymine]

The combinations *–ault* and *auld* sound as /o/:

Foucault [fuko]   **Clérambault** [klerãbo]   **Rochefoucauld** [rɔʃfuko]

M, MM

When Final

Final *m* or *m* before a final silent consonant results in a nasal vowel and is therefore silent:

daim [dẽ]   **parfum** [parfœ̃]   **thym** [tẽ]   **temps** [tã]

Words of foreign origin will sound final *m*:

Jérusalem [ʒerysalɛm]

Initial/Medial

If *m* precedes a vowel, it does not cause a nasal vowel and is therefore /m/:

aime [ɛm(ə)]   **camembert** [kamãbɛːr]   **maman** [mamã]

m is silent in the combination *–mn–* in some common words:

automne [otɔn(ə)]   **damner** [dane]   **damnation** [danasjõ]

but not in others:

hymne [imn(ə)]   **calomnie** [kalɔmni]   **amnésie** [amnezi]

double *mm* normally sounds as /m/:

femme [fam(ə)]   **commencer** [kɔmãse]

but words with initial -*emm* have /ãm/:

>   **emmener** [ãm(ə)ne]   **emmêler** [ãm(ə)le]

and initial -*imm* has lengthened double /mm/:

>   **immense** [immãs(ə)]   **immortel** [immɔrtɛl]

N, NN

When Final

Final *n* or *n* before final silent consonants results in a nasal vowel and is therefore silent:

>   **soudain** [sudɛ̃]   **jambon** [ʒãbõ]   **artisan** [artizã]
>   **dans** [dã]   **dent** [dã]   **charmant** [ʃarmã]

Words of foreign origin will sound final *n*: **Carmen** [karmɛn].

Initial/Medial

When *n* precedes a vowel, it does not cause a nasal vowel and is therefore /n/:

>   **soudaine** [sudɛn(ə)]   **inutile** [inytil(ə)]   **neige** [nɛːʒ(ə)]

Exceptions: A few words with initial -*en* have /ãn/:

>   **enivrer** [ãnivre]   **enamourer** [ãnamure]   **enorgueiller** [ãnɔrgœje]

Double *nn* is usually /n/:

>   **mienne** [mjɛn(ə)]   **sonner** [sɔne]

but initial *inn*- has /nn/ (lengthened sound):

>   **innombrable** [innõbrabl(ə)]   **innocent** [innɔsã]

and initial *enn*- is [ãn]:

>   **ennui** [ãnɥi] (see p. 173)

P, PP

When Final

Final p is normally silent:

trop [tro]   **beaucoup** [boku]   **champ** [ʃɑ̃]

but it is sounded in a few words: **cap** [kap].

Initial/Medial

p and pp usually sound as /p/:

porte [pɔrt(ə)]   **après** [aprɛ]   **approcher** [aprɔʃɛ]

including initial *ps*:

psaume [psom(ə)]   **Psyché** [psiʃe]   **psychologie** [psikɔlɔʒi]

p before *t* is often silent:

sept [sɛt]   **compter** [kõte]   **baptême** [batɛm(ə)]
prompt [prõ]   **prompte** [prõt(ə)]   **sculpture** [skyltyːr(ə)]

but is sounded in some words:

septembre [sɛptɑ̃br(ə)]   **crypte** [kript(ə)]
somptueux [sõptyø]   **rédempteur** [redɑ̃ptœːr]
(Always check a reliable dictionary for the combination *-pt-*.)

The combination *ph* sounds as /f/:

philosophe [filɔzɔf(ə)]   **philtre** [filtr(ə)]

Q

The letter q sounds as /k/ wherever it falls in the word:

quelque [kɛlk(ə)]   **coq** [kɔk]   **coquin** [kɔkɛ̃]   **querelle** [kərɛl(ə)]

The *q* in **cinq** is sounded when the word is standing alone or when it is
followed by a word beginning with a vowel or *h*. The *q* is silent when
cinq is followed by a word beginning with a consonant:

cinq [sɛ̃ːk]   **cinq ans** [sɛ̃ːkɑ̃]   **cinq hommes** [sɛ̃ːkɔm(ə)]
cinq femmes [sɛ̃ fam(ə)]

R, RR

In the singing of French art songs and opera, *r* has traditionally been pronounced as a flip of the tongue: /r/. In speech and popular singing the
uvular sound /ʀ/ is used. Judicious use of the uvular sound, however, has

recently become accepted in some circles for "classical" singing. It is advisable for singers with moderate experience with French to use the flipped /r/ sound. The uvular sound may be considered at some future point if stylistic trends call for it, but only if it is recommended by experts in French vocal music.

Double *rr* is lengthened (tongue roll) only in initial *irr-*:

irrésolu [irrezɔly]   **irréel** [irreɛl]

Double *rr* in other contexts normally sounds as /r/ (one flip of the tongue):

erreur [ɛrœːr]   **horreur** [ɔrœːr]   **arranger** [arɑ̃ʒe]

although a rolled *rr* is not inappropriate in moments of high intensity.

When Final

As one of the "careful" consonants, the letter *r* is often sounded at the end of a word, but there are frequent and common exceptions.

- Final *r* is sounded in all monosyllables:

mer [mɛːr]	**pour** [puːr]	**cher** [ʃɛːr]	**air** [ɛːr]
sur [syːr]	**par** [paːr]	**ver** [vɛːr]	**hier** [jeːr]
voir [vwaːr]	**fuir** [fɥiːr]	**coeur** [kœːr]	**fleur** [flœːr]

- Final *r* is sounded in many nouns and adjectives of two syllables:

amer [amɛːr]	**amour** [amuːr]	**enfer** [ɑ̃fɛːr]
hiver [ivɛːr]	**miroir** [mirwaːr]	**espoir** [ɛspwaːr]

- Final *r* is sounded in many proper names:

    Auber [obeːr]   **Honegger** [ɔnegeːr]   **Jupiter** [ʒypitɛːr]

- Final *r* is sounded in all verb infinitives in *-ir*:

    mourir [muriːr]   **venir** [vəniːr]   **découvrir** [dekuvriːr]

- Final r is silent in polysyllabic words ending in *-ier*, *-yer*, and *-iller* (/je/):

premier [prəmje]	**dernier** [dɛrnje]	**cahier** [kaje]
métier [metje]	**foyer** [fwaje]	**loyer** [lwaje]
oreiller [ɔreje]		

- Final *r* is silent in nouns and adjectives ending *-ser*, *-cher*, and *-ger*.

baiser [beze]	**clocher** [klɔʃe]	**rocher** [rɔʃe]
archer [arʃe]	**léger** [leʒe]	**boucher** [buʃe]
berger [berʒe]	**Roger** [rɔʒe]	**boulanger** [bulɑ̃ʒe]

- Final *r* is silent in all verb infinitives in *-er*.

aller [ale]	**parler** [parle]	**aimer** [eme]
chercher [ʃerʃe]		**trouver** [truve]

Initial/Medial

r is always sounded in these positions, including before final silent consonants:

mettre [metr(ə)]	**boucherie** [buʃ(ə)ri]
bergère [berʒeːr(ə)]	**première** [prəmjeːr(ə)]
dernière [dernjeːr(ə)]	**tort** [tɔːr]
vers [veːr]	**regard** [rəgaːr]
accord [akɔːr]	

Exception: **gars** [gɑ].

S, SC, SS

When Final

Final *s* is usually silent:

bas [bɑ]	**pas** [pɑ]	**lilas** [lilɑ]	**suis** [sɥi]
gens [ʒɑ̃]	**temps** [tɑ̃]	**vous** [vu]	**sous** [su]
sans [sɑ̃]	**corps** [kɔːr]	**alors** [alɔːr]	

including final *s* that indicates plurality of nouns and adjectives:

belles filles [bel(ə) fiːj(ə)]
charmantes choses [ʃarmɑ̃ːt(ə) ʃoːz(ə)]
hautes branches [ot(ə) brɑ̃ːʃ(ə)]
les haricots verts [le ariko veːr]

and final *s* in *all* verb forms:

tu aimes [ty em(ə)]   **je meurs** [ʒə mœːr]   **nous chantons** [nu ʃɑ̃tõ]

Liaison results in a normally silent *s* sounding as /z/. See section on liaison.

Final *s* is sounded as /s/ in a number of words:

fils [fis]	**lys** [lis]	**ours** [urs]	**hélas** [elɑːs]
iris [iris]	**sus** [sys]	**jadis** [ʒadis]	**angélus** [ɑ̃ʒelys]
prospectus [prɔspɛktys]			

There are some individual words requiring special explanation:

- The word **sens** may be a noun or a verb form, with different pronunciations.
  As a verb (from **sentir**), it is [sɑ̃], as in this line from *Faust*:

  Je sens l'amour s'emparer de mon être.
  [ʒə sɑ̃ lamuːr sɑ̃pare də mõ nɛtr(ə)]

  As a noun, meaning *sense,* it is [sɑ̃ːs]. Verlaine's poem "En sourdine" contains the line . . . **Et nos sens extasiés,** in which the noun is in the plural, still pronounced [sɑ̃ːs]. There is no liaison with /z/.

- When the word **tous** modifies a noun, it is [tu]:

  tous les deux [tu lɛ dø]

  When it is a pronoun (not modifying a noun), it is [tus]:

  entre tous [ɑ̃ːtr(ə) tus]

  Mais la lune, compatissante à tous [tus]
  De Grève, Debussy

  Dans ce fleuve à tous [tus] **étranger**
  Le Pont, Apollinaire, Poulenc

- The word **plus** usually has silent *s*:

  rien ne va plus [rjɛ̃ nə va ply]

  It has sounded *s* when the meaning is translated (or implied) as *more than* (**plus que**):

  Il en a plus que toi [il ɑ̃ na plys kə twa]

- The word **os** (*bone*) in the singular is [ɔs]. The plural is spelled the same but pronounced [o].

Final *s* is sounded in many proper names:

Francis [frɑ̃sis]   **Thaïs** [tais]   **Vénus** [venys]
Damis [damis]   **Tircis** [tirsis]   **Bacchus** [bakys]
Atlas [atlas]   **Cérès** [serɛs]   **Baucis** [bosis]
Reims [rɛ̃ːs]   **Mars** [mars]   **Saint-Saëns** [sɛ̃ sɑ̃ːs]

though it is silent in others:

Charles [ʃarl(ə)]   **Chartres** [ʃartr(ə)]   **Thomas** [tɔma]

Initial/Medial

As in other languages, s in French has two sounds: unvoiced /s/ and voiced /z/.

- Unvoiced *s* occurs initially before a vowel:

    soir [swar]   **silence** [silɛ̃ːs(ə)]

    It occurs initially or medially before or after an unvoiced consonant:

    aspect [aspɛ]   **structure** [stryktyːr(ə)]   **tocsin** [tɔksɛ̃]

    Unvoiced s occurs medially after nasal vowels:

    danser [dɑ̃se]

    Although the prefix **trans-** has /z/ when it is followed by a vowel:

    transir [trɑ̃ziːr]   **transitif** [trɑ̃zitif]

    it has /s/ when it is followed by a consonant or mute e:

    transmettre [trɑ̃smetr(ə)]   **transborder** [trɑ̃sbɔrde]   **transe** [trɑ̃ːs(ə)]

    In the combinations *sce* and *sci*, the *c* assimilates with the *s* to sound as /s/:

    descendre [desɑ̃dr(ə)]   **piscine** [pisin(ə)]   **science** [sjɑ̃ːs(ə)]

    Double *ss* is /s/:

    classe [klɑːs(ə)]   **laisser** [lese] or [lese]   **poisson** [pwasõ]

    In contrast to Italian, s preceding a voiced consonant in French is *unvoiced*:

    svelte [svɛlt(ə)] **transborder** [trɑ̃sbɔrde] **jasmin** [ʒasmɛ̃] **Israël** [israɛl]

- Voiced *s* occurs between vowel-letters (intervocalic):

    rose [roːz(ə)]   **croiser** [krwɑze]   **hasard** [azaːr]

    and in liaison (see "liaison"): **mes amis** [mɛzami].

- When *s* appears intervocalic but begins the second part of a compound word, it is unvoiced:

    susurrer [sysyre]

T, TT, TH

When Final

Final *t* is usually silent:

mot [mo]	**chat** [ʃa]	**doigt** [dwa]	**vient** [vjɛ̃]
petit [p(ə)ti]	**effet** [efɛ]	**effort** [efɔːr]	**aspect** [aspɛ]
argent [arʒɑ̃]	**Albert** [albeːr]	**Hamlet** [amlɛ]	

but it is sounded in a few words:

dot [dɔt]	**est** (meaning east) [ɛst]	**ouest** [wɛst]
huit [ɥit]	**brut** [bryt]	**direct** [dirɛkt]
exact [egzakt]	**Ernest** [ɛrnɛst]	**Tybalt** [tibalt]

The word **Christ** is [krist], but **Jésus-Christ** is [ʒezy kri]. The word **soit** when standing alone as an interjection sounds the *t*: **Soit!** [swat]. Otherwise it is silent, though it may sound in liaison:

> **Soit par hasard, soit à dessein** [swa par azaːr swa ta dɛsɛ̃]
> (*Vieille chanson*, Bizet/Millevoye)

Initial/Medial

The sound /t/ should be pronounced with no aspiration. The front of the tongue must contact the back of the upper front teeth. It is the same sound as in Italian:

tête [tɛːt(ə)]	**artiste** [artist(ə)]	**petite** [p(ə)tit(ə)]

Double *tt* and *th* also sound as /t/:

étiquette [etikɛt(ə)]	**attendre** [atɑ̃ːdr(ə)]
théâtre [teɑːtr(ə)]	**thé** [te]

In the suffixes -*tion*, -*tience*, -*tien(ne)*, -*tient(e)*, -*tiel(le)*, -*tieux(se)*, and -*tiable*, (after a vowel) the *ti* sounds as /sj/:

nation	[nasjõ]	**déploration**	[deplɔrasjõ]
patience	[pasjɑːs(ə)]	**patient**	[pasjɑ̃]
patiente	[pasjɑ̃ːt(ə)]	**vénitien**	[venisjɛ̃]
vénitienne	[venisjɛn(ə)]	**essentiel**	[esɑ̃sjɛl]
torrentiel	[tɔrɑ̃sjɛl]	**minutieux**	[minysjø]
insatiable	[ɛ̃sasjabl(ə)]		

(Compare this pronunciation with that of English, which has /ʃ/ or /tʃ/ in these words.)

Final -*tie* sounds as /si/:

Helvétie [ɛlvesi]

But other suffixes with *ti* have /tj/, including sometimes -*tien(ne)*

chrétien [kretjɛ̃]   **antienne** [ɑ̃tjɛn(ə)]   **entretien** [ɑ̃trətjɛ̃]
sentier [sɑ̃tje]   **cimetière** [simitjɛːr(ə)]

Also -*tion* following *s* is /tj/:

question [kɛstjõ]   **digestion** [diʒɛstjõ]

V

The letter *v* is found only in initial and medial positions and is always /v/. It is never doubled.

venir [vəniːr]   **vingt** [vɛ̃]   **vieux** [vjø]
avoir [avwaːr]   **naïveté** [naiv(ə)te]

W

This is essentially a foreign letter to French and is therefore found in foreign words, in initial positions only. Words from German use /v/, and words from English use /w/, though some English-derived words use /v/:

wagon [vagõ]   **whiskey** [wiski]   **Watteau** [vato]

X

When Final

The letter *x* is usually silent when final:

deux [dø]   **voix** [vwa]   **faux** [fo]

In a few words, final *x* sounds as /ks/:

index [ɛ̃dɛks]   **lynx** [lɛ̃ːks]   **sphinx** [sfɛ̃ːks]   **syrinx** [sirɛ̃ːks]
Béatrix [beatriks]   **Aix** [ɛks]   **Cadix** [kadiks]

When standing alone, the numbers **six** and **dix** sound the *x* as /s/: [sis], [dis]. When immediately modifying a word beginning with a consonant, the *x* is silent:

six mois [si mwa]

When immediately modyfying word beginning with a vowel or mute *h*, the *x* is in liasion, sounding as /z/:

dix heures [dizœːr(ə)], **six ans** [sizã]

Initial/Medial

As in English, initial x is rare. It usually sounds as /ks/:

xylophone [ksiləfɔn]

Sometimes it sounds as /gz/:

Xavier [gzavje]

Medial x is usually /ks/:

fixer [fikse]   **extrème** [ɛkstrɛm(ə)]   **mixte** [mikst(ə)]
The proper name **Bruxelles** is [brysɛl].

Initial *ex* followed by a vowel or *h* is /ɛgz/:

exemple [ɛgzãːpl(ə)]   **exercice** [ɛgzɛrsis(ə)]
exhaler [ɛgzale]   **exhiber** [ɛgzibe]

In numerical words, *-xième* has /z/:

deuxième [døzjɛm(ə)]   **sixième** [sizjɛm(ə)]   **dixième** [dizjɛm(ə)]
and **soixante** has /s/: [swasãːt(ə)].

In liaison, x sounds as /z/:

deux amis [dø zami] (see Liaison)

Z

When Final

Final *z* is usually silent, including all second person plural verb forms:

chez [ʃe]   **nez** [ne]   **dormez** [dɔrme]   **allez** [ale]

In several proper names it is sounded as /z/:

Berlioz [bɛrljoːz]   **Boulez** [bulɛːz].

Initial/Medial

In any position other than final, z sounds as /z/:

zéro [zero]   **zèle** [zɛl(ə)]   **azur** [azyːr]
seize [sɛːz(ə)]   **treize** [trɛːz(ə)]

LIAISON

Liaison is the sounding of an *otherwise silent* final consonant when the word following it begins with a vowel or unaspirated *h*. In IPA transcription, either the two words are written as one, or the consonant in liaison is shown as beginning the second word, to indicate the legato flow of pronunciation.

un [œ̃]   **arbre** [aːrbr(ə)]   **un arbre** [œ̃naːrbr(ə)] or [œ̃ naːrbr(ə)]

Liaison is to be distinguished from *elision*, which is the linking of an already sounded final consonant to a vowel sound beginning the next word, usually over a mute *e*.

elle [ɛl(ə)]   **est** [ɛ]   **elle est** [ɛlɛ] or [ɛl ɛ]

Sound Changes Resulting from Liaison

Four consonant-letters change sound when they are in liaison.

- *d* sounds as /t/:

    quand il pleut [kã til plø]   **grand arbre** [grã taːrbr(ə)]

- *g* sounds as /k/:

    long hiver [lõ kivɛːr]   **sang impur** [sã kẽpyːr]

- *s* sounds as /z/:

  tes yeux [tɛ zjø]   **mes amis** [mɛ zami]

- *x* sounds as /z/:

  six heures [si zœːr(ə)]   **je veux aller** [jə vø zale]

In the case of *s* in liaison, the situation is essentially that of an intervocalic *s* sounding as /z/. Occurrences of *d* and *t* in liaison are rare, those of *s* and *x* are common.

The letter *f* is normally sounded when final, so it technically cannot be in liaison. However, when the word **neuf** [nœf] is followed by **heures** or **ans**, the *f* changes sound to /v/:

  neuf heures [nœ vœːr(ə)]   **neuf ans** [nœ vɑ̃]

The remaining consonant-letters that may be sounded in liaison are *n*, *r*, *t*, and *z*. They retain their normal sounds.

When nasal vowels are involved in liaison by sounding *n* (note that *m* is never in liaison), sometimes nasality is eliminated. The most commonly accepted such situations are:

- **bon** loses nasality and the vowel is opened:

  bon anniversaire [bɔ nanivɛrsɛːr(ə)]

- The endings *-ain* and *-ein* lose nasality:

  vain espoir [vɛ nɛspwaːr]   **plein air** [plɛ nɛːr]

- The three adjectives **ancien**, **divin**, and **moyen** lose nasality:

  ancien ami [ɑ̃sjɛ nami]   **divin enfant** [divi nɑ̃fɑ̃]
  moyen age [mwajɛ naːʒ(ə)]

In a very few instances, non-nasal vowels change quality in liaison:

- The adverb **trop** [tro] has an open vowel sounds in liaison:

  trop heuruex [trɔ pørø]

- Adjectives with final *-er* open the vowel in liaison:

  premier amour [prəmjɛ ramuːr]
  léger appetit [leʒɛ rap(ə)ti]

However, verb infinitives in *-er* retain closed /e/:

  aimer et loiser [eme re lwaziːr]

Liaison does not occur in every instance where it might appear to apply. There are three categories to be aware of, obligatory liaison, forbidden liaison, and optional liaison.

Obligatory Liaison

In general, liaison must occur between grammatically closely related words.

- Article to noun:

    un homme [œ̃nɔm(ə)]   **les oiseaux** [lɛ zwazo]

- Adjective to noun:

    petit enfant [pəti tɑ̃fɑ̃]   **deux amis** [dø zami]

- Adverb to word modified:

    très utile [trɛ zytiːl(ə)]   **bien entendu** [bjɛ̃ nɑ̃tɑ̃dy]

- Pronoun to verb:

    ils ont [il zɔ̃]   **vous avez** [vu zave]

- Preposition to object:

    en hiver [ɑ̃ nivɛːr]   **dans un bois** [dɑ̃ zœ̃ bwa]

- Conjunction to next word:

    quant à [kɑ̃ ta]   **mais avant** [mɛ zavɑ̃]

- Two-part verb forms:

    il est allé [il ɛ tale]   **ils sont arrivés** [il sɔ̃ tarive]

- Various combinations of verb to object, or verb connecting subject and predicate:

    je dis un mot [ʒə di zœ̃ mo]   **nous sommes ici** [nu sɔm(ə) zisi]

- Inverted verb-subject forms:

    vont-ils? [vɔ̃ til]   **disaient-elles?** [dizɛ tɛl(ə)]

- *Plural* noun to modifier:

    États-Unis [eta zyni]   **désirs inapaisés** [deziːr zinapeze]

Forbidden Liaison

In certain situations liaison is not allowed.

- *Singular* noun to next word (some exceptions, see below):

  le printemps est venu [lə prɛ̃tɑ̃ ɛ vɛny] not [prɛ̃tɑ̃zɛ]
  la nuit immense [la nɥi immɑ̃ːs(ə)] not [nɥi timmɑ̃ːs(ə)]
  le vent a changé [lə vɑ̃ a ʃɑ̃ʒe] not [vɑ̃ ta]
  de paix et de douceur [də pɛ e də dusœːr] not [pɛ ze]

- After the word **et**:

  lui et elle [lɥi e ɛl(ə)]
  (but into the word **et** is allowed and common: **frais et si blanc**
  [frɛ ze si blɑ̃])

- After a proper noun:

  Paris est beau [pari ɛ bo]

- Before words beginning with aspirate *h*:

  les héros [lɛ ero]   **des haies** [dɛ ɛ]
  les hauts talons [lɛ o talõ]

- Before the word **oui** and the numbers **huit** and **onze**:

  il a dit oui [il a di wi]   **les onze** [lɛ õːz(ə)]
  except compound numbers with **huit**: **dix-huit** [dizɥit].

- Before or after the word **un** as a number or pronoun:

  j'en vois un [ʒɑ̃ vwa œ̃]
  plus d'un aurait donné sa vie [ply dœ̃ ɔrɛ dɔne sa vi(ə)]
  but liaison after **un** as an article normally does occur, as above.

- After the words **chacun** and **quelqu'un** (versions of **un**):

  chacun a son goût [ʃakœ̃ a sõ gu]

Although liaison is generally avoided after nouns in the singular, some
common or traditional phrases allow it:

  Bois épais [bwa zepɛ]
  quand leur voix appelle [kɑ̃ lœːr vwa zapɛl(ə)]
  nuit et jour [nɥi te ʒuːr]
  de temps en temps [də tɑ̃ zɑ̃ tɑ̃]

For those inexperienced with French, a problematic situation is presented
by words ending in *-rd*, *-rs*, and *-rt*. Since the *r* is sounded in such words,
liaison of the silent final letter is not called for. The *r* is linked to the word
following.

> **Son regard est doux** [. . . rəgaːr ɛ . . .]
> **Dans ton coeur dort un clair de lune** [. . . dɔːrœ̃ . . .]
> **Me penchant vers elle** [. . . vɛːr ɛl(ə)]

Exceptions may occur with final -rs when the s indicates plurality:

> **Si mes vers avaient des ailes** [. . . vɛːr zavɛ . . .]
> **leurs yeux** [lœːr zjø]
> **chers instants** [ʃɛːr zɛ̃stɑ̃]

The word **toujours** requires special comment. Normally the s is silent: [tuʒuːr]. It may be sounded in liaison, however, if it modifies the word following:

> **toujours heureux** [tuʒuːr zørø]
> **toujours ouvertes** [tuʒuːr zuvɛːrt(ə)]
> but not in other situations: **toujours à ses côtes** [tuʒuːr a sɛ koːt(ə)].

More generally, when words are adjacent but not closely related grammatically, liaison should be avoided:

> **Le jour qui luit est le meilleur** (*Lydia*, Fauré/Leconte de Lisle)
> In this case there is no liaison between the words **luit** and **est**; the subject of the verb **est** is **jour**.

> **Les cieux pour nous entr'ouvraient leurs nues** (*Après un rêve*, Fauré/ Bussine)
> There is no liaison after **nous**; the subject of **entr'ouvraient** is **cieux**.

There is also no liaison if there is a lift or break between the two words, often indicated by punctuation:

> **Les houles, en roulant les images . . .** (*La Vie antérieur*, Duparc/ Baudelaire)
> In this case there is no liaison after **houles**.

> **Vois, il souffle juste assez d'air . . .** (*Sérénade italienne*, Chausson/Bourget)
> Here there is no liaison after **vois**.

In the aria *Je veux vivre* from Gounod's *Roméo et Juliette* the words **longtemps encore** are separated by a rest in the music. Liaison is maintained, nevertheless, since the brief separation is purely musical and not indicated by the text alone.

Liaison is sometimes avoided for reasons of euphony or textual clarity:

> **tant de baisers et de tendresse** (*Chanson triste*, Duparc/Lahor)
> There is no liaison after **baisers**, in order to avoid [zeze].

Optional Liaison

In conversational French, some of the situations described in the preceding section, "Obligatory Liaison," are in fact optional. The heightened nature of singing requires more frequent observation of liaison than in speech. When the relation between adjacent words is not very close but also not remote, liaison may be a matter of choice. In vocal texts, such situations often present themselves in the form of prepositional phrases.

> **Fleurit avec la marjolaine** (*La Belle au Bois dormant*, Debussy/Hyspa)
> Liaison between **fleurit** and **avec** is optional.

> **Demandez à la mer immense** (*Toujours*, Fauré/Grandmougin)
> Liaison between **demandez** and **à** is optional.

> **La route qu'il poursuit en dansant** (*Voici que le printemps*, Debussy/Bourget)
> Liaison between **poursuit** and **en** is optional.

> **Ces cris au loin multipliés** (*Les cigales*, Chabrier/Gérard)
> Liaison between **cris** and **au** is optional.

Liaison is a complex matter, and confusing to the beginner. Pierre Bernac's book *The Interpretation of French Song* is an excellent resource for many reasons, but particularly because his annotations of song texts indicate when liaison should occur. Unfortunately, he does not explain his choices in cases of optional liaison, and many songs are not in the book. Careful study of his examples, however, will lead the student to a clearer understanding of this phenomenon.

MUSICAL SETTINGS OF MUTE *E* [ə]

When a syllable with mute e is given its own pitch by a composer, and elision does not apply, the /ə/ is sung and is equivalent to the vowel sound /œ/. This is the most common way in which vocal music treats mute e:

Manon

É - pou - se quel-que bra - ve fil - le
[epuːzə kɛlkə braːvə fiːjə]

Nuit
d'Étoiles
—Debussy

Nuit d'é - toi – les   Sous - tes voi – les
[nɥi det walə su te vwalə]

When a mute *e* ends a word and the next word begins with a vowel, the mute *e* is usually not pronounced. This is "elision" as defined on p. 148.

Voici que le printemps
—Debussy

flot te‿u-ne‿om-bre va-gue‿et   ten – dre
[flɔt yn õ:brə vag e tã:drə]

Recueillement
—Debussy

U - ne‿at-mos-phè-re‿ob - scu- re‿en-ve-lop-pe la   vil - le
[yn atmɔsfɛ:r ɔpskyːr ãvəlɔpə la vilə]

In the following example note the slur, indicating that the syllable [lõ] is to be sung on both the A and G, with elision causing [ʒy] to be sung on the F sharp. It is wrong to sing schwa on the G, as at least one edition of this song implies:

Voci que le printemps
—Debussy

pro - lon   -   ge u - ne   chan-son
[prɔlõːʒ ynə ʃãsõ]

When mute *e* follows a vowel, it is, as usual, silent in speech:

soie [swa]	**joie** [ʒwa]	**joue** [ʒu]	**queue** [kø]
vie [vi]	**amie** [ami]	**gaieté** [gete]	
rue [ry]	**vues** [vy]	**gaiement** [gemã]	

When mute *e* follows a vowel and is final in the poetic line, it will usually be set musically as schwa:

mais‿la vi   -   e
[mɛ la viə]

—Faust

J'allais par des chemins
perfides—Fauré

dans la joi - - e
[dɑ̃ la ʒwaə]

La Damnation de Faust

D'or, de ve - lours, de soi - e
[dɔr də vəluːr də swaə]

When the vowel-mute *e* pattern is final in a word but internal in a phrase, usually the *e* is not set; there is no schwa:

Réponse d'une épouse
sage—Roussel

froi de - ment sur la soie de ma ro - be
[frwadəmɑ̃ syːr la swa də ma rɔbə]

La flûte
enchantée
—Ravel

Vers ma joue comme un my - sté - ri - eux bai - ser
[ver ma ʒu kɔ mœ̃ misterjø beze]

When mute *e* is medial after a vowel in the same word, it is always silent, even in singing:

Carmen—Bizet

et nous **joue-rons** la bel - le
[e nu ʒurɔ̃ la bɛl(ə)]

Carmen—Bizet

Soit!   on **paie - ra**_____
[swat ɔ̃ pera]

Chanson Triste—Duparc

Je   me **noie-rai**
[ʒe mə nware]

C'est   la   **bos-sue**   de   ma cour
[sɛ la bɔsy də ma kuːr]

La pintade—Ravel

A common pattern involving schwa is the feminine ending *-ée(s)*. The most usual type of musical setting separates it into two sounds: /eə/. The singer must be careful that no intervening /j/ sound occurs when one is moving from one sound to the next. This is of course true in any instance of a vowel sound preceding schwa, but it seems to be a particular problem with this combination.

Re-viens,   re - viens,__   ma bien - ai - mé - e
[rəvjɛ̃ rəvjɛ̃ ma bjɛ̃ nemeə]

L'Absence
—Berlioz

sous   la   ra - mé - - - e__
[su la rameə]

La lune blanche
—Fauré

Soie   verte i - ri - sé - e
[swa vɛrt irizeə]

De grève—Debussy

When this pattern is internal in the phrase, it is usually set as /e/ only:

el - les se sont ré- fu - giées   du   cô - té   de
[ɛlə sə sõ refyʒje dy kote də]

Pelléas et
Mélisande

l'om - bre
[lõːbrə]

Le paon—Ravel

du   reste__   de   la   jour - née
[dy rest(ə) də la ʒurne]

De soir—Debussy

Où   mes   pen- sées   tris   –   te
[u mɛ pãse tristə]

Tied Note Notation with Mute *e*

When a composer sets a mute *e* as the second of a pair of tied notes, and elision does not apply, there are various possibilities of execution:

- If the tied note value is of short duration and the mute *e* is preceded by a consonant, the note is used to articulate the consonant with a brief (often very brief) /ə/ sound following.

La caravane
—Chausson

La_____   su - eur_____   qui__   l'i - nonde___
[la syœr ki linõːd(ə)]

L'Ombre des arbres
—Debussy

Se   plaign - ent   les   tour - te - relles____
[sə plɛɲə lɛ turtərɛl(ə)]

Carmen—Bizet

que   rien   ne   m'é- pou - van   –   te
[kə ɽjɛ̃ nə mepuvãt(ə)]

- If the tied note value is sufficiently long, the /ə/ may be more sustained (as /œ/).

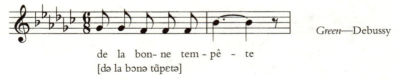

Green—Debussy

de   la   bon- ne   tem - pê - te
[də la bɔnə tãpɛtə]

Nuit   fré- mis- san - te,   mys - ti - (que)
[nɥi fremisã:tə mitikə]

- If the mute *e*, preceded by a vowel, is not separated syllabically in the text underlay, it is silent. No schwa is pronounced.

Il pleure dans mon coeur—Debussy

de   la   pluie!___
[də la plɥi]

Carmen—Bizet

J'al-lais   ê - tre   la proie___
[ʒalɛ zɛːtrə la prwa]

- If it is separated syllabically, the tied note will sound as schwa.

Il pleure dans mon coeur—Debussy

qui s'en- nui - e
[ki sãnɥiə]

In settings by twentieth-century composers, particularly Ravel, mute *e* is often not pronounced. There is either no note for the schwa, or there is a tied note of short duration that suggests the articulation of the consonant following with little or no vowel sound after it.

Le martin- pêcheur —Ravel

Com-me je   te- nais ma per - che   de   ligne ten - due
[kɔm(ə) ʒə tənɛ ma perʃ(ə) də liɲ(ə) tãdy]

Placet futile —Debussy

ni   du   rouge,   ni jeux   miè - vres
[ni dy ruːʒ(ə) ni ʒø mjeːvr(ə)]

This can even lead in some instances to complete elision of mute *e*'s as in speech:

Le cygne—Ravel

mais q'est-ce que je   dis?
[mɛ kɛs kə ʒ di]

Compare these two settings of the word **paysage**:

Le son du cor—Debussy

un pa – y – sa – ge   lent
[œ̃ peizaːʒə lɑ̃]

à loi – sir   des pa – y – sa – ges peints
[a lwa‿ziːr de pe(i)zaːʒ(ə) pɛ̃]

Shéhérazade—Ravel

The first clearly sets four syllables, while the second suggests two.

Remember that some forms of the verb **faire** pronounce *ai* as schwa:

Shéhérazade
—Ravel

Me fai– sant un der –nier geste a – vec   grâ – ce
[mə fəzɑ̃ tœ̃ dɛrnje ʒɛst avɛk graːs(ə)]

Carmen
—Bizet

De   leurs in – struments fai–saient   ra – ge
[də lœr ʒɛ̃strymɑ̃ fəze raːʒə]

MUSICAL SETTINGS OF GLIDES

/j/

In patterns of *i* plus vowel, musical settings often treat /j/ as /i/:

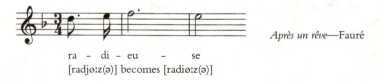

Après un rêve—Fauré

ra – di – eu – se
[radjøːz(ə)] becomes [radiøːz(ə)]

Manon—Massenet

plein de dis-cré-ti-on
[diskresjõ] becomes [diskresiõ]

although similar situations sometimes find the musical setting keeping the glide:

Jazz dans la nuit—Roussel

ir - ra - diés
[irradje]

Pelléas et Mélisande

et ce ma-riage al - lait met - tre fin
[et sə marjaːʒ alɛ mɛtrə fɛ̃]

Le paon
—Ravel

C'est ain- si qu'il ap-pelle sa fian-ceé
[sɛ tɛ̃si kil apɛl sa fjãse]

Remember that *i* followed by mute e medially in a word is just /i/. There is no glide.

Faust—Gounod

Tu - re nie - ras, pour vie - vre
[ty rənira pur viːvrə]

Chanson triste—Duparc

J'ou - blie-rai les dou- leurs pas (sées)
[ʒublire lɛ dulœːr pɑse]

De rêve—Debussy

Nul ne leur **dé - diera** plus
[nyl nə lœr **dedira** ply]

Faust
—Gounod

Non! tu ne **prie-ras** pas!
[nõ ty nə **prira** pɑ]

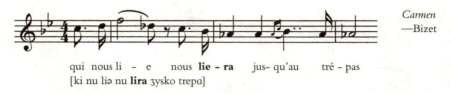

Carmen
—Bizet

qui nous li – e   nous **lie – ra**   jus- qu'au   tré – pas
[ki nu liə nu **lira** ʒysko trepɑ]

/w/

When /w/ is spelled *ou*, composers usually set it as the vowel /u/:

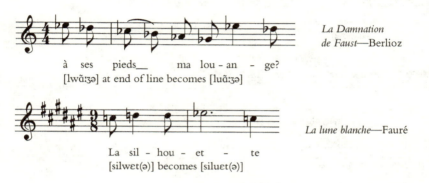

*La Damnation
de Faust*—Berlioz

à   ses   pieds__   ma lou – an – ge?
[lwɑ̃ːʒə] at end of line becomes [luɑ̃ːʒə]

La lune blanche—Fauré

La sil – hou – et   –   te
[silwɛt(ə)] becomes [siluɛt(ə)]

although sometimes such words will be set with the glide retained:

Pelléas et Mélisande

Ne   jouez pas ain – si
[nə ʒwe pɑ zɛ̃si]

Carmen—Bizet

Quant   au   doua – nier
[kɑ̃ to dwanje]

Recueillement—Debussy

Sous   le   fouet   du   Plai – sir____
[su lə fwe dy pleziːr]

/ɥ/

When *ui* follows a single consonant, such as in **lui, fui, nuit, suivi, puissance**, and many other words, musical settings always retain the glide-vowel pattern. The /ɥi/ combination occurs as one syllable on one note.

When *ui* follows a consonant plus *l* or *r*, they divide into two syllables as /yi/:

La Damnation
de Faust—Berlioz

Le   long   bru - is - se - ment____
[lə lõ bryisəmã]

Lydia—Fauré

L'or flu - i - de____   que tu   dé - nou - es
[lɔr flyidə kə ty denuə]

When /ɥ/ is followed by vowels other than /i/, musical settings usually treat /ɥ/ as the vowel /y/, creating another syllable:

Aprés un
rêve—Fauré

lu - eurs   di - vi - nes en - tre - vu - és
[lɥœːr] becomes [lyœːr]

Venise—Gounoud

D'un   nu - age   é - toi - lé
[nɥaːʒ(ə)] becomes [nyaːʒ(ə)]

Carmen—Bizet

Pour tu - er   le   temps____
[tɥe] becomes [tye]

although sometimes such words are set with the glide retained:

Pelléas et Mélisande

ce   grand   nua - ge
[sə grã nɥaːʒ(ə)]

Le Paon—Ravel

Les vo - lailles   ha - bi - tuées ne   lèvent
[le vɔlaj(ə) zabitɥe nə levə]

Remember that final *-ue* never results in a glide but is either /y/ or /yə/, depending on the musical setting:

Elle est per - due . . .   per - du - e!
[ɛl ɛ pɛrdy pɛrdyə]

Pelléas et Mélisande

Je   le   tue - rai!
[ʒə lə tyre]

Faust—Gounod

FRENCH DICTIONARIES

Fortunately, most French dictionaries of recent publication, whether French–English or French only, use the International Phonetic Alphabet for all entries. Any dictionary that does not use the IPA is to be avoided. Most of them do not indicate vowel length or word stress, but since these points can be consistently deduced, their absence is not important.

There are some discrepancies from one dictionary to another, virtually all of them involving differences regarding /e/ and /ɛ/ in certain situations. One of them concerns the combination *ai*, normally pronounced open /ɛ/. This combination may be considered closed /e/ when the next syllable has a closed vowel:

> **baiser** is transcribed [beze] or [bɛze]
> **baisser** is [bese] or [bɛse]
> **maison** is [mezõ] or [mɛzõ]
> **raison** is [rezõ] or [rɛzõ]
> **plaisir** is [pleziːr] or [plɛziːr]
> **aisé** is [eze] or [ɛze]
> **pays** is [pei] or [pɛi]
> **paisible** is [pezibl(ə)] or [pɛzibl(ə)]

Since this situation is similar to vocalic harmonization, and vocalic harmonization is considered an option rather than a rule, it is best to consider the alternative pronunciations to the above words as equally valid options. For the purpose of singing, this text prefers the closed pronunciation, just as it prefers observing vocalic harmonization.

Other inconsistencies between dictionaries concern initial *ess*. Some dictionaries have /e/ while others have /ɛ/. **Essaim** is [esɛ̃] or [ɛsɛ̃], **essor** is [esɔːr] or [ɛsɔːr]. This text uses the closed version, as do most dictionaries of recent publication.

There are also discrepancies with /a/ and /ɑ/. The word **croire**, for example, is usually given with /ɑ/, but some dictionaries give it with /a/. Also, for initial *irr-* some dictionaries give /rr/, implying a lengthened sound, while others do not.

Sometimes one encounters pronunciations in one dictionary that are not found in others. For example, one dictionary gives initial *ex* plus a vowel or *h* as /egz/: **exemple** [egzɑ̃ːpl(ə)], while the customarily accepted pronunciation of all words with initial *ex* is with /ɛ/: [ɛgzɑ̃ːpl(ə)].

SAMPLE TEXTS

Below are two sample texts with IPA transcription. The first is relatively simple; the second is more difficult and contains several challenging spellings. The IPA reflects the musical setting, such as elisions, schwas, and glides becoming vowels.

LE CHARME [lə ʃarm(ə)]
Poem by Armand Silvestre
Music by Ernest Chausson

> **Quand ton sourire me surprit,**
> [kɑ̃ tõ suriːrə mə syrpri]
>
> **Je sentis frémir tout mon être,**
> [ʒə sɑ̃ti fremiːr tu mõ nɛtrə]
>
> **Mais ce qui domptait mon esprit,**
> [mɛ sə ki dõtɛ mõ nɛspri]
>
> **Je ne pus d'abord le connaître.**
> [ʒə nə py dabɔːr lə kɔnɛtrə]
>
> **Quand ton regard tomba sur moi,**
> [kɑ̃ tõ rəgaːr tõba syr mwa]
>
> **Je sentis mon âme se fondre,**
> [ʒə sɑ̃ti mõ naːmə sə fõːdrə]

Mais ce que serait cet émoi,

[mɛ sə kə sərɛ sɛt emwa]

Je ne pus d'abord en répondre.

[ʒə nə py dabɔːr ɑ̃ repõːdrə]

Ce qui me vainquit à jamais,

[sə ki mə vɛ̃ki ta ʒamɛ]

Ce fut un plus douloureux charme;

[sə fy tœ̃ ply dulurø ʃarmə]

Et je n'ai su que je t'aimais,

[e ʒə ne sy kə ʒə tɛmɛ]

Qu'en voyant ta première larme.

[kɑ̃ vwajɑ̃ ta prəmjɛːrə larmə]

LA VAGUE ET LA CLOCHE [la vag e la klɔʃ]
Poem by François Coppée
Music by Henri Duparc

Une fois, terrassé par un puissant breuvage,

[ynə fwa, tɛrase par œ̃ pɥisɑ̃ brœvaːʒə]

J'ai rêvé que parmi les vagues et le bruit   Bernac recommends

[ʒe rɛve kə parmi le vagə e lə brɥi]   no liaison after **vagues**.

De la mer je voguais sans fanal dans la nuit,

[də la mɛr ʒə vɔge sɑ̃ fanal dɑ̃ la nɥi]

Morne rameur, n'ayant plus l'espoir du rivage.

[mɔrnə ramœːr nejɑ̃ ply lɛspwaːr dy rivaːʒə]

L'océan me crachait ses baves sur le front,

[lɔseɑ̃ mə kraʃe sɛ bavə syːr lə frõ]

Et le vent me glaçait d'horreur jusqu'aux entrailles,

[e lə vɑ̃ mə glase dɔrœːr ʒysko zɑ̃traːjə]

Les vagues s'écroulaient ainsi que des murailles   No liaison into

[le vagə sekrule ɛ̃si kə dɛ myraːjə]   **ainsi** because
                                                                 of rest.

Avec ce rythme lent qu'un silence interrompt.

[avɛk sə ritmə lɑ̃ kœ̃ silɑ̃ːs ɛ̃tɛrõ]

Puis, tout changea. La mer et sa noire mêlée
[pɥi tu ʃɑ̃ʒa la mɛːr e sa nwaːrə mɛleə]

Sombrèrent . . . sous mes pieds s'effondra le plancher
[sõbrɛːrə su mɛ pje sefrõdra lə plɑ̃ʃe]

De la barque. Et j'étais seul dans un vieux clocher,
[də la barkə e ʒetɛ sœl dɑ̃ zœ̃ vjø klɔʃe]

Chevauchant avec rage une cloche ébranlée.
[ʃəvoʃɑ̃ tavɛk raːʒ ynə klɔʃ ebrɑ̃leə]

J'étreignais la criarde opiniâtrement,
[ʒetrɛɲe la kriard ɔpiniɑtrəmɑ̃]

Dictionaries
may have [krijard]

Convulsif et fermant dans l'effort mes paupières,
[kõvylsif e fɛrmɑ̃ dɑ̃ lefɔːr mɛ popjɛːrə]

Le grondement faisait trembler les vieilles pierres,
[lə grõdəmɑ̃ fəze trɑ̃ble lɛ vjɛːjə pjɛːrə]

Note
faisait [fə . . .]

Tant j'activais sans fin le lourd balancement.
[tɑ̃ ʒaktive sɑ̃ fɛ̃ lə luːr balɑ̃səmɑ̃]

Pourquoi n'as-tu pas dit, o rêve, où Dieu nous mène?
[purkwa na ty pɑ di o rɛːv u djø nu mɛnə]

Pourquoi n'as-tu pas dit s'ils ne finiraient pas
[purkwa na ty pɑ di sil nə finirɛ pɑ]

L'inutile travail et l'éternel fracas
[linytilə travaːj e letɛrnel fraka]

No dark /ɑ/
in **fracas**.

Dont est fait la vie, hélas, la vie humaine!
[dõ tɛ fɛ la vi elaːs la vi ymɛnə]

Bibliography

Bernac, Pierre. *The Interpretation of French Song.* New York: Norton, 1970.

Booth, Trudie Maria. *French Phonetics.* Lanham, Md.: University Press of America, 1997.

Camilli, Amerindo. *An Italian Phonetic Reader.* London: University of London Press, 1921.

———. *Pronuncia e Grafia dell'Italiano.* Florence: Sansoni Editore, 1943.

Canepari, Luciano. *Dizionario di Pronuncia Italiana.* Bologna: Zanichelli, 1999.

Carton, Fernand. *Introduction à la Phonétique du Français.* Paris: Bordas, 1974.

Castel, Nico. *The Complete Puccini Librettos.* Geneseo: Leyerle Publications, 1993.

———. *A Singer's Manual of Spanish Lyric Diction.* New York: Excalibur, 1994.

———. *Three Wagner Opera Libretti.* Geneseo: Leyerle Publications, 2006.

Castiglione, Pierina Borrani. *Italian Phonetics, Diction and Intonation.* New York: S. F. Vanni, 1957.

Colorni, Evelina. *Singer's Italian.* New York: Schirmer Books, 1970.

Cox, Richard G. *The Singer's Manual of German and French Diction.* New York: Schirmer Books, 1970.

Duden Aussprachewörterbuch. Mannheim: Dudenverlag, 1990.

Fouché, Pierre. *Traité de Prononciation Française.* Paris: Librairie C. Klinckrieck, 1957.

Gartside, Robert. *Interpreting the Songs of Gabriel Fauré.* Geneseo: Leyerle Publications, 1996.

Glass, Beaumont. *Schubert's Complete Song Texts.* Geneseo: Leyerle Publications, 1996.

Grubb, Thomas. *Singing in French.* New York: Schirmer Books, 1979.

Hall, Christopher. *Modern German Pronunciation.* 2nd ed. Manchester: Manchester University Press, 2003.

Léon, Pierre R. *Prononciation du Français Standard.* Paris: Didier, 1978.

Lepschy, Anna Laura, and Giulio Lepschy. *The Italian Language Today.* London: Hutchinson, 1977.

Malécot, André. *Introduction à la Phonétique Français.* The Hague: Mouton, 1977.

Martinet, André, and Henriette Walter. *Dictionnaire de la Prononciation Française dans son Usage Réel.* Paris: France—Expansion, 1973.

Moriarty, John. *Diction.* Boston: SchirmerMusic Company, 1975.

Nitze, William, et al. *A Handbook of French Phonetics.* New York: Henry Holt, 1913.

Odom, William. *German for Singers*. 2nd ed. New York: Schirmer Books, 1997.

Rothmüller, Marko. *Pronunciation of German and German Diction*. Bloomington, Ind.: published by author, 1978.

Schane, Sanford. *French Phonology and Morphology*. Cambridge: M.I.T. Press, 1968.

Sheil, Richard F. *A Singer's Manual of Foreign Language Dictions*. 6th ed. New York: YBK Publishers, 2004.

Siebs, Theodor. *Deutsche Aussprache*. Berlin: Walter de Gruyter, 1969.

Stapp, Marci. *The Singer's Guide to Languages*. San Francisco: published by author, 1991.

Valdeman, Albert. *Introduction to French Phonology and Morphology*. Rowley, Mass.: Newbury House, 1968.

Wall, Joan, et al. *Diction*. Dallas: Pst...Inc., 1990.

Walter, Henriette. *La Phonologie du Français*. Paris: Presses Universitaires de France, 1977.

Warnant, Léon. *Dictionnaire de la Prononciation Française*. Gembloux: Éditions J. Duculot, S. A., 1962.

Index of Sounds by Spelling

A

a   Italian, 5, 6, 12; German, 85–86, 88–89, 121–122, 125; French, 157–159

à   Italian, 9–10, 39; French, 147, 157

â   French, 147, 158

ä   German, 85–86, 92, 94

aa   German, 87, 88, 89

äu   German, 100

ae   Italian, 16; German, 101

aen, aën   French, 148, 174

ai   Italian, 16, 18; German, 100; French, 150, 160–163, 172, 208, 212

aî   French, 147

aï   French, 147, 151, 153, 177

aie(s)   French, 160

aient   French, 160, 172

ail, aill   French, 161

aim   French, 175

ain   French, 175

aio   Italian, 19

ais   French, 160

ait   French, 160

aiu   Italian, 19

am   French, 174

an   French, 174

ao   Italian, 16; French, 158

aon   French, 158, 174

aou, aoû   French, 167

au   Italian, 16, 18; German, 100; French, 164, 165

aû   French, 147

auld   French, 187

ault   French, 187

ay   German, 100; French, 151, 160, 163–164

B

b   Italian, 21, 22; German, 106–107; French, 181

bb   Italian, 35; French, 181

C

c   Italian, 28–29, 32; German, 111–112; French, 181–182

ç   French, 148, 182–183

cc   Italian, 28–29, 35; French, 181,183

ch   Italian, 29; German, 102–103, 109–110, 121, 134; French, 153, 183

chs   German, 103–104

ck   German, 112, 114

cq   Italian, 35

ct   French, 182

cueil   French, 169

D

d   Italian, 21, 22; German, 106–107; French, 183, 197

dd   Italian, 35; French, 183

desc   French, 161, 163

dess   French, 161, 163, 172

E

e   Italian, 5, 12, 28; open and closed, Italian, 7, 35–38, 66–81; German, 86, 91, 92–94, 121; French, 148, 159–163

é   Italian, 9; French, 147, 150, 153, 159, 162

è   Italian, 9, 39; French 147, 153, 159

ê   French, 147, 156, 159

ë   French, 147–148, 153, 159

ea   Italian, 16; German, 101; French, 185

ean   French, 174

eau   French, 165

ee   Italian, 41; German, 87, 91, 92

ée   French, 205–206

eff   French, 161, 163

ei   Italian, 16, 18; German, 100; French, 160

eil, eill   French, 160

eim   French, 175

ein   French, 175

el   Italian, 76

em   Italian, 76; French, 174

emm   French, 157, 161, 173

en   Italian, 76–77; French, 174

enn   French, 157, 161, 173

ent   French, 172

eo   Italian, 17; German, 101

er   Italian, 77; French, 160, 162–163, 190–191, 198; German, 105, 124

es   Italian, 77

ess   French, 161, 163

eu   Italian, 17; German, 100; French, 169–170

ex   German, 111; French, 196

ey   Italian, 16; German, 100; French, 160

ez   French, 162

F

f   Italian, 22; French, 184

ff   Italian, 35; French, 184

G

g   Italian, 28–29, 32; German, 106; French, 184–185, 197

gea   French, 185

geais   French, 185

geait   French, 185

geo   French, 185

gg   Italian, 28–29, 35; French, 184–185

gh   Italian, 29

gl, gli   Italian, 5, 11, 20, 22, 31–32, 35, 71–72; French, 185

gn   Italian, 11, 20, 22, 30–31, 35, 71; German, 112, 121; French, 185

gue   Italian, 9; French, 168, 171, 185

gueil   French, 169

gueu   French, 169

gui   Italian, 9; French, 185

H

h   Italian, 29–30; German, 87, 110–111; French, 149, 153, 185, 200

I

i   Italian, 5, 6, 8, 10, 12, 28–29, 30, 31–32, 38–41; German, 86, 89–91, 121; French, 166, 177, 208 ì, í   Italian, 9, 38

î   Italian, 10; French, 147, 166

ï   Italian, 10; French, 147, 153,
         166, 177

ia, ià   Italian, 9, 13, 17, 18, 38–41,
             French, 152

ie, iè   Italian, 9, 13, 17, 18; German,
             86, 87, 90, 102, 127–128;
             French, 166

iei   Italian, 19

ien   German, 128; French, 175

ig   German, 107–108, 134

ii   Italian, 10, 41

il   French, 156, 169, 177, 186

ilh   French, 177, 187

ill   German, 112; French, 152, 154,
          156, 171, 177, 186–187

im   French, 175

in   French, 175

io, iò   Italian, 9, 10, 13, 17, 18, 38;
             French, 152; German, 102

iu, iù   Italian, 9, 17

J

j   Italian, 8; German, 101–102;
        French, 186

K

kk   German, 114

kn   German, 112

L

l   Italian, 11, 13, 15, 21, 22, 27,
        45; French, 186

lh   French, 177, 187

ll   Italian, 35; German, 112;
         French, 152, 154, 171, 177,
         186–187

lz   Italian, 27

M

m   Italian, 11, 15, 22; French,
         173–174, 187

mm   Italian, 35; French, 187–188

mn   French, 187

N

n   Italian, 11, 15, 22, 27, 31,
        61–62; French, 173–174, 188,
        198

nb   Italian (phrasal), 61–62

nc   Italian, 32; French, 174, 181

nf   Italian (phrasal), 62; German,
          134

ng   Italian, 32; German, 112–113;
          French, 174, 184

nh   French, 153

nk   German, 113

nm   Italian (phrasal), 61–62

nn   Italian, 35; French, 188

np   Italian (phrasal), 61

nq   Italian, 32

nv   Italian, 62

nz   Italian, 27

O

o   Italian, 5, 12; open and closed,
        Italian, 7, 35–38, 66–81;
        German, 86, 91, 94–96,
        121–122;
        French, 164–165

ò   Italian, 9

ö   German, 85, 99–100, 122

ô   Italian, 10; French, 147, 165

oa   Italian, 17

oe   Italian, 17; German, 101;
         French, 158, 169

oeil   French, 169

oeu   French, 169–170

oi   Italian, 17, 18; French, 157,
         178

oî   French, 147

oia   Italian, 19

oie   French, 178

oin   French, 175, 178

ol   Italian, 77
om   Italian, 77–78; French, 176
on   Italian, 78; French, 176
oo   Italian, 41; German, 87, 94–95
or   Italian, 78
os   Italian, 78
ou   French, 167, 178
où, oû   French, 147, 167
oue   French, 167
ouill   French, 167
ow   German, 95, 111
oy   French, 151, 157, 176, 179

P

p   Italian, 32, 21, 22; French,
            188–189
pf   German, 113
ph   German, 113; French, 189
pp   Italian, French, 188–189
ps   Italian, 32; German, 113;
            French, 189
pt   French, 189

Q

q, qu   Italian, 32; German, 113;
            French, 168, 179, 189
qq   Italian, 35
que   French, 171
queu   French, 169

R

r   Italian, 11, 12, 13, 15, 21,
            23–24, 27; German,
            104–106; French, 189–191,
            198
ress   French, 161, 172
rr   Italian, 23, 35; French, 180, 190
rz   Italian, 27

S

s   Italian, 11, 24–25, 32; German,
            108–109, 135; French,
            191–194

sc   Italian, 11, 20, 22, 30, 35;
            French, 182, 193
sch   Italian, 30; German, 109–110
sh   German, 110
sp   German, 110
ss   Italian, 24, 35; German, 121–
            122, 124; French, 191–194
st   German, 110
sz   German, 112
ß   German, 121–122

T

t   Italian, 21–22; French,
            194–195
th   German, 113, French 194
ti   German, 113; French, 178, 195
tia, tie French, 178, 195
tient   German, 101; French, 178,
            195
tion   German, 101, 102, 115; French,
            178, 195
tsch   German, 113
tt   Italian, 35; French, 194
tz   German, 111–112

U

u   Italian, 5, 6–7, 8–9; German,
            86, 96–97, 121, 122, 123,
            124; French, 167–168
ù, ú   Italian, 9
ü   German, 86, 98–99, 122,
            123–124
ua   Italian, 18; French, 152, 179
ue   Italian, 18; German, 101;
            French, 152, 168, 169
uei   Italian, 19
ueu   French, 169–170
ui   Italian, 18
uio   Italian, 19
um   French, 176
un   French, 176
uo   Italian, 18
uoi   Italian, 19

uoio   Italian, 19

uu   German, 97

uy   French, 151, 179

V

v   Italian, 22; German, 111;
            French, 195

vv   Italian, 35

W

w   German, 111, French, 195

X

x   German, 111; French, 195–196,
            198

Y

y   German, 98; French, 151,
            157, 160, 163, 166, 175, 177,
            179

ÿ   French, 166

yen   French, 175, 176

ym   French, 175

yn   French, 175

Z

z   Italian, 20, 25–27; German,
            111–112; French, 197, 198

zz   Italian, 27–28, 35

General Index

A

Acute accent
Italian, 9
French, 147
Apocopation, 15
Aspirated *h,* 149
Assimilation
of consonant sounds, German,
136–139
of *n,* Italian, 32, 61–62, 63

B

Breakdown of mixed vowels, 100, 170

C

Cedilla, 148, 182–183
Circumflex
French, 147, 156
Italian, 10
Closed vowels. *See* Vowel quality
Compound words
German, 115, 129
Italian, 21, 25, 36
Consonant length
French, 154, 180
German, 114
Italian, 22
Consonants
articulating double in singing Italian,
44–45

consonant clusters, Italian, 11, 12
dental (forward) pronunciation of
French, 146
dental (forward) pronunciation of
Italian, 4, 21
de-voicing of German, 106–107, 111
French, 180–197
French double, 154, 180
German, 102–114
German double, 114
Italian, 21–35
Italian single and double, 11, 21, 32–35
non-aspiration of French, 146
non-aspiration of Italian, 4, 21
phrasal clusters in German, 133–136
possible assimilation of sounds in
German, 136–139
singing clusters in Italian, 45–46

D

De-voicing of consonants. *See* Conso-
nants
Diacritical marks
French, 147–148
German, 85
Italian, 9–10
Dictionaries
French, 212–213
German, 139–140
Italian, 62–63

225

Dieresis
    French, 147
    Italian, 10
    See also Tréma
Diphthongs
    English, 7–8, 91, 95, 101
    German, 100–101
    inappropriate, 3, 8
    Italian, 9, 12, 15–18, 20, 38–41
    musical settings of Italian, 46–48
    phrasal, Italian, 19, 51–57
    vowel distribution in singing, Italian,
        48–50
Double consonants. *See* Consonants

E
Elision, 148–149, 203

F
Flipped *r*
    French, 189–190
    German, 104–105
    Italian, 21, 23–24
    See also Index of Sounds by Spelling

G
Glides
    French, 151, 176–180
    German, 101–102
    Italian, 5, 8–9, 12, 13, 17–19, 32, 38–41
    musical settings of French, 208–212
Glottal attack (separation), 19, 89, 92,
        101, 128–133, 149
Grave accent
    French 147
    Italian, 9–10

I
International phonetic alphabet (IPA)
    French, symbols for, 146
    German, symbols for, 84
    Italian, symbols for, 4

L
Liaison, 149, 197–202

M
Mixed vowels
    breakdown of, 100, 170
    French, 167–172
    German, 97–100
Mute *e*, 148, 151, 171
    musical settings of, 202–208

N
Nasal vowels, 156, 172–176. *See also* Index
    of Sounds by Spelling

O
Open vowels. *See* Vowel quality

P
Phrasal consonant clusters. *See* Conso-
    nants
Phrasal diphthongs. *See* Diphthongs
Phrasal doubling
    German, 114
    Italian, 41–44
Phrasal triphthongs. *See* Triphthongs
Prefixes
    German, 91, 92, 93, 96, 116–118, 129
    Italian, 12, 25, 75

R
Rolled *r*
    French, 190
    German, 105
    Italian, 21, 23–24

S
Schwa
    French, 170–172
    German, 93–94, 105
    musical settings of French, 202–208
Semiconsonant, 8

Semivowel, 8

Stressed monophthongs, 55, 57

Strong vowels, 53

Strong verbs, German, 120

Suffixes
    German, 88, 95, 96, 107–108, 109,
        118–119
    Italian, 14, 68–69, 73, 77–80

Syllabification
    French, 150–155
    German, 126–127
    Italian, 11–13, 19

T

Tréma, 10, 147. *See also* Dieresis.

Triphthongs
    Italian, 18–19, 20
    musical settings of Italian, 50–51
    patterns of phrasal, Italian, 19,
        57–60

U

Umlaut, 10, 85

Unaspirated *h,* 149

V

Verb endings
    French, 171–172, 191
    German, 119–120
    Italian, 80–81

Vocalic harmonization, 149–150, 162,
    164, 169, 212

Vowel length
    French, 155–156
    German, 86–87, 115
    Italian, 20–21
    words of non-Germanic origin,
        127–128

Vowel modification, 6, 37, 90–91, 97

Vowel quality
    German, 86, 120–122
    Italian, 7, 35–38, 66–81
    monosyllables, German, 122–125
    words of non-Germanic origin,
        126–127
    See also Index of Sounds by Spelling

Vowels
    French, 155–176
    German, 86–101, 121–125, 126–128
    Italian, 4–8, 35–41, 66–81
    See also Diphthongs; Index of Sounds
        by Spelling; Mixed vowels;
        Triphthongs

W

Word (syllabic) stress
    French, 155
    German, 87, 115–118, 126
    Italian, 9, 13–14, 20–21

Word origin
    German, 85–86, 125–128
    Italian, 66–67

Word structure, German, 87, 116–120,
    125–128

Word underlay in scores, Italian, 60–61